'A crash course in self-awareness for leaders. In an era when too many executives are oblivious to their own limitations, Kirstin Ferguson reveals how to take an honest look in the mirror. It's filled with vivid, practical lessons.'
Adam Grant – #1 *New York Times* bestselling author of *Think Again* and *Hidden Potential*, and host of the podcast *Re:Thinking*

'A clear-eyed, compelling guide to uncovering the biases you don't even know you have. Think you're self-aware? Think again. *Blindspotting* will shake up the way you see yourself and others in all the right ways.'
Dan Harris – *New York Times* bestselling author of *10% Happier* and host of the *10% Happier* podcast

'*Blindspotting* will change the way you see yourself – and the world. This book offers a masterclass that will help you find your blind spots, before they find you. A must-read for anyone who wants to lead with impact.'
Sukhinder Singh Cassidy – CEO, Xero

'In today's world, leadership isn't about what you know – it's about how fast you can learn. In *Blindspotting*, Ferguson shows that the best leaders are Seekers, challenging their assumptions, embracing uncertainty, and seeing what others miss. A must-read for those who want to lead with greater clarity and impact.'
Liz Wiseman – *New York Times* bestselling author (*Multipliers, Rookie Smarts, Impact Players*)

'Who would have guessed that your leadership superpower could be what you don't know? Australia's foremost leadership expert, Kirstin Ferguson, of course! *Blindspotting* is practical, insightful, compelling – a must-read for every modern leader.'
Kate Jenkins AO – Chair, Australian Sports Commission

'*Blindspotting* masterfully subverts what we think we know and gives us permission to benefit from the magic that happens when we come to know ourselves.'
Marcus Collins – Marketing professor and bestselling author of *For the Culture*

'You, literally, don't know what you're missing. This book will help you change that. It guides you on how to stay curious longer, rush to answers more slowly, and get smarter and more effective.'
Michael Bungay Stanier – Author of *The Coaching Habit* and host of *Change Signal*

'*Blindspotting* is a must-read for anyone who wants to supercharge their and their team's effectiveness. My proudest career moments have always been as part of a team, the power of collective wisdom to achieve great ambitions or overcome complex challenges. Great leaders have the humility and vulnerability to recognise that they create the space for others to do their best work. Earlier in my career I thought leading teams was about knowing the most and having the answers, but I learned the hard way that is not at all what it is about. If I had access to *Blindspotting*, I know I would have got there sooner.'
Pip Marlow – Company Director and former Managing Director, Microsoft Australia

'In an unpredictable world, we should expect the unexpected. Yet, too often, we don't. One of the greatest risks of rigid, righteous thinking is that it blinds us to what is right in front of us and what lies ahead. Ferguson masterfully combines people-focused leadership with brilliant storytelling and thought-provoking case studies. *Blindspotting* isn't just a book about leadership, it's a mirror, helping readers uncover their own blind spots and rethink the way they engage with the world. More than that, it challenges us to seek out fresh perspectives and embrace the Seekers among us and within ourselves.'
Julie Inman Grant – Australia's eSafety Commissioner

'*Blindspotting* is a wake-up call to challenge the familiar and discover the insight lying just out of sight. By revealing the unconscious patterns that shape our choices, this book will help you break free from what's holding you back. A must-read for anyone ready to grow with clarity and self-awareness.'
Dr Tasha Eurich – Organisational psychologist and *New York Times* bestselling author (*Shatterproof, Insight, Bankable Leadership*)

'*Blindspotting* is leadership gold – offering exactly what today's leaders need to navigate complexity and uncertainty. Ferguson takes the essential skills of honesty, curiosity and flexibility and transforms them from abstract concepts into actionable practices. A refreshing antidote to leadership hubris that will help you recognise your intellectual limitations, challenge assumptions and embrace different perspectives.'
Amy Gallo – Co-host of *Harvard Business Review's Women at Work* podcast and author of *Getting Along: How to work with anyone (even difficult people)*

'Once again, Ferguson has provided an insightful and pragmatic resource for leaders who want to have an impact. Her in-depth research, experience and accessible style of writing make this book a must-have for leaders who are wrestling with the challenges of leading in today's world.'
Lucy Adams – CEO, Disruptive HR

'We all have blind spots, but in *Blindspotting*, Ferguson shows us how to recognise and overcome them. Through real-world examples and actionable insights, she teaches leaders how to embrace intellectual honesty, question assumptions and navigate uncertainty with confidence.'
Dorie Clark – Executive education faculty at Columbia Business School and *Wall Street Journal* bestselling author of *The Long Game*

'Honesty, curiosity and flexibility are the cornerstones of *Blindspotting* and these elements drive Ferguson's thinking and practice. Ferguson's work is as persuasive and practical as it is important. Read *Blindspotting* and you will see!'
Stuart Crainer and Des Dearlove – Founders, Thinkers50

'Admitting you don't have all the answers used to be seen as a leadership weakness but is now universally understood to be a strength. Leaders with the courage to fail fast and pivot in response to new information will likely be leading a culture that is honest and transparent. *Blindspotting*, Ferguson's latest must-read business book, highlights how flexibility, honesty and curiosity are critical success factors in the modern business environment. I highly recommend it.'
Marina Go – Chair, Adore Beauty

'In a world obsessed with answers, *Blindspotting* reveals how embracing uncertainty and questioning our assumptions can unlock extraordinary leadership potential. A masterful guide to turning our blind spots into breakthrough moments.'
Holly Ransom – CEO, Emergent Global

'Great leaders are not no ego, but low ego. They don't fear what they don't know – they embrace it. Blindspotting is a masterclass in turning intellectual honesty into an advantage, helping leaders see what others miss.'
Cassandra Kelly – Founder, C-Change, and Chair, FutureFeed

'How masterful to take a noun we all know so well and turn it into a verb that we can all do something about. I realised in reading this book that I'd just taken the first critical step towards understanding my own blind spots. This is a simultaneously humbling and empowering read full of practical tools and illuminating case studies. This book is a guide in challenging assumptions, identifying red flags and

surfacing hubris, whilst gifting us tools on how to exercise intellectual honesty, curiosity and flexibility. In a world of extraordinary ambiguity and complexity, the concept of blindspotting could well be the critical unlock for modern-day leadership.'
Jenelle McMaster – Oceania Deputy CEO and People & Culture Leader, Ernst & Young

'There is no more powerful book than *Blindspotting* for insights and guidance on how to lead in a world that lacks certainties – it is not only recommended but required reading! Rather than wondering how to survive, Ferguson lays out the mindset and practices to lead and thrive, as well as find beauty and hope in a world full of possibilities. A must-read.'
Chris Havrilla – Vice President, Product Strategy, Oracle

'In a time when people seem to look only to confirm what they already believe, Ferguson encourages us to seek what we don't know, and to engage with that discomfort. This book is brilliant not just for leaders and aspirants, but anyone working with other humans.'
Daisy Turnbull – Author, *50 Risks to Take with Kids* and *50 Questions to Ask Teens*, and Director of Coeducation, Cranbrook School

'A much-needed spotlight on how we can all be more visionary leaders, from one of the most thoughtful, rigorous and pragmatic leaders I know.'
Reb Rebele – Senior Fellow, The Wharton School

'In *Blindspotting*, Ferguson not only makes it clear why a question mindset is crucial for leaders to succeed in uncertain times. She also provides powerful examples and advice on *how* to use honesty, curiosity and flexibility to achieve tangible results. *Blindspotting* gives leaders the key they have been missing to unlock the potential in themselves and their organisations.'
Pia Lauritzen – Philosopher and author of *Questions*

'Authentic leadership makes a comeback – if more leaders followed Kirstin Ferguson's advice, how much better would the world be! She weaves fascinating stories of leadership in with her no-nonsense, authentic leadership advice, creating a powerful narrative for today's leaders. In the style of Adam Grant, Malcolm Gladwell and James Clear, *Blindspotting* will leave you remembering the leadership stories and easily integrating the advice. Today, more than ever, the world is crying out for authentic leaders who admit their flaws. This is a blueprint for how to become the type of leader the world needs.'
Shirley Chowdhary – Non-executive director and public speaker

'*Blindspotting* is a powerful exploration of business brilliance through a cybernetic lens; emphasising adaptive intelligence, feedback loops and self-correcting decision-making. Ferguson's work here is a vital leadership roadmap to challenge assumptions, embrace uncertainty and build dynamic, resilient systems for innovation, growth and future-readiness.'
Dr Catherine Ball – Scientific Futurist and author of *Converge*

'*Blindspotting* offers a pathway through complexity with insights to empower you and your team using intellectual honesty as a foundation to unlock creative, collaborative solutions. The book is a roadmap to help you foster a culture of openness and innovation, where every team member can contribute to overcoming challenges and driving success.'
Allan English – Chair, English Family Foundation

Blindspotting

Dr Kirstin Ferguson AM is an author, columnist and an expert in leadership and culture. Honoured as one of the top fifty management thinkers globally, she received the prestigious Thinkers50 Distinguished Leadership Award in 2023.

Kirstin's career began as an officer in the Royal Australian Air Force. She has also been the chief executive officer of an international consulting firm, as well as acting chair and deputy chair of the Australian Broadcasting Corporation. Over fifteen years as a company director, Kirstin contributed her expertise to numerous public, private and non-profit boards.

Kirstin holds a PhD in leadership and culture, alongside honours degrees in Law and History. An adjunct professor at the Queensland University of Technology Business School, she was named Outstanding Alumnus of the Year in 2020. Her contributions to business and gender equality were recognised in 2023 when she was appointed a Member of the Order of Australia (AM). In 2024, she received the University of New South Wales Alumni Award for Professional Achievement.

Since 2021, Kirstin has written a popular nationally syndicated column in the *Sydney Morning Herald* and the *Age*, where she provides guidance on work, leadership and careers.

contact@kirstinferguson.com
kirstinferguson.com
@kirstinferguson

ALSO BY KIRSTIN FERGUSON

Head & Heart: The art of modern leadership

Women Kind: Unlocking the power of women supporting women
with Catherine Fox

Blindspotting

How to see what others miss

Kirstin Ferguson

PENGUIN BOOKS

UK | USA | Canada | Ireland | Australia
India | New Zealand | South Africa | China

Penguin Books is part of the Penguin Random House group of companies whose addresses can be found at global.penguinrandomhouse.com

First published by Penguin Books in 2025

Copyright © Kirstin Ferguson Pty Ltd 2025
Illustrations copyright © Kirstin Ferguson Pty Ltd 2025

The moral right of the author has been asserted.

All rights reserved. No part of this publication may be reproduced, published, performed in public or communicated to the public in any form or by any means without prior written permission from Penguin Random House Australia Pty Ltd or its authorised licensees.

Penguin Random House values and supports copyright. Copyright fuels creativity, encourages diverse voices, promotes free speech and creates a vibrant culture. Thank you for buying an authorised edition of this book and for complying with copyright laws by not reproducing, scanning or distributing any parts of it in any form without permission. You are supporting writers and allowing Penguin Random House to continue to publish books for every reader. Please note that no part of this book may be used or reproduced in any manner for the purpose of training artificial intelligence technologies or systems.

Cover design by Luke Causby, Blue Cork Design © Penguin Random House Australia Pty Ltd
Internal illustrations by Victoria Brown
Typeset in 12/16 pt Adobe Garamond Pro by Midland Typesetters, Australia

Printed and bound in Australia by Griffin Press, an accredited
ISO AS/NZS 14001 Environmental Management Systems printer

 A catalogue record for this book is available from the National Library of Australia

ISBN 978 1 76134 483 1

penguin.com.au

We at Penguin Random House Australia acknowledge that Aboriginal and Torres Strait Islander peoples are the Traditional Custodians and the first storytellers of the lands on which we live and work. We honour Aboriginal and Torres Strait Islander peoples' continuous connection to Country, waters, skies and communities. We celebrate Aboriginal and Torres Strait Islander stories, traditions and living cultures; and we pay our respects to Elders past and present.

*For my daughters – Emily and Zoe –
I love you to the moon and back. And back again; infinity.*

CONTENTS

Prologue 1
Introduction 7

Part 1 The Power of Blindspotting 19
 1 See What Others Miss 21
 2 Discover Seekers and Knowers 41
 3 Unmask Your Thinking Traps 59

Part 2 The Three Blindspotting Mindsets 83
 4 Be Honest 85
 5 Be Curious 117
 6 Be Flexible 150

Part 3 Put Blindspotting into Practice 183
 7 Become a Better Seeker 185
 8 Build Teams of Seekers 219
 9 Cultivate a Blindspotting Culture 243

Conclusion 263
Epilogue 270

Appendix Blindspotting Self-Assessment Tool 276
Notes 281
Acknowledgements 290
Index 293

Interviews

Leaping into the unknown *Wendy McMahon, President of CBS News and Stations*	35
Leveraging doubt for success *Sukhinder Singh Cassidy, CEO of Xero*	54
The perils of expertise *Richard Bistrong, anti-bribery compliance consultant*	77
Ripple effects of tragedy *David Epstein, investigative journalist and author*	112
From physics to business *Safi Bahcall, physicist, entrepreneur and author*	145
The Beyoncé blind spot *Marcus Collins, marketing professor and author*	177
Taking on a tycoon *Julie Inman Grant, Australia's eSafety Commissioner*	214
One shot to transform *Meg Bear, former President and Chief Product Officer of SAP SuccessFactors*	238
Landing on uncertainty *Robert Denney, Air Vice Marshal, Royal Australian Air Force*	259

Tables

Table 1	Mindsets of Seekers and Knowers	49
Table 2	Blindspotting Self-Assessment Tool Data Analysis	278
Table 3	Blindspotting Self-Assessment Tool	280

PROLOGUE

On a chilly, overcast day in February 1993, three men huddled around a booth in a Denny's restaurant in San Jose, California. It was Jensen Huang's thirtieth birthday. As he and his fellow co-founders, Chris Malachowsky and Curtis Priem, signed the founding documents for their new company, they ordered Super Bird sandwiches and bottomless coffee. They chose to call their new company NVIDIA, after the Latin word for envy, and decided the corporate colours would be green.

The trio of electrical engineers had every reason to be confident – each had a stellar reputation within the electronics industry, and with $2 million in seed funding secured, they were primed for success. But the journey ahead would be far more treacherous than any of them anticipated.

In the early 1990s, video games were mostly confined to consoles such as the Super Nintendo and the Sega Mega Drive (or the Genesis, as it was known in North America). Graphics were two-dimensional (2D), and though enjoyable for their time, they were a far cry from the sophisticated visual experiences we enjoy today. Huang, NVIDIA's chief executive officer (CEO), and his co-founders could see a future where three-dimensional (3D) graphics would revolutionise gaming, and they were determined to be at the forefront of it.

The decision they made in that Denny's booth was bold – and it almost destroyed them.

Rather than entering the crowded 2D graphics-chip market, NVIDIA chose to gamble on 3D. Their first chip, the NV1, was designed to render images using quadrilaterals (quads), a novel approach that Huang believed was superior to the industry standard of using triangles. The logic was sound: quads could offer more flexibility in rendering complex shapes. But NVIDIA soon discovered they had severely misjudged the market.

Game developers, the lifeblood of NVIDIA's success, were accustomed to rendering images with triangles. The industry had standardised around this method, and there was no appetite to shift to quads, regardless of their potential. The result? The NV1 was a commercial disaster. NVIDIA shipped 250,000 units of their new graphics chip. All but 1,000 were returned. Huang would later admit, 'It was a great technology achievement. It was a terrible product. The list of mistakes that we made, and that I made, in the company's first three years, you really could write a book.'[1]

Huang and his co-founders had assumed their technical expertise would be enough to lead the market towards a new standard. But they failed to see a critical blind spot: while their approach might have been theoretically superior, it was out of sync with what their target market wanted. The NV1 debacle should have been a wake-up call. But instead of pivoting, NVIDIA doubled down on the same approach.

Their next chip, the NV2, also rendered images using quads, and once again, they banked on the hope that game developers would eventually come around. But in August 1995, Microsoft released Windows 95, igniting the personal computer (PC) revolution Huang had anticipated. A month later, Microsoft introduced DirectX, a suite of tools that set the standard for how software and games would interact with PC hardware – and it standardised the use of triangles for rendering graphics.

NVIDIA had misjudged the market.

Huang realised the gravity of their situation: 'The architecture we chose was clever at the time, but it turned out to have been the wrong architecture completely. And so the question is: what do we do?'[2]

The answer lay in honesty and an unexpected lifeline.

By this point, NVIDIA had caught the attention of gaming giant Sega, who was hoping to use NVIDIA's NV2 technology for their forthcoming console. But with DirectX now dominating the market and NVIDIA's graphics chip incompatible with the triangle rendering standard, the partnership was on the verge of collapse. Huang knew he had to act quickly if he wanted to save his company.

In the summer of 1996, just three years after NVIDIA's founding, Huang sat down with the CEO of Sega America, Shoichiro Irimajiri, for one of the most important meetings of his career. Humbled by the failures of the NV1 and NV2, Huang admitted to Irimajiri that NVIDIA had made a critical error with their architecture. The product they had been contracted to deliver was doomed.

Huang then made a bold request: he asked Sega to pay out the contract in full, even though NVIDIA had failed to deliver a viable product. 'I needed Sega to pay us in whole or NVIDIA would be out of business,' Huang later recounted.[3]

To his surprise, Irimajiri did not shut the door on NVIDIA. Instead, he admired Huang's honesty and saw potential in Huang and his team, despite their setbacks. 'I wanted to make NVIDIA successful,' Irimajiri recalled years later. 'Somehow.'[4]

Against all odds, Irimajiri convinced Sega's headquarters to not only pay out the contract but to invest an additional $5 million into NVIDIA, buying the fledgling company six more months to survive. 'It was all the money that we had,' Huang said. '[Irimajiri's] understanding and generosity gave us six months to live.'[5]

'Confronting our mistake, and with humility asking for help, saved NVIDIA,' Huang said in a commencement address to National Taiwan University in 2023. 'These traits are the hardest for the brightest and most successful.'[6]

That moment marked a turning point for NVIDIA. With his back against the wall, Huang knew the only way forward was to abandon the company's flawed approach and realign with the industry standard.

Armed with Sega's financial lifeline and newfound clarity, NVIDIA went back to the drawing board. They scrapped their quad-based architecture and committed to rendering images using triangles, in line with DirectX and the rest of the industry. But time was not on their side. NVIDIA had only six months to develop a new graphics chip – an impossible task under normal circumstances, as it typically took two years to bring a new chip to market.

Huang, however, was determined. He had heard about a Silicon Valley startup, Ikos, that had developed an emulator – a massive piece of hardware that could simulate the functionality of another device.

When Huang contacted Ikos, he learnt they had just gone out of business. But there was one last emulator sitting in a warehouse, a large piece of hardware the size of a fridge and with a price tag of one million dollars at the time. With NVIDIA's future hanging in the balance, Huang purchased the emulator, hoping it would help them deliver their new product on time. It would also use up much of their rapidly depleting funds.

The gamble worked. NVIDIA's third graphics chip, the Riva 128, was developed and released in a record-breaking six months. And this time, it rendered images in triangles rather than quads.

The Riva 128 was a massive success. It sold one million units in its first four months, catapulting NVIDIA back into the spotlight and saving the company from certain collapse. Not only had NVIDIA managed to survive, but they had also learnt how to streamline their development process, allowing them to release new products at twice the pace of their competitors.

'The Riva 128 shocked the young market, put us on the map, and saved the company,' Huang said.[7]

From that moment on, NVIDIA built its entire corporate culture around the principle that had saved them: intellectual honesty. It became one of the company's five corporate values and is still in place today.

For Huang, the key to NVIDIA's long-term success wasn't just about creating cutting-edge technology. It was about recognising blind spots before they became fatal mistakes. 'The ability to call a spade a spade, to act as quickly as possible to recognise that we've made a mistake, and that we learn from it and quickly adjust,' Huang explained, became one of NVIDIA's core values.[8]

Huang's willingness as a leader to admit mistakes and seek help – both from Sega and from his own team – became a cornerstone of NVIDIA's culture. As the company grew, this mindset allowed them to innovate rapidly and adapt to the ever-changing landscape of technology.

NVIDIA's survival isn't only a story of technical innovation. It is a story of humility in the face of failure and the courage to pivot when it matters most.

'I think it's when the company faces adversity of extraordinary proportions – when there's no reason for the company to survive, when you're looking at incredible odds – that's when culture is developed, character is developed,' Huang reflected years later.[9]

NVIDIA should have failed, but because of these principles, they soared to unprecedented heights. As Huang put it, 'The company's success is built on a foundation of recognising when we've gone the wrong way and quickly adjusting. That's what keeps us moving forward.'[10]

Jensen Huang is currently the longest-serving CEO in Silicon Valley, described by Facebook founder Mark Zuckerberg as 'like Taylor Swift, but for tech'.[11] He has been listed as one of *Time* magazine's 100 most influential people, named the best CEO in the world by *Harvard Business Review*, and recognised as *Fortune* magazine's Businessperson of the Year. He is known for wearing his trademark black leather suit and leads a company that is transforming virtually every part of our lives.

Huang's story is a reminder that success doesn't come from avoiding mistakes but from learning from them. It's a lesson that resonates far beyond the world of technology, offering timeless wisdom for leaders in every industry: be honest about your blind spots, be curious about new possibilities and be flexible enough to change course when necessary.

INTRODUCTION

Imagine walking into a room filled with the brightest minds in your organisation, each person looking to you for direction. There's an implicit expectation that you, as the leader, will know exactly what to do. You've been trained for this. You've honed your skills for years, developed expertise and built a reputation as someone who always knows the answer. But what if, in that moment, the most important thing you could do was admit, 'I don't know'?

For most of us, this seems counterintuitive, if not outright dangerous. Isn't leadership about decisiveness? Isn't it about having the answers when no one else does? And yet, what if true leadership, the kind that drives innovation and resilience in today's fast-moving world, isn't about always knowing but about recognising and embracing what you don't know?

This book is about exactly that – shining a light on our blind spots, the hidden gaps in our thinking and decision-making that can have profound consequences, not just for ourselves but also for the teams and organisations we lead. It's about becoming aware of our intellectual limitations, questioning our assumptions and embracing the unknown with curiosity and flexibility. By practising blindspotting, leaders can develop the skills needed to navigate uncertainty, foster creativity and make better decisions.

In the past, leadership was often said to be about expertise. Leaders were seen as the people with the most knowledge and experience, the ones who could make decisions quickly and decisively. But the challenges leaders face today are more complex and interconnected than ever before, and they can't be solved with expertise alone – they require collaboration, creativity and an openness to learning.

We live in a world where complexity, ambiguity and disruption have become the norm. The rise of artificial intelligence is transforming education and employment, as well as raising challenging questions around ethics. Geopolitical tensions across the globe continue to blur the lines of traditional warfare and extend to economic sanctions, cyber attacks and disinformation. Fluctuating interest rates, inflation and market volatility make it difficult for individuals and businesses to plan ahead. The shift to remote work during the COVID-19 pandemic and the resistance to return to previous ways of working is causing lingering issues for employers and their workforce alike. Meanwhile, the widening polarisation of societal views on contentious issues is increasingly causing divisions not only in communities but also within organisations and between employees.

Traditional approaches to leadership – those based on hierarchical decision-making and controlling information flow – are no longer sufficient. Complex issues require complex solutions. The ambiguous world we need to navigate requires leaders to be aware of what they don't know, to be open to having their own biases challenged and to be willing to accept that their personal views may not reflect those of the people they lead.

The most effective leaders are those who can adapt to new realities, where the ability to learn, unlearn and pivot is far more valuable than holding all the answers. This is why blindspotting is so crucial: it empowers us to engage with uncertainty, to admit when we don't know something and, most importantly, to learn from our mistakes and grow.

INTRODUCTION

> The most effective leaders are those who can adapt to new realities, where the ability to learn, unlearn and pivot is far more valuable than holding all the answers.

This book is designed to guide you through the challenges facing any type of leader. Whether you're steering a large organisation or leading a small team, whether you're aspiring to corporate responsibility or managing a community sports club, this book is written for you. Teachers, parents and community leaders alike will be able to apply the practical tools within its pages, and they'll help you navigate the complexities of leadership. With a focus on growth and responsibility, *Blindspotting* will equip you to have the most positive impact possible, no matter your role or job title.

If you're tasked with influencing others and making tough decisions in any capacity, it is my hope that this book will become your guide. By embracing the practice of blindspotting, you will learn to see what others might overlook, empowering you to make smarter decisions and inspire those around you to do the same.

WHAT BLINDSPOTTING MEANS FOR YOU

So, what is blindspotting? I have coined this term to describe, at its core, the practice of recognising and addressing your intellectual blind spots. It's about being aware of the limitations in your knowledge and actively seeking out different perspectives and ideas that challenge your assumptions.

Blindspotting rests on three key mindsets:

Be Honest: Admit what you don't know and be transparent about your limitations. It involves being truthful not only with yourself but also with others about where your knowledge ends and when you need outside input.

Be Curious: Cultivate a deep desire to explore new ideas, ask questions and seek out alternative viewpoints.

Curiosity can drive you to be more innovative and creative, allowing you to discover possibilities you hadn't previously considered.

Be Flexible: Develop the capacity to adapt your thinking and decision-making when new information becomes available. This means being open to changing your mind when needed and not being rigidly attached to your initial assumptions or beliefs.

These three mindsets work together to help leaders become more effective in an increasingly complex world. If we embrace blindspotting we are better equipped to handle ambiguity, engage with a variety of different viewpoints and foster an environment where learning and experimentation are valued.

Blindspotting is not a weakness; it's a strength. It requires humility, but it also builds resilience. When we are willing to admit our blind spots and actively seek out new perspectives, we are more likely to make better decisions, avoid costly mistakes and inspire others to do the same.

As you read through this book, you might start recognising some of your own blind spots – moments when you made decisions based on incomplete information, failed to question your assumptions, or missed opportunities because you were too focused on what you thought you knew.

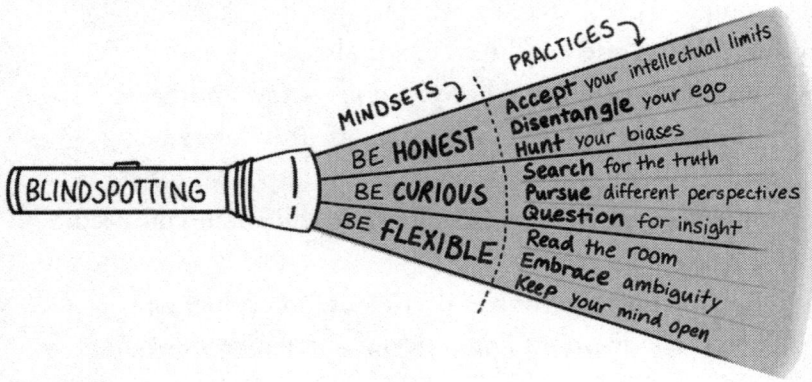

Failing to practise blindspotting can have serious consequences for us, our organisations and our teams. Leaders who are unwilling to admit their blind spots might inadvertently create cultures of closed-mindedness, where team members are discouraged from questioning the status quo or sharing new ideas. This stifles innovation and can lead to workplace cultures where those we lead feel unable to speak up.

Driving along the highway one day, I caught sight of a large, illuminated sign that would normally warn of an accident ahead. But instead of the usual warning, this sign flashed a different message: 'Blind spot check – better safe than unseen.' It was a simple, yet powerful reminder. Just as we're urged to consider our blind spots when driving, we should also reflect on the blind spots in our thinking. It's about more than avoiding accidents – it's about being proactive, aware and deliberate in how we navigate through our thoughts and decisions. Better safe than unseen.

In a world where artificial intelligence and machine learning are reshaping industries and revolutionising decision-making at a record pace, our greatest advantage lies in something uniquely human: the ability to pause, reflect and question where we might be wrong. The courage to confront our intellectual blind spots is what truly sets us apart in this age of technology.

MOMENTS OF IMPACT

As leaders, we all have moments that define us – moments where we lift others up and moments where, perhaps unknowingly, we let others down. If you reflect on your life, you can probably recall leaders who have had a positive impact on you – a teacher or a coach who believed in your potential before anyone else did, or maybe a manager who truly listened to your ideas and gave you the confidence to succeed.

On the flip side, it's also likely you remember leaders who stifled your creativity or ignored your feedback, leaving you feeling unheard or undervalued.

These moments of leadership, both positive and negative, stick with us. But here's the challenge: while it's easy to recall how others have impacted us, it's much harder to recognise when we've been the leader who created those memorable moments for someone else. The truth is, we all have blind spots – gaps in our perception of how we are seen and how we affect others.

Blindspotting is a powerful framework that can help us avoid these negative moments of impact by encouraging us to be intellectually honest, curious and flexible. It challenges us to acknowledge our limitations and biases and to recognise that we don't always see the full picture. By embracing the idea that we don't know everything and that we might be wrong, we become more open to learning and growing as leaders. In doing so, we're far more likely to have a positive, lasting impact on the people we lead.

The best leaders are those who understand that leadership is not about having all the answers but about being willing to listen, learn and adapt. By practising blindspotting, we create an environment where our teams feel valued and heard, where everyone's perspective is taken into account, and where creativity and innovation can thrive.

> **The best leaders are those who understand that leadership is not about having all the answers but about being willing to listen, learn and adapt.**

THE ORIGINS OF BLINDSPOTTING

You might be wondering why I am so passionate about blindspotting and why I believe it is an essential practice for today's leaders. The truth is, my own leadership journey has been shaped by moments of recognising my blind spots – moments where I thought I had all the answers, only to realise that I didn't.

I've had the privilege of leading in a wide range of environments, from serving in the military to navigating the complex world of corporate boardrooms. I've led teams through times of crisis, been involved with large-scale transformations and challenging mergers and acquisitions. Through these experiences, I've learnt that leadership is not about having all the answers – it's about asking the right questions.

My interest in what makes a great leader began early in my career when I served in the Royal Australian Air Force (RAAF). As a young officer, I was thrust into leadership roles that required me to make important decisions in high-pressure environments. I quickly learnt that my success as a leader depended not on my ability to project confidence or certainty, but on my ability to listen, learn and adapt. In the military it is especially obvious that the best leaders are those who can remain calm under pressure, acknowledge what they don't know and seek input from those around them.

This lesson was reinforced throughout my corporate career. I've worked in industries ranging from law to business, and in each role I've encountered situations where my initial assumptions were challenged and I had to adapt my thinking. Leadership is not about always being right – it's about being willing to change your mind when new information comes to light.

My academic background has also shaped my understanding of leadership. I hold a PhD in leadership and culture, and I've spent years studying the factors that contribute to making a person an effective leader. One of the most important insights I've gained is that leaders who are willing to engage in blindspotting – those who can admit their limitations, remain curious and adapt to change – are more likely to succeed in today's complex world.

Throughout my career, I've had the privilege of working with and learning from some of the world's most creative and inspiring leaders.

I've seen firsthand how leaders who practise blindspotting can create cultures of innovation, foster high-performing teams and drive meaningful change. This book is my way of sharing those lessons with you.

WHAT YOU WILL LEARN IN THIS BOOK

Blindspotting is designed to be a practical guide for leaders who want to develop the skills needed to navigate today's complex world. Whether you're leading a small team or a large organisation, the concepts in this book will help you become a more effective leader. Here's a preview of what you'll learn:

- **Part 1: The power of blindspotting** is where we'll explore the concept of blindspotting in depth. You'll learn about intellectual honesty, curiosity and cognitive flexibility – and why they are essential qualities for leaders. We'll also discuss the common thinking traps that prevent us from seeing our blind spots and how to avoid them.
- **Part 2: The three blindspotting mindsets** will introduce us to the foundations of blindspotting – how to be honest, be curious and be flexible. You will explore each of these mindsets to understand what they involve, the benefits they can offer you and those you lead, and the best time to put them into action.
- **Part 3: Putting blindspotting into practice** is all about action – the 'how to' of blindspotting. In the final section of this book, you will learn practical strategies for implementing blindspotting as a leader and creating a culture of blindspotting within your team or organisation. We'll also explore real-world case studies of companies that have successfully used blindspotting to drive innovation, growth and success.
- **Appendix: The blindspotting self-assessment tool** has been designed to accompany your reading of this book. You will be able to receive a free, personalised report on your

blindspotting abilities. The appendix explains how the tool was developed and where you can access it online.

Between every chapter in this book you will also find an interview with an extraordinary leader about how they have used the principles of blindspotting in their career. These stories are designed to bring the concept of blindspotting to life, providing real-world examples of how intellectual honesty, curiosity and cognitive flexibility can be applied in leadership. I had the privilege of speaking with leaders about their experience of blindspotting, including: Wendy McMahon, President of CBS News and Stations; Sukhinder Singh Cassidy, CEO of Xero; Richard Bistrong, anti-bribery, ethics and compliance consultant and former anti-bribery offender; David Epstein, investigative journalist and author; Safi Bahcall, physicist, entrepreneur and author; Marcus Collins, marketing professor and author; Julie Inman Grant, Australia's eSafety Commissioner; Meg Bear, former President and Chief Product Officer of SAP SuccessFactors; and Air Vice Marshal Robert Denney of the RAAF. Each of these leaders offers a unique perspective on how they have used blindspotting to challenge assumptions, navigate complexity and lead with openness and adaptability in their lives and careers. It is my hope their stories will inspire you to embrace honesty, curiosity and flexibility in your leadership practice, as well as help you discover actionable strategies that you can implement as a leader today.

In addition to these detailed stories, I also had the opportunity to interview impressive leaders and experts from various fields, each of whom has shared valuable insights for this book. These include: Cindy Hook, CEO of the Brisbane 2032 Olympic and Paralympic Games; Chris Havrilla, Vice President of Oracle Cloud Human Capital Management Product Strategy; Duncan Mavin, international financial journalist and author; Marlene Poynder, Managing Director of the Carlyle Hotel; Megan Reitz, Associate Fellow at Saïd Business School, University of Oxford; and Pia Lauritzen, philosopher and tech entrepreneur. Their perspectives, incorporated within the chapters of this book, further enrich the conversation of how blindspotting plays a critical role in leadership across different industries and disciplines.

INTELLECTUAL HUMILITY vs INTELLECTUAL HONESTY

The foundation of blindspotting hinges on the often overlooked theory of intellectual humility. While this concept has seen a surge of interest in academic circles over the last decade, particularly among psychologists and philosophers, it remains largely unfamiliar to the corporate world. And this isn't entirely surprising. The term 'humility' can be a stumbling block for many leaders. It evokes unease, partly because humility is often misunderstood as a sign of weakness. Many leaders hear the word 'humility' and mistakenly think it requires diminishing themselves or displaying meekness in a way that detracts from their authority or confidence.

Standard dictionary definitions don't help clear this up. The Oxford English Dictionary, for example, defines humility as 'the quality of having a low opinion of oneself; meekness, lowliness, humbleness: the opposite of pride or haughtiness'. And Merriam-Webster describes humility as 'freedom from pride or arrogance'. It's no wonder many leaders, particularly those in high-pressure, high-stakes environments, view humility as something incompatible with the confidence and decisiveness their roles demand.

However, peeling back these definitions shows that humility – especially intellectual humility – is anything but a weakness. On the contrary, it's a powerful tool for growth, innovation and adaptability. It allows us to acknowledge our limitations and gaps in knowledge, creating space for learning, collaboration and better decision-making. But even for those who recognise the value of humility, it can be an awkward term to embrace. After all, how often do we hear someone openly aspire to have humility? Or worse, boast about how humble they are? It's jarring, to say the least.

That's why in this book I have chosen to frame the conversation around intellectual honesty rather than intellectual humility. Not just because it's more comfortable to use, but also because it's more actionable. Where humility can feel abstract or even passive, honesty is something any leader can actively practise and demonstrate. It's a way of engaging with the world, your team and yourself that demands transparency, self-awareness and a genuine commitment to seeking the truth.

That said, it's important to clarify that we're not simply swapping one term for another. Intellectual humility and intellectual honesty are distinct concepts, and both play crucial roles in the practice of blindspotting.

> **Intellectual humility and intellectual honesty are distinct concepts, and both play crucial roles in the practice of blindspotting.**

While the two concepts are distinct, they do overlap in important ways. Humility allows us to step back, question our assumptions and acknowledge we don't have all the answers. Honesty, on the other hand, pushes us forward – to critically engage with new information, challenge our biases and pursue the truth with integrity.

Both intellectual humility and intellectual honesty ask us to recognise our cognitive limitations and the biases that influence our thinking. Both require us to approach new information with an open mind and a willingness to be proven wrong. And both challenge us to seek truth over comfort, learning over ego.

In the context of blindspotting, intellectual humility and intellectual honesty are the twin pillars underpinning the Be Honest mindset to support our ability to see what others might miss. Together, they form a powerful, practical framework for decision-making, innovation and leadership in fast-moving, decision-driven environments.

In the chapters that follow, we'll dive deeper into how you can master the mindset of intellectual honesty in your leadership and your organisation. We'll explore how to identify and overcome the biases that cloud your judgement, how to cultivate intellectual humility without undermining your authority, and how to create environments where truth, learning and innovation can thrive. Together, these practices will help you master the art of blindspotting.

LET'S BEGIN THE JOURNEY OF BLINDSPOTTING

The journey you're about to embark on will challenge you to think differently about leadership. It will ask you to question your assumptions, embrace ambiguity and remain open to learning. But in doing so, it will help you become a more effective leader – one who is better equipped to navigate the complexities of today's world.

As you read through the following chapters, I encourage you to reflect on your own leadership journey. What assumptions have you made that need to be questioned? How can you foster a culture of curiosity and intellectual honesty within your organisation? Where do you think your blind spots might hide?

By the time you finish this book, you'll not only understand the importance of blindspotting, but you'll also have the tools to put it into practice. Whether you're leading a team of two or two thousand, blindspotting empowers you to make smarter choices that will benefit you and those you impact.

Once you unlock the transformative power of blindspotting, it won't just change the way you approach your work – it will redefine how you interact with the world around you and, most importantly, how you see and understand yourself.

It's time to delve deeper into how this mindset can reshape your leadership, your decision-making and your ability to thrive in a rapidly changing world. So, let's get started: the world of blindspotting is waiting, and the rewards are endless.

PART 1

THE POWER OF BLINDSPOTTING

1

SEE WHAT OTHERS MISS

Imagine you're walking through a forest at night with a torch in your hand. At first, you're using the torch on its dimmest setting, just enough to see a few steps ahead of you. You feel safe. You trust the torch's light, even though it doesn't show you the full picture of your surroundings. You walk cautiously, hoping that nothing unexpected lies in the darkness beyond.

But then something changes – you turn up the power, the beam brightens. Suddenly, it doesn't only light the path ahead but also illuminates the trees, the landscape and everything you couldn't see before. You realise how much you were missing with your dimmed beam – hidden paths, obstacles that would have made you stumble, and opportunities you might have passed by. You can see further and more clearly. With the full power of the torch, you have a better understanding of where you're going.

This is the essence of blindspotting. Each of us walks through life using a dim light to navigate the complex world around us, seeing only a fraction of what's there. But when we learn to use the power of our metaphorical torch – when we embrace the blindspotting mindsets of honesty, curiosity and flexibility – we can light up the full picture, revealing the hidden paths and potential stumbling blocks in our way. Only by using the full power of that torch can we see clearly and make the best decisions for ourselves and the people we lead.

Let's begin by diving into the practice of blindspotting and the mindset shifts that can elevate our leadership and decision-making.

First, we will explore the power of blindspotting and what exactly blindspotting entails – how to see what others miss. The core idea is simple yet profound: by acknowledging that we don't know everything, we open ourselves to new perspectives, ideas and innovation.

UNDERSTANDING BLINDSPOTTING

Blindspotting is the practice of being honest about the ways our thinking can be flawed, being curious in order to understand what we may be missing, and being flexible of mind so as to see the whole picture.

In 1938, some of the most powerful figures in the automobile industry gathered for lunch at the Waldorf Astoria in New York. Seated among the titans of industry, executives and leading suppliers, attendees eagerly awaited the keynote speaker – a man who had revolutionised the world of cars, engineering and beyond. His name was Charles F. Kettering, a prolific inventor whose work had shaped modern life in ways few could rival. By this time, Kettering had racked up over 300 patents, including lead gasoline, the electrical starter motor for cars and advances in refrigeration and air conditioning. He was a legend in his field and a true figure of influence. So, when Kettering took the stage, the room fell silent.

What came next, however, stunned the audience.

Instead of delivering a speech filled with certainties and predictions about the future of the automobile industry, Kettering said something almost unthinkable for a leader of his stature: 'If we could get this idea that we know very much about anything out of our minds,' he said, 'we have a wonderful future ahead of us – in any line of business – if we will just lift the lid and say we know so little about anything.'[1]

This was blindspotting in its most powerful form – acknowledging what you don't know. It's the key to embracing intellectual honesty and allowing curiosity to guide you into uncharted territory. At a time when gasoline powered every vehicle on the road, Kettering challenged the automotive industry's brightest minds to consider a radical new idea: cars powered by the sun. 'I haven't the slightest idea how to do it,' Kettering admitted to a room filled with executives and industrialists.[2] But that didn't matter. What mattered was that he was willing to entertain the possibility. And that, he believed, was the key to unlocking innovation.

Kettering's message was clear – real progress would come not from clinging to what you already know, but from opening your mind to what you don't.

Less than twenty years later, General Motors (GM) – the very company where Kettering was once the long-time vice president of research – unveiled the world's first solar-powered vehicle. It was called the Sunmobile, a tiny 15-inch model Corvette fitted with eight solar cells on the hood. Invented by GM engineer William G. Cobb, the Sunmobile made its debut at a car convention in Chicago in 1955. Though small, this working model was a breakthrough. To the rapturous applause of onlookers, Cobb drove the miniature Sunmobile across the stage, showcasing the power of harnessing solar energy.

Kettering's willingness to embrace his blind spots and admit that he didn't have all the answers had paved the way for possibilities that had once seemed far-fetched. By publicly calling for intellectual honesty, Kettering had role-modelled blindspotting. His openness to uncertainty created a culture where innovation could thrive in the automobile industry, and ideas that were once unimaginable became reality.

In a world where leaders are often pressured to have all the answers, Kettering showed the real key to success lies in our willingness to question, to doubt and to see the world with fresh eyes. His legacy reminds us that when we embrace blindspotting – when we are intellectually honest, curious and flexible – we open ourselves up to a future where anything is possible.

The more we commit to practising blindspotting, the more it will become second nature – an instinctive part of how we see ourselves, engage with others and interpret the world around us. Just as Charles F. Kettering demonstrated, acknowledging what we don't know is not a weakness but a strength. Blindspotting acts as the engine that drives individual leaders and entire organisational cultures towards greater creativity and a lasting positive impact.

Rather than saying 'I don't know', Kettering would have been more accurate to say, 'I don't know . . . yet.'

Blindspotting transforms how we think about ourselves, what we believe we know and the kinds of information we actively seek out. It sharpens our mental agility, equipping us with the tools to navigate uncertainty – whether that's technological, financial or social – and helps us tackle these complex challenges. By integrating blindspotting into our leadership, we're more likely to make more informed, thoughtful decisions and create environments where flexibility and curiosity thrive.

> **Blindspotting transforms how we think about ourselves, what we believe we know and the kinds of information we actively seek out.**

Blindspotting also encourages us to actively seek out a variety of perspectives and to collaborate with individuals different from ourselves. It's a practice that enables us to value the contributions of others, even when their views diverge from our own. It helps us approach difficult conversations with an open mind. In doing so, blindspotting fosters more inclusive, innovative environments where differences are seen as opportunities, not obstacles.

As we dive deeper into the benefits of blindspotting in the chapters ahead, remember Kettering's lesson: true progress comes from being open to the unknown, challenging what we think we know and embracing the possibilities we might not yet see. This is the foundation on which blindspotting is built.

THE THREE BLINDSPOTTING MINDSETS

Blindspotting is based around three powerful theories – intellectual honesty, intellectual curiosity and cognitive flexibility. Put more simply, the three mindsets of blindspotting are: Be Honest, Be Curious and Be Flexible. These aren't abstract ideas; they're practical ways of thinking and leading that, when embraced, can help you see what others miss.

When we operationalise these three mindsets, blindspotting becomes a practice that equips us with actionable tools for making better decisions and cultivating healthier, more resilient organisational and team cultures. Leaders who draw on honesty, curiosity and flexibility are able to adapt to the fast-changing world around them, spotting opportunities and challenges others might overlook. More importantly, they create environments where innovation and critical thinking can thrive.

The foundations of blindspotting are drawn from the latest research in psychology and philosophy. These fields provide a scientific and philosophical backbone to the practice, but what makes blindspotting truly transformative is how it applies these theories in a practical, action-oriented way – one that leaders can immediately

use to boost their effectiveness and guide their organisations through rapid change.

When writing my previous book, *Head & Heart: The art of modern leadership*, I collaborated with Queensland University of Technology to develop the Head & Heart Leader Scale (headheartleader.com), a tool designed to measure eight key attributes of modern leadership. Since its launch in 2023, tens of thousands of people from around the world have completed the scale, and the data generated supports the three mindsets that underpin blindspotting. The research I have undertaken to develop the eight attributes of head and heart leadership, and the three mindsets of blindspotting, share many interrelated characteristics.

The modern leadership attribute of curiosity, specifically intellectual curiosity, is reflected in the blindspotting mindset Be Curious. What we know from the data of the Head & Heart Leader Scale is that curiosity is consistently the highest scored modern leadership attribute – most people self-assess themselves as being highly curious.

The modern leadership attribute of humility, or more accurately, intellectual humility, is reflected in the blindspotting mindset Be Honest. The data confirms what we would intuitively expect: there is a close relationship between intellectual humility and intellectual curiosity. It is only when we are able to humbly accept the limits of our knowledge that we are likely to be curious enough to search for answers.

Finally, the modern leadership attribute of perspective, which requires us to demonstrate cognitive flexibility, is represented by the blindspotting mindset Be Flexible. Leading with perspective means 'reading the room' and constantly reading the signals around us, whether in our team, organisation or industry. It involves assessing new information and adjusting our course of action accordingly. The survey results showed that perspective is a truly special quality and those who self-assess themselves as having this trait were much more likely to score higher than average in all eight of the modern leadership attributes.

The data is clear: when leaders embody the mindsets of honesty, curiosity and flexibility, something remarkable happens. It is this research and experience that helped develop the blindspotting mindsets. Be Honest. Be Curious. Be Flexible.

The magic of blindspotting lies in the synergy of these three mindsets working together. When we embrace honesty, curiosity and flexibility, we unlock a new level of awareness and insight, empowering ourselves and our teams to make better decisions and drive meaningful change.

WHAT BLINDSPOTTING IS NOT

Blindspotting isn't about second-guessing yourself or constantly wavering in your decisions. It doesn't mean abandoning the confidence you've developed through years of expertise, nor does it require you to doubt your abilities or undermine your own judgement. It is not indecisiveness or a lack of conviction. Blindspotting is about calibration, not hesitation. It's about being clear-headed and methodical in how you align your confidence with the strength of the evidence and information you have available, without falling prey to overconfidence or rigid thinking.

> **Blindspotting is about calibration, not hesitation.**

Many leaders, especially those in high-pressure environments where quick decisions are critical, might fear that adopting the practice of blindspotting could be seen as a sign of weakness or uncertainty. But blindspotting does not mean you should avoid making bold decisions or never hold strong convictions. It doesn't mean becoming wishy-washy or flip-flopping on your opinions whenever new data arises. On the contrary: it is about making sure your convictions are rooted in reality and that your decisions are well grounded, not based on outdated assumptions or unchecked biases.

What blindspotting teaches us is that true strength lies in being adaptable, not inflexible. As a leader, holding strong views can be crucial – the people we lead often look to us for direction and confidence. However, practising blindspotting ensures that those views are aligned with the reality we're facing, not rooted in the comfort of what we've always believed to be true.

Blindspotting is not about abandoning your instincts or erasing your leadership experience. It doesn't mean disregarding your expertise, nor does it suggest that you shouldn't trust yourself when making tough decisions. Blindspotting helps you recognise when your expertise might have reached its limits, when it's time to seek new perspectives, and when it's essential to acknowledge that you don't have all the answers . . . yet. It's not doubting yourself; it's having the wisdom to know when you need to listen to learn. This is the hallmark of a truly great leader – someone who knows when to lead with conviction but who is also astute enough to adapt when circumstances change.

At its core, blindspotting is about aligning the strength of your beliefs with the evidence you've gathered. It's about holding your beliefs lightly – not abandoning them at the first sign of contradiction but being ready to revise them when compelling new information comes to light. It's a disciplined way of thinking that ensures you are not blindly charging ahead with outdated ideas or assumptions. It encourages you to ask: 'Do I have enough information to make this decision? Am I relying on what I've always known, or am I considering new evidence?'

The beauty of blindspotting is that it allows you to be both confident and curious, both decisive and flexible. You can still lead with conviction, but you do so with the awareness that conviction should be proportional to evidence. If new data challenges your thinking, you don't ignore it out of pride or fear of being seen as weak – you adjust, recalibrate and move forward even stronger than before. It's this agility that makes blindspotting such a powerful tool for leaders in fast-moving, complex environments.

> **The beauty of blindspotting is that it allows you to be both confident and curious, both decisive and flexible.**

Leaders who practise blindspotting develop a unique advantage. We become skilled at identifying when our assumptions need to be questioned, when more information is needed and when it's time to stick to our convictions. We also cultivate a culture of intellectual honesty within our teams – where questions are encouraged, where a variety of perspectives are valued and where flexibility is seen as a strength, not a weakness.

Blindspotting won't weaken your leadership – it will make your leadership stronger. It will equip you to lead with confidence not because you have all the answers, but because you know how to find them.

BENEFITS OF BLINDSPOTTING

When we embrace blindspotting in our everyday leadership practices and in our approach to solving complex issues, the benefits are far-reaching. Blindspotting results in more effective decision-making, as we are open to challenging assumptions and seeking wide-ranging perspectives before arriving at conclusions. The three mindsets – Be Honest, Be Curious and Be Flexible – also make us more adaptable, strategic and innovative when it comes to navigating complex challenges, enhancing our leadership capabilities.

Leaders who practise blindspotting become more attuned to the needs and ideas of others, too, fostering better interpersonal relationships and encouraging openness and collaboration. This also promotes psychological safety, allowing team members in organisations of any size and in pursuit of any purpose to feel confident in sharing their ideas without fear of judgement. Finally, by practising blindspotting, we will likely experience improved life satisfaction, as we'll gain a deeper understanding of ourselves and the impact we have on those around us, creating a more fulfilling and rewarding leadership journey.

BENEFITS FOR LEADERS
More effective decision-making
Blindspotting equips us with the ability to pause and critically assess our decisions before acting. This deliberate pause is crucial in today's fast-paced environments where decisions are often made quickly and under pressure. Leaders who practise blindspotting understand that certainty doesn't always equate to accuracy. By recognising we might not have all the answers, we become more aware of potential gaps in our reasoning, biases that could cloud our judgement, and assumptions that might not hold up under scrutiny. This results in more balanced and comprehensive decisions that consider all angles.

Enhanced leadership capabilities
Blindspotting encourages us to approach challenges with resilience and curiosity. Rather than seeing failure as a reflection of our abilities or as something to be avoided, we view failure as a learning opportunity. This resilience allows us to continually evolve, ensuring we remain adaptable in rapidly changing environments. Leaders who can absorb setbacks without being paralysed by them also set an important example for their teams, fostering a culture of continuous improvement and growth. By constantly learning from our experiences, we can refine our strategies, making them more effective over time.

Stronger interpersonal relationships
By practising blindspotting, we will be able to build deeper, more meaningful relationships with our teams. Leaders who engage in blindspotting are not just open to receiving feedback, they actively seek it. We listen to others' perspectives without defensiveness and recognise the value of differing opinions. This fosters an environment of trust and respect, where employees feel appreciated and understood,

which not only increases engagement but also encourages more open communication. When team members believe their views are valued, they are more likely to contribute their ideas freely and collaborate more effectively.

Improved life satisfaction
On a personal level, blindspotting can greatly enhance our emotional wellbeing. By acknowledging that we don't need to know everything or be right all the time, we will likely experience less stress and anxiety. This mindset shift frees us from the pressure of constantly needing to validate our worth through our knowledge or decision-making abilities. Instead, we tie our self-worth to continuous learning and growth, which results in greater self-confidence and emotional resilience.

BENEFITS FOR ORGANISATIONS AND TEAMS
Promotes psychological safety
Regardless of the size of the team you lead or the industry you are working within, teams and organisations that embrace blindspotting cultivate a culture of psychological safety, where team members feel comfortable sharing their ideas, raising concerns and offering constructive feedback without fear of judgement or punishment. In such environments, leaders model the mindset of honesty by openly admitting when they don't know something or when they have made a mistake. This creates an atmosphere where team members feel empowered to speak up about issues important to them and their team, allowing them to contribute to decision-making processes without fear of retribution.

Encourages collaboration and inclusivity
Blindspotting promotes a culture of collaboration and inclusivity by encouraging us to actively seek out and value viewpoints other than our own. Differences in perspective are seen as opportunities for learning rather than obstacles. We understand the best

solutions often come from engaging people with different skills, backgrounds and expertise. This inclusivity leads to more creative problem-solving and enhances the organisation's ability to confront challenges in innovative ways.

Fosters continuous learning and innovation

Organisations that embrace blindspotting allow a culture of continuous learning and innovation to thrive. In these organisations, curiosity is encouraged at every level, and team members are motivated to seek out new knowledge, challenge assumptions and explore alternative solutions. Blindspotting ensures that the organisation doesn't become complacent or rigid in its thinking but instead remains agile and adaptable in the face of change.

> **Blindspotting ensures that the organisation doesn't become complacent or rigid in its thinking but instead remains agile and adaptable in the face of change.**

Strengthens organisational culture

Blindspotting enhances an organisation's culture by promoting transparency, trust and open communication among team members at all levels. Leaders who model blindspotting behaviours create an environment where people feel safe to share their ideas and express concerns without fear of criticism or exclusion. This leads to stronger relationships within teams and promotes a culture of continuous improvement.

As we wrap up the first chapter on the power of blindspotting, we've uncovered the many benefits the practice can have for leaders, our teams and our organisations. In the next chapter, we will be introduced to two archetypes you may recognise in yourself and others: Seekers and Knowers. Let's dive in.

KEY TAKEAWAYS

- **The power of admitting 'I don't know . . . yet.'** Inventor and engineer Charles F. Kettering's bold admission of how little he knew exemplifies the strength that comes from a leader acknowledging their intellectual limits. This openness to uncertainty and curiosity to explore unknown possibilities fuels innovation. Real progress comes from embracing what you don't know and seeking new insights rather than clinging to certainty.
- **Blindspotting fosters innovation.** The practice of blindspotting – being honest about knowledge gaps, curious about new possibilities and flexible in thinking – creates a culture where innovation thrives. Leaders who acknowledge their blind spots and actively seek different perspectives are more likely to uncover new solutions and drive creativity within their organisations.
- **Psychological safety is a catalyst for growth.** Blindspotting promotes psychological safety within organisations, where employees feel safe to share ideas without fear of judgement. This open environment encourages creative risk-taking and experimentation, which are essential for innovation. Leaders who model intellectual humility foster trust and collaboration, leading to high-performing, innovative teams.
- **Continuous learning is the key to adaptability.** Organisations that embrace blindspotting cultivate a culture of continuous learning, where employees and leaders alike are encouraged to challenge assumptions and seek out new knowledge. This mindset allows organisations to remain adaptable and agile in fast-changing environments, ensuring long-term competitiveness and growth.

- **Blindspotting can improve emotional wellbeing.** Practising blindspotting not only enhances decision-making and leadership capabilities but also improves life satisfaction. Leaders who are comfortable admitting their limitations experience less stress, develop stronger relationships and are more emotionally resilient. This mindset shift from needing to be right to valuing continuous learning leads to greater fulfilment both personally and professionally.

FURTHER READING

Mark Alfano, Michael P. Lynch and Alessandra Tanesini (ed), *The Routledge Handbook of Philosophy of Humility* (2021).

Kirstin Ferguson, *Head & Heart: The art of modern leadership* (2023).

Franziska Frank, *The Power of Humility in Leadership: Influencing as a role model* (2023).

Edgar H. Schein and Peter A. Schein, *Humble Leadership: The power of relationships, openness, and trust* (2018).

Daryl Van Tongeren, *Humble: Free yourself from the traps of a narcissistic world* (2022).

LEAPING INTO THE UNKNOWN

> 'Leaders often feel they need to have all the answers.
> But the truth is, we don't.'
> Wendy McMahon, President and CEO, CBS News and Stations

Wendy McMahon never set out to become a trailblazing leader. But in the competitive world of broadcasting and digital media, she rose through the ranks, driven by an unrelenting curiosity and a willingness to admit when she didn't know something.

Wendy and I first connected after I learnt that she had bought copies of my previous book for her leadership team. As a modern leader, Wendy believed strongly in leading with the head and heart, and she wanted to encourage this culture at her workplace.

I wanted to understand more about Wendy's journey and her rise to the top of the broadcast news industry – going from a small newsroom in Savannah, Georgia, to becoming the head of CBS News and Stations. Wendy's decades of experience offer invaluable lessons for corporate leaders grappling with their own blind spots.

'Leaders often feel they need to have all the answers,' Wendy shared with me when we met via Zoom. She was seated in her large sunny office inside the CBS headquarters in Hollywood, Los Angeles. I listened attentively from my own home office on the other side of the Pacific Ocean from Wendy, on the Sunshine Coast, Australia. She continued, 'But the truth is, we don't. And when you're honest about that, it opens space for real growth and collaboration.'

The practice of blindspotting – being intellectually honest, curious and flexible – has become a cornerstone of Wendy's leadership style.

When Wendy accepted a role as senior vice president of digital content for television stations owned by the American Broadcasting Company (ABC) in 2015, it was a leap into the unknown. 'There was nothing on my CV that suggested I was right for that role,' she admitted. 'But I pitched a vision centred on audience engagement and digital storytelling, and I guess it worked.'

At the time, the television industry was on the cusp of seismic changes. Streaming services were emerging as serious competitors to traditional TV networks, but many in the industry remained sceptical. 'The business was split,' Wendy recalled. 'Half held on to the belief that digital was just a blip, while the other half knew it was the future.'

Stepping into the world of digital media was an uncomfortable pivot for Wendy. She had spent her entire career up to that point in television newsrooms, but now she was surrounded by tech experts who knew far more about digital content and streaming platforms than she did. 'It was the most humbling experience of my career,' she told me. 'But it was also the most formative.'

In this new role, Wendy had to lean on her intellectual honesty, a key element of blindspotting. As she wisely recognised, 'When you go into a role where you're the leader, and hundreds of people are looking to you for guidance, it's uncomfortable to admit you don't know everything. But it's also essential if you want to succeed.'

This level of humility, coupled with Wendy's natural curiosity, allowed her to build trust with her team. Rather than dictating every decision, she encouraged collaboration by asking probing questions and actively listening to the experts around her. 'I was deeply curious, always asking why and how,' Wendy explained. 'It wasn't about having all the answers – it was about defining the vision and then letting the people in the room figure out the why and the how.'

Throughout her career, Wendy has leant heavily on her natural curiosity – a trait that was cultivated early in her life. 'I've always been someone who asks questions and seeks to understand,' she said. 'It's why I got into journalism in the first place.'

In the corporate world, this same sense of curiosity has allowed Wendy to stay ahead of the curve and adapt to changing industry trends. This included introducing digital, mobile and streaming videos for each of the ABC-owned television stations in cities such as Chicago, Houston and New York City. 'If you're not constantly curious about what's coming next, you're going to be left behind,' she warned. 'Leaders need to be asking questions all the time: Why are we doing it this way? What if we tried something different? What are we missing?'

This intellectual curiosity also drives Wendy to surround herself with a range of voices and opinions. 'I've always believed that the best ideas come from people who see the world differently than you do,' she explained. 'If you're only listening to people who think like you, you're never going to grow.'

One of Wendy's key insights during her time in digital media was the importance of user-centric thinking. In an era where data-driven decision-making was becoming the norm, Wendy championed the idea that audiences, not executives, should determine the success of a product.

'This idea of A/B testing – putting a product out there and letting the audience decide whether it succeeds or fails – was still fairly new in television,' Wendy said. 'But for those of us in the digital space, it became clear that we were in service to the audience, not the other way around.'

Wendy's team at ABC launched streaming platforms and digital products that brought traditional TV storytelling into the digital realm such as streaming videos from news stations so they could be watched on a mobile phone. 'We didn't know how things would land,' Wendy said. 'But we trusted the audience to show us what was working and what wasn't.'

This willingness to experiment – and fail – became a critical part of Wendy's leadership philosophy. 'I always told my team that failing fast was better than sticking with something that wasn't working,' she said. 'It's all part of being flexible in your thinking and being open to changing direction when the data shows you're wrong.'

Wendy's experiences are a powerful example of intellectual honesty in leadership – a key mindset of blindspotting. As organisations face unprecedented challenges – whether from technology disruptions, market volatility or global crises – leaders who cling to their egos or insist on being the smartest person in the room will find themselves quickly outpaced by more adaptable competitors.

'People think that leadership is about having all the big ideas,' Wendy explained, 'but really, the most successful leaders are the ones who are constantly gathering data, listening to their teams and testing their ideas against reality.' In other words, the best leaders are the ones who aren't afraid to admit what they don't know – and are aware of their intellectual blind spots.

Another big challenge Wendy faced in her leadership journey was fostering a culture where others felt comfortable admitting their own intellectual limitations. In many corporate environments there's pressure to always have the right answer, and leaders who express uncertainty can be seen as weak or indecisive.

But Wendy believes the most effective organisations are those where leaders create an environment of psychological safety, where admitting what you don't know is not just accepted but encouraged. And this attitude starts at the top, as she pointed out: 'If I don't model intellectual honesty, how can I expect my team to be honest with me about their own blind spots?'

This culture of openness became especially important during the COVID-19 pandemic, especially at the beginning of the crisis in 2020. With so many unknowns about the virus and its impact on the world, leaders across all industries were forced to confront their intellectual limitations. 'There were so many times during the pandemic when the only answer to a question was, "I don't know",' Wendy recalled. 'But that's okay. Admitting that uncertainty allowed us to stay flexible and adapt as new information came in.'

For Wendy, being honest about what she didn't know created a stronger bond with her team. 'When you're transparent about your own blind spots, it gives others permission to do the same,' she said. 'It fosters collaboration and ensures that decisions are made based on the best available information – not just on one person's opinion.'

Perhaps the most critical aspect of Wendy's leadership philosophy is her commitment to thinking flexibly and being able to change her mind when new evidence presents itself. 'If you're not willing to change your mind, you're not really listening,' she said. 'And if you're not listening, you're not leading.'

Wendy's flexibility has been a key driver of her success, particularly in an industry as fast changing as media. For example, she was able to think about how mobile phones could be used to consume video news content before others considered the possibility. 'There's no room for rigidity in this business,' she explained. 'You have to be comfortable with constant change and be willing to pivot when things don't go as planned.'

This lesson is particularly relevant for corporate leaders as industries across the board face disruption from technology, globalisation and shifting consumer preferences. The ability to adapt, pivot and stay open to new possibilities separates successful leaders from those who get left behind.

Wendy McMahon's story offers a powerful reminder that leadership isn't about having all the answers. It's about embracing the practice of blindspotting by being intellectually honest, curious and flexible in the face of uncertainty. As industries continue to evolve, leaders who embrace these qualities will be better equipped to navigate complexity, foster innovation and build resilient organisations or teams.

As Wendy put it, 'Leadership isn't about being the smartest person in the room. It's about creating a culture where everyone feels empowered to contribute, ask questions and learn. That's how you build something truly great.'

For leaders looking to thrive in today's ever-changing world, Wendy's advice is clear: accept your intellectual limitations, stay curious and be flexible enough to adapt when new information comes to light. That's the key to lasting success.

2

DISCOVER SEEKERS AND KNOWERS

Think about the people you've encountered in your life: there are some who are constantly asking questions, always curious and eager to dig deeper to learn. And there are others who believe they already know everything, certain their perspective is the only one that matters. Most of us can recognise these two distinct types: people who are genuinely seeking the truth, and people who have stopped looking because they think they've already found it.

In the practice of blindspotting, I call these two archetypes Seekers and Knowers. Seekers are those who embrace the pursuit of objective

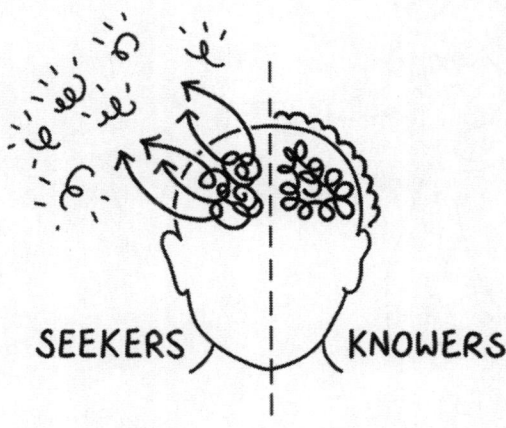

truth, who actively seek to understand and who value the opinions of others to fill in gaps in their knowledge. On the other side of the coin are the Knowers – those who believe they already have all the answers, who feel they possess all the necessary information and who don't see a need to change their mind or question their assumptions.

The difference between Seekers and Knowers is profound, and understanding which archetype you might be at any point in time can transform how you approach leadership, problem-solving and growth.

SEEKERS

We all know those rare individuals who are comfortable admitting what they don't know – people who don't shy away from saying, 'I don't have the answer, but I'm eager to find out.' These people are Seekers and have the courage to admit their limitations when faced with new information or complex situations. Seekers are not only willing to ask for help but also embrace learning from anyone, including the people they lead. For them, the pursuit of knowledge is far more important than the need to appear knowledgeable.

What sets Seekers apart is their unwavering focus on the facts. They're driven by the desire to find the objective truth, not by a need to protect their own ideas or prop up their egos. Seekers take the time to think critically about the sources of information they rely on, rigorously assessing whether the data is relevant, credible and unbiased. When faced with complex issues, they dive in, trying to understand the facts and the motivations behind why someone might hold a particular perspective. Their curiosity isn't limited to validating their own theories – they thrive on discovering new information that challenges what they already think is true.

Instead of worrying about how they might appear to others, Seekers are focused on figuring things out. They find excitement in learning something new, especially if it disrupts their previous understanding. This constant search for truth drives them forward.

> **Instead of worrying about how they might appear to others, Seekers are focused on figuring things out.**

Seekers understand cognitive biases can cloud their judgement and create blind spots, so they actively work to uncover and neutralise them. When they recognise a gap in their knowledge, they eagerly look for other perspectives to fill that void. Their questions aren't designed to win an argument or bolster their own position but to deepen their understanding. Because of this, Seekers listen to different opinions without becoming defensive. They are comfortable engaging with other people's beliefs and can keep their ego in check when their views are challenged. This openness makes them agile thinkers – able to rethink ideas and adjust accordingly when new information surfaces.

Seekers are also better able to tolerate ambiguity. They are at ease with the fact that not every question has a definitive answer, and they can live in that space of uncertainty while still pursuing clarity. They know that life doesn't always present clear-cut solutions and they are okay with that.

Importantly, Seekers have a balanced understanding of their intellectual limits. They're neither trapped by their limitations nor overconfident in what they know. They have an appropriate level of confidence in their beliefs while remaining open to other viewpoints that might challenge those beliefs. Seekers don't doubt themselves at every turn, and they don't allow their convictions to blind them to new insights either. They aren't constantly deferring to others for validation but are aware of when to reconsider their stance in light of fresh perspectives.

> **ARE YOU A SEEKER?**
> To identify whether you tend to adopt the mindset of a Seeker, reflect on the following questions:
> 1. Do you regularly question your own opinions and beliefs, knowing there's a chance you could be wrong?
> 2. When presented with new evidence, are you willing to reconsider and possibly change your stance on an issue?
> 3. Do you value opinions that differ from your own, seeing them as opportunities to expand your understanding rather than threats to your beliefs?
> 4. Are you comfortable admitting that your beliefs or attitudes might be incorrect, even in front of others?
> 5. In the face of conflicting evidence, do you remain open to changing your opinion rather than stubbornly defending your original view?
> 6. Do you actively seek out new information that may challenge or even contradict what you already think is true?
> 7. Do you make a conscious effort to explore opposing viewpoints, rather than surrounding yourself with people or information that confirm your existing beliefs?

> 8. When someone disagrees with you, do you invite them to explain their perspective so that you can fully understand their point of view, rather than shutting down the conversation?
> 9. Are you comfortable admitting when you don't know something and seeking help or advice from others, regardless of their position or status?
> 10. Do you enjoy being proven wrong or learning something new that shifts your thinking, because it means you've grown in knowledge and understanding?

KNOWERS

We've all encountered someone who seems to believe they already know the answer, no matter the situation. These individuals rarely seek out alternative perspectives, convinced they have all the information they need. In the practice of blindspotting, I call these people Knowers. And be warned: we can all be Knowers from time to time.

Knowers tend to hold firm to their opinions, even when faced with clear evidence to the contrary. To them, being right is paramount, and they'll do whatever it takes to defend their position. This unwavering certainty can be comforting in some situations but can also lead to serious blind spots in thinking and decision-making.

For Knowers, questions aren't tools for learning but for winning. Where a Seeker will ask questions out of curiosity, a Knower asks questions to reaffirm their own position – or, at the more extreme end of the spectrum, to trap, dismiss or undermine others. Knowers

tend to overlook the role of bias in their thinking and rarely reflect on how their ingrained assumptions may shape their personal views. Ambiguity makes them uncomfortable; they crave definitive answers and rely on certainty, even when none exists.

There are times when the focus and determination of a Knower can be an asset. For instance, when faced with an urgent task that requires immediate action, a Knower's single-minded focus can help cut through distractions and get the job done. In situations that demand confidence and clarity, especially in times of crisis or in the face of tight deadlines, the assertiveness of a Knower can be useful. However, over time, this approach can limit growth and innovation, particularly when dealing with complex problems that require flexibility and open-mindedness.

> **There are times when the focus and determination of a Knower can be an asset.**

One of the key characteristics of a Knower is their tendency to overestimate their intellectual strengths. They often tie their ego to what they know, and because of this they deprive themselves of opportunities to learn and grow. When their knowledge or opinions are questioned, Knowers frequently feel threatened, latching even more tightly to their beliefs. This defensiveness makes them resistant to feedback and less likely to engage in conversations that challenge their ideas. Instead of seeing these moments as opportunities for growth, Knowers view them as threats to their self-esteem, which leads them to double down on their original views.

Knowers struggle with a deep-seated belief that others have little to teach them. Their worldview is not just a perspective – it's tied to their sense of self-worth and superiority. Whether it's their social status, intelligence, race, gender, religion or political affiliation, they often believe they are right simply because of who they are. For Knowers, the objective truth isn't something to be uncovered through exploration or dialogue; it's something they believe they already possess. This mindset limits the capacity for self-reflection and makes Knowers blind to their own biases.

While the confidence and decisiveness of Knowers can be beneficial in situations that demand quick thinking, these traits can backfire when long-term success and adaptability are needed. Leaders who fall into the Knower mindset risk stifling creativity, alienating their teams and missing out on valuable insights.

Recognising Knower tendencies in ourselves – such as the need to be right or a reluctance to listen to opposing views – can be a first step towards embracing a more open, Seeker-like approach. Blindspotting encourages a combination of both archetypes. By balancing the strengths of the Knower with the humility of a Seeker, we can navigate challenges more effectively, with a clearer perspective and a more collaborative spirit.

> **ARE YOU A KNOWER?**
> To identify whether you tend to adopt the mindset of a Knower, reflect on the following questions:
> 1. Would you rather be right than try to understand why someone else might think you're wrong?
> 2. Do you find it difficult to admit when you're wrong and correct a mistake?
> 3. Do you feel defensive when people disagree with your point of view?
> 4. Do you believe your ideas are usually better than others'?
> 5. Do you think you know all there is to know in a particular area?
> 6. Do people ever comment that you always seem to know the answer?

> 7. When someone challenges your opinion, do you feel the need to prove them wrong?
> 8. Do you often dismiss alternative viewpoints as uninformed or irrelevant?
> 9. Are you uncomfortable when there isn't a clear-cut answer or when you're forced to navigate grey areas?
> 10. Do you avoid asking for help because you assume you know what needs to be done?

These descriptions of Seekers and Knowers are intentionally framed as extremes, representing two distinct archetypes that shape how we approach our understanding of ourselves, others and the world around us. In reality, we all shift between these mindsets depending on the situation, and we exist somewhere along a spectrum between the two. Sometimes we may think more like Seekers – open, curious and willing to admit we don't know everything – while at other times, we may fall into the Knower category, feeling certain and defensive about our beliefs.

The key to blindspotting is recognising when you are leaning more towards being a Seeker or a Knower and choosing the appropriate mindset for the context you're in. This awareness and adaptability are essential skills in blindspotting, allowing you to approach situations with the right balance of confidence and openness.

> **The key to blindspotting is recognising when you are leaning more towards being a Seeker or a Knower and choosing the appropriate mindset for the context you're in.**

A SEEKER MINDSET	A KNOWER MINDSET
Accepts their intellectual limitations	Downplays or denies their intellectual limitations
Able to admit what they don't know	Believes they already have the answer
Keen to understand their biases	Unaware of their biases
Asks questions to learn	Uses questions to win
Values different perspectives	Gets defensive when ideas are challenged
Willing to rethink their ideas	Holds firm to their views
Comfortable with ambiguity	Needs definitive answers

Table 1 – Mindsets of Seekers and Knowers

WHEN KNOWING IS NEEDED

It's easy to think of Seekers as 'good' and Knowers as 'bad', but the reality is far more nuanced. There are situations where being a Knower – confident, decisive and full of conviction – is exactly what's needed. Imagine you are leading your team through a crisis, performing a delicate surgery or handling an emergency where quick, definitive action is required. In those moments, a Knower's mindset is critical. You can't afford to waver, question or explore every option; you need to act and lead with certainty. This is when being a Knower is essential.

However, the art of blindspotting lies in identifying when to be a Seeker and when to lean into being a Knower. It's about reading the room and assessing whether certainty or curiosity is the best approach for the moment.

> The art of blindspotting lies in identifying when to be a Seeker and when to lean into being a Knower.

Earlier in my career, when I was in my mid-thirties, I was promoted to become chief executive of the consulting firm where I was employed. While I had been in senior leadership roles before, this was the first time I was leading an organisation. I remember during this period having two very different experiences of needing to end someone's employment – a tough situation many leaders might find themselves facing at one point or another. In one case, the individual had been underperforming for some time, despite being given numerous chances to improve. I adopted a Seeker's mindset, spending months trying to understand what might be holding them back. I asked questions, provided support and explored different ways to help them succeed. When it was clear there was no change in the employee's performance, the final conversation – while difficult – came as no surprise to the person concerned. It was the culmination of a thoughtful, measured process, and the individual understood why the decision had been made.

In contrast, another situation arose where, as the result of a single, very serious incident, an employee's behaviour was in clear violation of company values and potentially the law. There was no time for multiple discussions or a lengthy process. I had to act swiftly. In this instance, I took on a Knower's mindset and made a swift decision to terminate their employment. The conversation was short, decisive and without room for ambiguity. In that moment, being a Knower was not only appropriate but necessary.

Had I approached the first scenario with a Knower's mindset – immediately telling the underperforming employee they weren't measuring up without seeking to understand their perspective – I would have likely missed important factors that could have potentially changed the outcome. It would have also signalled to my team that I was a leader unlikely to listen to them or to seek understanding, fostering a culture of fear and reducing psychological safety. People I was leading would have learnt to keep their struggles hidden, afraid of the consequences.

Being a Knower is also entirely necessary in certain situations. It's knowing when to adopt that mindset that is the key. Imagine someone walking into a meeting with a fully formed solution, dismissing all other ideas because they believe their approach is correct. They ignore the non-verbal cues of frustration from their colleagues and use questions not to understand but to debate and disprove others' suggestions. This is a Knower who is operating in the wrong context, potentially stifling creativity and disengaging the team. When knowing leads to an inability to listen and learn, it is a clear problem.

Contrast this with a Seeker, who comes into the same meeting with a potential solution but acknowledges its limitations. They actively listen to other ideas, ask thoughtful questions to enhance their understanding and remain open to adapting their approach based on new insights. Instead of viewing disagreement as a challenge to their authority, they see it as an opportunity to learn more and find the best way forward.

Ultimately, we all embody both Seekers and Knowers in different situations. The key is recognising which mindset will serve you best in any given moment. In a high-pressure scenario where immediate action is required, being a Knower is crucial. But in most other instances, adopting a Seeker's mindset – one of curiosity, openness and collaboration – will lead to more effective leadership and long-term success.

The power of blindspotting lies in our ability to recognise when to adopt a Seeker's humble mindset and when to step into the decisive certainty of a Knower. By developing the skills to shift between these mindsets depending on the situation, we create opportunities for greater collaboration, better decision-making and stronger leadership. However, while this awareness is crucial, it's not always easy to maintain. Often, our blindspotting ability is challenged by deeper cognitive traps embedded in the way we think, biases we aren't even aware exist. These traps can pull us into a rigid Knower mindset or cloud our judgement, making it harder to engage as Seekers even when we intend to.

In the next chapter, we will explore some of the most common cognitive traps that undermine our ability to practise blindspotting. Understanding these mental pitfalls is critical to ensuring we can stay balanced between being Seekers and Knowers, and ultimately become more effective leaders.

> **KEY TAKEAWAYS**
> - **The balance between being a Seeker and a Knower.** Effective leadership requires both the open-minded curiosity of a Seeker and the decisive certainty of a Knower. Seekers embrace learning, admitting they don't know everything, while Knowers rely on conviction and certainty when action is required. Recognising when to adopt each mindset is crucial for navigating complex leadership situations.
> - **Seekers thrive on curiosity and critical thinking.** Seekers actively search for new information, different perspectives and contradictory evidence. They question their own assumptions and remain flexible, adapting their beliefs when relevant information emerges. Their focus is not protecting their ego or being right but finding the objective truth.
> - **The dangers of stubbornly holding onto beliefs.** Knowers tend to hold on to their views rigidly, often seeing challenges to their opinions as personal attacks. This stubbornness can lead to conflict, stifle creativity and limit innovation within their teams. Knowers' reluctance to reconsider their views can prevent them from seeing blind spots in their thinking.
> - **The importance of context in adopting a mindset.** When to be a Seeker or a Knower is highly dependent on context. For example, a crisis may demand a Knower's

certainty and rapid decision-making skills, while most other situations benefit from the open-minded and collaborative approach of a Seeker. Effective leadership involves switching between these mindsets as the situation calls for it.
- **Self-reflection is key when blindspotting.** The practice of blindspotting involves recognising when you're leaning towards being a Seeker or a Knower. When you engage the blindspotting mindsets of honesty, curiosity and flexibility you can consciously choose the one that best serves the moment, ensuring a more balanced and effective approach to leadership, learning and growth.

FURTHER READING

Carol Dweck, *Mindset: Changing the way you think to fulfil your potential* (2006).

Tasha Eurich, *Insight: The surprising truth about how others see us, how we see ourselves, and why the answers matter more than we think* (2017).

Julia Galef, *The Scout Mindset: Why some people see things clearly and others don't* (2021).

Adam Grant, *Think Again: The power of knowing what you don't know* (2021).

Liz Wiseman, *Multipliers: How the best leaders make everyone smarter* (2010).

LEVERAGING DOUBT FOR SUCCESS

'I get far more joy from being the person who can drive impact than I do from being the person who is right 100 per cent of the time.'

Sukhinder Singh Cassidy, CEO, Xero

Imagine stepping into a room full of seasoned executives, all waiting to hear your vision as their new leader. The pressure is immense. Yet, instead of delivering a bold strategy or a list of definitive answers, you simply say, 'I don't know . . . yet.'

For most leaders, admitting uncertainty is unthinkable. But for Sukhinder Singh Cassidy, it's the key to unlocking true leadership. 'I remember joining StubHub,' Sukhinder explained, reflecting on the moment she became the ticket exchange and resale company's president, 'and I got invited to a leadership offsite before I even started. They asked me for my views, and I said, "I don't know . . . yet." Saying "I don't know" was the most powerful thing I could have said.'

This philosophy has defined her remarkable career with tech giants including Google, Tripadvisor, StubHub and Xero, companies where she helped shape the future of digital business. It's a powerful lesson for corporate leaders: the willingness to say 'I don't know' can be a strength, not a weakness. It opens the door to perspectives different from your own, and it shows that you are open to learning, just as much as leading.

In a world where leaders are expected to have all the answers, Sukhinder challenges that notion. Her approach is grounded in blindspotting – the willingness to admit what you don't know, to actively seek out new perspectives, and to adjust your thinking as you learn more. This philosophy not only transformed her leadership style but also empowered the teams she led to innovate, question assumptions and thrive in uncertainty.

In a corporate environment where making fast decisions with incomplete information is often the norm, Sukhinder's leadership style shows us that what makes you a great leader isn't knowing everything – it's knowing when to listen, when to learn and when to pivot. Throughout her career, she has role-modelled blindspotting – constantly questioning her assumptions, seeking out various viewpoints, and being willing to change direction when the evidence calls for it. In doing so, she has not only led by example but also fostered environments where her teams can thrive.

In keeping with the practice of blindspotting, one of Sukhinder's key strategies when stepping into a new leadership role is committing to what she calls a 'listening tour'. This is a period where, instead of rushing in to a new role with preconceived ideas, she first gathers input from everyone around her.

'When you enter a new situation, you have to be committed to listening,' Sukhinder told me when we met via Zoom, speaking to me from Xero's office in San Mateo, California, just south of San Francisco.

After joining Xero in 2022, Sukhinder continued this approach by engaging in hundreds of one-on-one meetings with her new team members. In those meetings she collects data points, observes patterns, and only then does she form an opinion. 'The minute you present people with a truth they've already told you, you quickly get buy-in,' she said.

This practice of gathering collective wisdom before making decisions is an example of role-modelling blindspotting at its finest.

For leaders in any field, the lesson is clear: intellectual curiosity is the gateway to innovation. By first suspending their own judgement and engaging in active listening, leaders can foster a culture of open dialogue, which will ultimately result in better decisions and stronger team collaboration.

Despite her willingness to listen to others, Sukhinder isn't afraid to form a hypothesis herself and test it. She describes this decision-making framework as 'gut–data–gut': first, she uses her instincts to form an initial hypothesis; then, she gathers data to test that hypothesis; and lastly, she returns to her gut feeling to make the final decision. 'If I don't have a gut feeling, it's all about gathering,' she explained.

Gut–data–gut is not about being right from the outset but about being flexible enough to adapt based on the evidence. This is where cognitive flexibility – the Be Flexible mindset – comes into play. Sukhinder isn't tied to her initial ideas; she's willing to pivot if new information calls for it, ensuring that her final decision is informed by a balance of instinct and hard data. In today's fast-paced business environment, the ability to adapt and change direction when necessary is a competitive advantage for any type of leader.

But for Sukhinder, it's not enough for leaders to engage in blindspotting. She believes leaders must encourage these behaviours within their teams, creating a culture where intellectual honesty, curiosity and flexibility are encouraged at all levels.

'I think people learn different ways,' she explained. 'Some people are more deductive, others more instinctive.' She acknowledges that her leadership style – being both opinionated and willing to be proven wrong – can sometimes make people think she's too fixed in her views. But she is clear about one thing: her opinions are loosely held, and she's always ready to change her mind based on good data.

'One of the risks of being a leader is people just serve you back what they think you want to hear,' she said. To counter this, she encourages her teams to speak up, to challenge assumptions, and to be intellectually honest about what they don't know. Creating this environment of transparency fosters innovation and allows her teams to uncover blind spots that might otherwise go unnoticed.

In today's business landscape, ambiguity is inevitable. But Sukhinder doesn't worry about having all the answers upfront: 'I'm comfortable leading through ambiguity because I believe you peel back the onion. You don't need to see the whole picture. You just need to find the iota or sliver of the thing that works, and you build from there.' Rather than seeing uncertainty as a roadblock, she views it as an opportunity to make incremental progress – an attitude all leaders can seek to emulate.

At Xero, Sukhinder used this approach to lead the company through a difficult period of restructuring. Faced with the challenge of needing to reduce costs while maintaining growth, she broke down the process into manageable steps for her team. 'The first thing we're going to do is fix our cost structure,' she told them. Once that was completed, they moved on to the next priorities: profitability and growth. By breaking down large, ambiguous goals into smaller, tangible steps, Sukhinder was able to lead her team through uncertainty and ambiguity without it becoming overwhelming.

One of the key elements of blindspotting is the ability to detach your ego from your decisions and remain open to change, and this has been a defining characteristic of Sukhinder's leadership style.

'My ego is tied up in being an agile CEO, not a perfect CEO,' she said. 'I get far more joy from being the person who can drive impact than I do from being the person who is right 100 per cent of the time.' This mindset allows Sukhinder to navigate difficult decisions without being weighed down by the fear of being wrong. She's not afraid to admit when her initial assumptions are incorrect, because her self-worth isn't tied to always being right.

This emotional agility is something she encourages in her teams as well. By creating a culture where it's okay to be wrong, Sukhinder helps her teams move past fear and embrace experimentation. 'I don't really care if I'm wrong. I mostly care that somebody cares enough to put out an opinion and that we get to the answer,' she explained. Leaders who can separate their ego from their decision-making process as Sukhinder does are better able to adapt to new information, make faster decisions and create an environment where their teams feel empowered to contribute.

Sukhinder's leadership journey is a masterclass in the power of blindspotting. By embracing its mindsets of honesty, curiosity and flexibility, she has not only achieved success but also inspired those around her to do the same. By role-modelling blindspotting, Sukhinder creates a ripple effect throughout the organisation she leads; her teams know that it's okay to admit they don't have all the answers, and they know that their ideas will be heard, even if they challenge the status quo.

3

UNMASK YOUR THINKING TRAPS

As leaders, we generally pride ourselves on our ability to make sound decisions based on our knowledge, experience and intuition. But what happens when our thinking is clouded by unseen biases and cognitive traps? In this chapter, we will delve into the most common thinking traps that can ensnare even the most seasoned leaders among us, such as the curse of expertise, the pull of hubris and the illusion of knowledge. These mental shortcuts can distort our judgement, leading us to ignore critical information, shut out alternative viewpoints or make decisions that seem right at the time but are ultimately flawed.

To understand the impact of these cognitive traps, we will explore real-world examples of how these rigid ways of thinking have led to disastrous consequences.

WHEN FORT KNOX FAILED

'The system was like Fort Knox.'[1]

When Paula Vennells was CEO of the United Kingdom (UK) Post Office Limited, she likely found comfort in these words uttered by Duncan Tait, who partnered closely with Vennells as head of Fujitsu UK. Tait reassured Vennells that Horizon – the Post Office's new branch accounting software installed by Fujitsu – was impenetrable. Tait compared it to Fort Knox, the US Army facility known for housing that nation's gold reserves, implying it was not just secure but infallible. So, when accounting shortfalls were reported each night from Post Office branches across the country, the Post Office was convinced the fault could only lie with the postmasters. It simply couldn't be the technology.

This belief would not only ruin the lives of hundreds of British postmasters, it would also bring down Vennells and tarnish the UK Post Office's reputation around the world.

The UK Post Office and Fujitsu's steadfast belief in the Horizon system's perfection became their blind spot. They refused to consider the possibility of a software failure, and over time, this rigid thinking entrenched itself at every level of leadership. The result? Incalculable harm to hundreds of innocent people.

The making of a scandal
In 1996, the Japanese technology company Fujitsu won a contract worth one billion pounds to install a computer software system – Horizon – throughout the UK Post Office's network. Originally, Horizon was designed as a swipe-card system to help pensioners and others collect benefits. However, when the logistics of that approach proved too difficult, the project was redirected to serve as an all-encompassing branch accounting system to handle the financial transactions of 20,000 Post Office branches across the UK.

It was a risky pivot. What had been intended as a narrowly focused system was now expected to handle the entire financial infrastructure of the Post Office – a huge task, even by modern standards.[2] Still, Horizon was launched that year.

Within weeks, individual postmasters began noticing financial discrepancies. Transactions weren't adding up and nightly balances were often short. When postmasters contacted the Post Office helpline to report these issues, they were met with a clear message: the system was flawless; if there were financial shortfalls, the problem had to be with the postmasters themselves. Time and again, postmasters were told they were the only ones experiencing these issues, leading them to believe they were at fault.

But this was far from the truth.

Over the next 15 years, more than 900 postmasters in the UK were prosecuted on charges of theft, fraud and false accounting.[3] Nearly 250 of them were sent to prison.[4] Postmasters who ran local branches were financially ruined, and, in at least four tragic cases, driven to suicide.[5] Meanwhile, the Post Office continued to assert Horizon's perfection, with Vennells vigorously defending the organisation throughout her tenure from 2012, when she was appointed chief executive, until she was forced to resign in 2019. For Vennells and her management team, there had been no room for doubt. The Post Office's internal narrative became absolute: the software was faultless, and any failures rested squarely on the shoulders of postmasters.

Cognitive traps at work

The UK Post Office scandal highlights several cognitive traps that distorted the leadership team's judgement. At the heart of the crisis was their failure to engage in blindspotting – failing to be honest, curious and flexible in their thinking. Blindspotting requires leaders to ask, 'What might we be missing?' and 'What don't we know yet?' Unfortunately, these questions seem to have never been asked by leaders at the Post Office during this time.

The Post Office's leadership team had invested heavily in Horizon; the system *had* to work perfectly. Instead of remaining open to evidence that might have contradicted this belief, they were blinded to the very real possibility of error. As time went on, they grew more confident that the issue lay not in the software, but in the integrity of the postmasters themselves. This sense of certainty – often fuelled by an unwillingness to admit fault – meant that the leaders failed to investigate alternative causes for the discrepancies.

By the time issues were first reported – almost as soon as Horizon was launched – hundreds of millions of pounds had already been spent on the software. To question the system would have been to admit that the investment had been flawed, a reality too difficult for the Post Office to face. So, they doubled down on their position, refusing to consider that Horizon could be faulty – refusing to consider what they didn't know.

The costs of errors in thinking
As reports of shortfalls continued and postmasters faced prosecution, the Post Office clung to its position. Even when whistleblowers within Fujitsu began to raise concerns in 2015, and legal actions started stacking up, the leadership team remained steadfast.[6] Their unwillingness to adapt to the emerging evidence or entertain the possibility of a flaw in Horizon was a classic case of cognitive rigidity – the inability to change one's perspective even in the face of contradictory information.

It wasn't until 2019, through legal battles and whistleblower testimonies, that the truth finally came to light: the shortfalls weren't the result of fraud or theft perpetrated by the postmasters. They were the result of a software glitch. Horizon wasn't flawless – it was deeply flawed.

The consequences of this failure were far-reaching. The Post Office was forced to compensate those wrongfully prosecuted, and Vennells, along with several other senior leaders, saw their careers end in disgrace. During the 2024 Post Office Horizon IT Inquiry, Vennells admitted, 'Individuals, myself included, made mistakes, didn't see things, didn't hear things.'[7]

But these admissions came far too late. For the postmasters who lost their livelihoods – and in some cases, their lives – the damage was irreparable.

At the core of this scandal was a leadership team that refused to be intellectually honest with themselves or others. Had they engaged in blindspotting, the outcome could have been vastly different.

If Vennells and her team had asked, 'What are we missing?' or 'What don't we know yet?' they might have acknowledged that even the most complex software systems can have flaws. They might have considered that Fujitsu's assurances of Horizon's perfection weren't enough; instead, they might have sought independent verification of the system's reliability.

A leadership team committed to blindspotting would have embraced curiosity and sought out different perspectives, questioning the comfortable narrative that Horizon was beyond reproach. They would have conducted an impartial investigation into the financial discrepancies and discovered the software's bugs much sooner, potentially sparing hundreds of people from wrongful prosecution.

Instead, the Post Office's leaders fell victim to their own blind spots and cognitive traps, allowing overconfidence and a need for certainty to cloud their judgement. Rather than seeking the truth, they sought to protect their reputation at all costs, leading to one of the biggest miscarriages of justice in the UK's history.

THE CURSE OF EXPERTISE

Imagine you've worked for years to become the go-to expert in your field. You've climbed the ranks and earned accolades, and you are relied upon for critical decisions within your organisation or team. But what if all that knowledge and confidence – the very things that propelled your career – are also what could lead to your biggest mistake? In many aspects of our lives, expertise is often treated like an unshakeable asset. Yet, the more we know, the more we can become blind to fresh insights, alternative strategies and critical errors lurking in plain sight.

This paradox is known as the curse of expertise.[8] It's a cognitive trap that leads even the smartest and most experienced leaders to overestimate their knowledge.[9]

David Dunning, a leading expert on cognitive biases, explains: 'The first rule of the Dunning-Kruger club is you don't know you're a member of the Dunning-Kruger club.'[10] The Dunning-Kruger effect, which Dunning co-discovered, shows that people of low ability tend to overestimate their skills.[11] But Dunning also warns that this bias extends to experts: experts are better at knowing when they are right, but they are also more confident than a non-expert and fail to show appropriate levels of doubt when they might be wrong.[12]

In other words, expertise doesn't just shield us from mistakes – it can also blind us to our own fallibility. The more knowledge we have, the harder it becomes to see where we might be going wrong.[13]

Double-edged sword of expertise

One of the most dangerous aspects of expertise is that it often feels like a superpower – an unassailable belief that you always know the right answer. Studies have consistently shown that experts not only possess more confidence in their knowledge but also are more certain about their convictions, even when they're wrong. As Dunning points out, 'Not knowing the scope of your own ignorance is part of the human condition. But the problem with it is we see it in other people, and we don't see it in ourselves.'[14]

Consider the case of Linus Pauling, one of the few two-time Nobel Prize winners. Pauling was a renowned chemist, but when he ventured into the field of oncology, he infamously championed mega doses of Vitamin C as a treatment for cancer.[15] Despite his immense knowledge of chemistry, he overstepped his expertise and his claims were discredited by medical professionals. The same phenomenon occurred during the COVID-19 pandemic when experts from unrelated fields, such as legal scholars and radiologists, made highly confident but deeply flawed public predictions about the virus.[16]

The problem is clear: expertise often comes with overconfidence, leading us to make assumptions that go unchallenged because we no longer question ourselves. Philosopher Nathan Ballantyne coined the term 'epistemic trespassing' to describe this dangerous behaviour – when experts in one field cross into another where they have no authority yet assert themselves as if they do.[17] It's a trap even the brightest minds can fall into.

> Expertise often comes with overconfidence, leading us to make assumptions that go unchallenged because we no longer question ourselves.

Why experts fail to see their own blind spots
As leaders, we trust our expertise to guide us through high-stakes decisions. But this very trust can lead to the illusion of knowledge – the belief that our understanding of a situation is complete when, in fact, we may be missing critical information. This is especially dangerous in industries where disruption is constant, and where existing assumptions can quickly become obsolete.

Air Vice Marshal Robert Denney, one of the Royal Australian Air Force's most senior pilots, warns that overconfidence is one of the biggest red flags in aviation. 'Overconfidence often manifests itself as a lack of honesty. If you are being honest with yourself, you appreciate you are going to make mistakes. If you are dishonest with yourself, you believe you are perfect. That will always cause problems,' Robert told me. His decades of experience taught him that being a successful pilot requires a continuous reassessment of one's skills and limitations.

All leaders should take his advice to heart, because overconfidence is a red flag in any field, not just aviation. Leaders who are too confident in their knowledge are more likely to overlook warning signs, miss key information or reject new ideas.

Derived from Zen Buddhism, the Japanese word 'shoshin', or beginner's mind, describes an open and curious mindset where one approaches every situation with eagerness and no preconceived notions – something we all could benefit from emulating. Liz Wiseman, author of *Multipliers*, argues that when we're in this 'rookie mode', we are most open to learning, exploring different ideas and challenging our assumptions.[18] In contrast, experts, weighed down by their prior knowledge, often lose this curiosity and become closed off to new possibilities.

Relying on what you already know
The curse of expertise is linked to a phenomenon called the Einstellung effect – when we approach problems in the same way repeatedly, even when new or better solutions are available. This cognitive trap can stifle innovation and prevent leaders from seeing opportunities right in front of them.

For example, consider the story of American multimedia brand Blockbuster. At its peak, Blockbuster was the dominant player in the video rental industry. But when Netflix emerged with a new business model based on streaming, Blockbuster's leadership failed to recognise the potential impact of digital disruption. In 2000, when Netflix approached Blockbuster with an offer to buy the video store company for $50 million, Blockbuster declined, convinced that its brick-and-mortar approach was the future. They were so focused on their existing business model that they missed the opportunity to pivot and adapt to the rapidly changing digital landscape. By the time Blockbuster realised the threat, it was too late. Netflix had already captured the market, and Blockbuster's business collapsed. By 2010, Blockbuster filed for bankruptcy.

This is a classic case of a blind spot created by the curse of expertise. Blockbuster's leaders were so entrenched in their existing assumptions, reinforced by their success in the field, that they failed to see the potential of new technology. Leaders who practise blindspotting, on the other hand, are constantly scanning for emerging trends and possibilities. They are willing to question their assumptions and adjust their strategies in response to new information.

Overcoming the curse of expertise

For all of us, the curse of expertise is a real and present danger. It's easy to become overconfident in your knowledge, assuming past successes will always guide you through future challenges. But as the example of Blockbuster shows, that very confidence can prevent you from seeing the bigger picture.

The antidote to the curse of expertise is blindspotting – recognising the limits of your knowledge, remaining curious and being open to new ideas. Real expertise isn't just about having all the answers – it's also about knowing when to ask the right questions.

> The antidote to the curse of expertise is blindspotting.

THE PULL OF HUBRIS

Success can be a powerful seduction. When we rise to the top, when we make a series of brilliant decisions, when our ideas come to fruition, it's easy to start believing we can do no wrong. That sense of invincibility – the overconfidence in our abilities and the conviction that our success is self-made – is the start of a dangerous downward spiral into hubris.

Take a moment to consider some of the most well-known corporate collapses in recent history: Theranos and the subsequent prosecution of its founder Elizabeth Holmes; the arrest and imprisonment of Sam Bankman-Fried, the founder of the FTX cryptocurrency exchange; the toxic culture at Uber and the removal of its CEO and co-founder Travis Kalanick; and the rise and fall of WeWork under Adam Neumann. In each of these cases, it wasn't just the leaders at the helm who succumbed to hubris – it was also the investors, partners and stakeholders who failed to engage in blindspotting. They were blinded by the allure of success.

As Duncan Mavin, investigative journalist and author of

The Pyramid of Lies: Lex Greensill and the billion-dollar scandal, told me: 'Hubris is at the absolute core of corporate collapse. You see it every time – leaders come into a position, and they think, "It's all about me." Their ego takes over. They stop listening to the people around them, and they push ahead with decisions that ultimately lead to failure. And when things go wrong, they don't learn.'

Duncan's investigative work reveals the dangers of unchecked hubris in corporate environments. In his research on the collapse of Greensill Capital, he observed how leaders often confuse confidence with competence. 'There's a fine line between being a visionary with the genius to get you out of a difficult situation and someone who foolishly doubles down on mistakes,' he explains.

Greensill Capital, once a high-flying finance firm, fell from grace in 2021 when its business model was revealed to be unsustainable and riddled with risks.[19] Its founder, Lex Greensill, had charmed investors, political leaders and even the former British Prime Minister David Cameron, all of whom failed to see the cracks forming in the company's foundation. Lex Greensill's hubris, his refusal to consider that his model might be flawed, ultimately led to the collapse of a multi-billion-dollar company.

So why do smart, capable leaders fall into the trap of hubris? The answer lies in the seductive nature of success itself. When we experience a series of victories, it's natural to start believing in our own infallibility. Over time, our past achievements become the foundation of our confidence. We trust our instincts – and why wouldn't we? They've worked for us before.

However, success breeds complacency. It can narrow our field of vision, making it harder to see our own limitations or consider the possibility that we could be wrong. Instead of seeking out other perspectives or questioning our own assumptions, we become convinced our way is the right way. Hubris feeds off this certainty. The more successful we are, the more likely we are to double down on our past approach, even when the world around us is changing and that approach might no longer be the best option. It's not that we don't see the red flags – it's that we don't believe they apply to us.

This pattern is evident in the story of health technology company Theranos. During the period of 2014 – 2015, founder and CEO Elizabeth Holmes was hailed as a visionary, praised for her bold ambition to revolutionise the healthcare industry through her company's blood-testing devices. She secured millions of dollars in funding, and for a time, it seemed that nothing could stand in her way. Holmes graced the covers of *Fortune* and *Forbes* magazine in 2014 and was named as one of *Time* magazine's '100 Most Influential People' in 2015.[20]

But beneath the glossy image of success was a company built on deception. Holmes refused to acknowledge the technological flaws in her company's blood-testing device. Her confidence in her vision blinded her to the reality of the situation. She ignored warnings from engineers and medical experts, pushing forward with promises she couldn't keep. Her hubris not only led to the collapse of her company but also landed her in prison.

In Holmes' case, hubris prevented her from practising intellectual honesty – one of the key theories underpinning blindspotting. As a leader, she failed to be transparent about what she knew and, more importantly, about what she didn't know.

Hubris is the antithesis of blindspotting: it tells you that you already know everything you need to know. It convinces you that your vision is flawless and that anyone who disagrees with you is simply wrong. But as history has shown time and time again, hubris rarely leads to long-term success.

The fine line between visionary and blind

There is a delicate balance between visionary leadership and blind arrogance. Many of the world's most successful companies were built by leaders who were unafraid to take risks and think outside the box. But the problem arises when that risk-taking becomes reckless – when we become so consumed by our own narrative of success that we stop listening to others.

Consider Travis Kalanick, the former CEO of transportation company Uber. Kalanick's bold leadership style helped Uber become one of the fastest-growing companies in the world. But his unchecked ego and aggressive approach to competition also created a toxic culture within the company, leading to numerous scandals, lawsuits and, ultimately, his removal as CEO. Kalanick's inability to reflect on the impact of his leadership style and his refusal to take accountability for Uber's internal problems is a classic example of how hubris can derail even the most promising ventures.

As Duncan told me, 'There's a fine line between being the genius who gets things done and the leader who pushes too far and too fast without stopping to consider the consequences. It's that inability to pause and reflect that often leads to collapse.'

Overcoming the pull of hubris

The temptation of hubris lies in its simplicity. It tells us that success is straightforward, that the path forward is clear, and that no course corrections are needed. But blindspotting requires the opposite mindset. It asks us to remain vigilant, to continuously question our assumptions and to look for various perspectives that challenge our thinking.

So, how do we resist the pull of hubris? The answer lies in cultivating intellectual honesty and embracing the principles of blindspotting. Remaining open to feedback, being willing to admit when we're wrong, and actively seeking out perspectives different to our own means we are far more likely to succeed in the long run.

Blindspotting is kryptonite for hubris.

> **Blindspotting is kryptonite for hubris.**

THE ILLUSION OF KNOWLEDGE

One of the most dangerous traps in decision-making is not ignorance, but the illusion of knowledge. As historian and author Daniel J. Boorstin once observed, 'The greatest obstacle to discovery is not ignorance – it is the illusion of knowledge.'[21] This phenomenon, where we believe we know more than we actually do, is one of the most insidious cognitive biases because it operates quietly and subtly. It isn't about a lack of information; rather, it's an overconfidence in what we think we know, which then blinds us to reality.

Many of us like to think we are Seekers – people who approach life with curiosity, honesty and flexibility. We might even believe we engage in blindspotting, regularly scanning our own biases and assumptions. Yet, when we take a closer look at decisions that haven't gone well, it's often clear that one or more of the three key blindspotting mindsets – Be Honest, Be Curious, Be Flexible – were missing. The illusion of knowledge traps us into becoming Knowers, convinced we already possess all the relevant information to make sound decisions. This false sense of security can lead to costly mistakes, both in personal and organisational contexts.

It's important to distinguish the illusion of knowledge from similar cognitive traps, such as the pull of hubris and the curse of expertise. Hubris involves overconfidence rooted in ego, where someone believes they are infallible simply because of their past successes. It's the belief that you're always right because you've been right before. The curse of expertise refers to a scenario where true experts in a particular field become so entrenched in their knowledge that they fail to see new or alternative approaches. They are confident in their narrow domain but miss opportunities for innovation or new solutions.

The illusion of knowledge, however, is a more universal problem. It doesn't require true expertise or an inflated ego to take hold. Instead, it manifests when we overestimate our understanding of a topic, believing we have sufficient information or insight to make decisions without ever fully grasping the complexities we're facing. It's the assumption that because we've read a few articles or listened to a few informed opinions, we are equipped to make sound judgements.

We all think we know more than we do

Psychologist Steven Sloman and philosopher Philip Fernbach delve into this issue in their book *The Knowledge Illusion*, arguing that human beings are 'built to collaborate' and thus often confuse the knowledge of others for their own. This phenomenon, called 'the community of knowledge',[22] suggests we often overestimate our understanding of how things work because we assume the expertise of others in our social or professional networks fills in the gaps. We feel like we know more than we do simply because we are aware that someone else understands the details.[23]

For example, if you ask someone how a toilet works, they might give a confident answer about flushing and pipes but are likely to falter when pressed on the specifics. This initial confidence reflects the illusion of knowledge – they think they understand because they have a general sense of the process, even if they don't understand the mechanics.

This same pattern plays out in leadership contexts. Being near experts or having access to consultants doesn't make us experts ourselves. Yet the illusion of knowledge can make us feel as though we fully grasp a complex situation when, in reality, we are relying on incomplete or second-hand information.

The consequences of the illusion of knowledge can be severe in corporate environments, where leaders must make high-stakes decisions quickly. Overconfidence stemming from the illusion of knowledge can lead to missed opportunities, miscalculations and even failure. We may feel that we have all the necessary data, that we've done our due diligence and that our understanding of the situation is complete. But we often miss critical blind spots simply because we are convinced we already know everything we need to know.

In the case of Theranos, investors, board members and business partners believed the claims of the company without sufficient scientific validation. The technology being promoted by Holmes never worked as advertised, ultimately leading to the company's collapse. In the case of Greensill Capital, stakeholders believed in the company's ability to manage risks and sustain innovative financial practices, despite significant warning signs. Once the business model was closely scrutinised and the truth emerged, the company went into administration and a criminal investigation was launched.

The illusion of knowledge not only hampers our decision-making but also makes us more susceptible to confirmation bias – the tendency to seek out information that supports our pre-existing beliefs while ignoring any evidence to the contrary. When we are convinced that we already know the truth, we gravitate towards echo chambers, surrounding ourselves with people and information that reinforce our views. This narrowing of perspective only deepens the illusion, making it harder to engage in blindspotting.

> **When we are convinced that we already know the truth, we gravitate towards echo chambers, surrounding ourselves with people and information that reinforce our views.**

The antidote to this cognitive trap is intellectual honesty, the cornerstone of blindspotting. To dispel the illusion of knowledge, we need to cultivate the ability to say, 'I don't know . . . yet,' and mean it. This requires being honest with ourselves and others about the limitations of our knowledge. Being open and flexible is essential if we want to avoid the pitfalls that might follow.

Overcoming the illusion of knowledge requires a commitment to continuous learning and self-awareness. We need to actively seek out new information, challenge our assumptions and remain open to the idea that we might be wrong. This isn't a sign of weakness;

rather, it is the mark of strong, intellectually honest leadership. In the end, leaders who can recognise and overcome the illusion of knowledge are those best equipped to navigate the complexities of the modern world.

As we've explored the common thinking traps that can cloud our judgement – the curse of expertise, the pull of hubris and the illusion of knowledge – it's clear that avoiding these pitfalls requires more than just awareness of them. It demands a fundamental shift in how we approach the way we think. The cognitive traps we fall into often stem from an overconfidence in our understanding, a refusal to admit when we don't know something, or an attachment to being right at all costs. To truly overcome these challenges, we need to ground ourselves in intellectual honesty. Blindspotting isn't just about recognising where we might be wrong; it's about actively pursuing truth and being willing to adjust our beliefs in the face of new information.

This brings us to the first mindset of blindspotting: Be Honest. In the next chapter, we'll dive deeper into what it means to be honest – with others, but more importantly with ourselves. By incorporating this mindset into our approach, we build the foundation for thoughtful, open-minded leadership. Let's explore how embracing honesty can transform the way we think and lead.

> ### KEY TAKEAWAYS
> - **Thinking traps will cloud our judgement.** Even experienced leaders are susceptible to cognitive traps such as the illusion of knowledge, the curse of expertise and the pull of hubris. These traps can distort judgement and lead to poor decisions by causing leaders to ignore critical information or alternative perspectives.

- **Expertise can blind us to our own fallibility.** The curse of expertise shows that deep knowledge in one area can prevent us from seeing new opportunities or innovations in others. Experts, confident in their domain, often fail to remain curious or open to different solutions, leading to mistakes that could have been avoided with a beginner's mindset.
- **Hubris can be seductive yet destructive.** As seen in the examples of Theranos and Greensill Capital, a leader's hubris – a dangerous overconfidence in one's abilities and vision – can lead to corporate collapse. Success often causes leaders to believe their past achievements guarantee future success, blinding them to warning signs and dissenting perspectives.
- **The illusion of knowledge is subtle and dangerous.** Unlike overt arrogance or the hubris that accompanies success, the illusion of knowledge is more insidious. It's not a lack of information but rather an overconfidence in what we think we know that leads us astray. Leaders often believe that having surface-level understanding is enough to make informed decisions, only to realise too late that their knowledge was incomplete.
- **Intellectual honesty is a remedy for cognitive traps.** One of the core remedies to both the illusion of knowledge and the curse of expertise is intellectual honesty. Leaders must be willing to admit what they don't know and actively seek out additional perspectives. This willingness to say, 'I don't know . . . yet,' is a key element of blindspotting and helps avoid cognitive traps that lead to poor decision-making.

FURTHER READING

Joe Aston, *The Chairman's Lounge: The inside story of how Qantas sold us out* (2024).

Eliot Brown and Maureen Farrell, *The Cult of We: WeWork and the great startup delusion* (2021).

John Carreyrou, *Bad Blood: Secrets and lies in a Silicon Valley startup* (2018).

Mike Isaac, *Super Pumped: The battle for Uber* (2019).

Duncan Mavin, *The Pyramid of Lies: Lex Greensill and the billion-dollar scandal* (2022).

Duncan Mavin, *Meltdown: Scandal, sleaze and the collapse of Credit Suisse* (2024).

Nick Wallis, *The Great Post Office Scandal* (2021).

THE PERILS OF EXPERTISE

> 'The worst part of a blind spot is that they convince us we don't have any.'
>
> Richard Bistrong, anti-bribery, ethics and compliance consultant and former anti-bribery offender

In the fast-paced world of corporate leadership, where every decision can make or break a company, success often hinges on expertise and confidence. But for senior executive Richard Bistrong, his rise to the top was followed by the ultimate fall. The often painful lessons he learnt prove that even the most seasoned leaders are not immune to the thinking traps that can cloud judgement, foster unethical behaviour and derail a career.

When Richard and I first met in London at a conference being held in the stunning fifteenth-century Guildhall in 2023, I was impressed by his reputation as a leader in the field of preventing bribery and corruption. I didn't learn until later that his commitment was rooted in personal experience, and I became eager to speak with Richard about his life and the fascinating leadership insights it might offer.

Richard is a born-and-bred New Yorker who is always immaculately dressed in a sports coat and tie. His great-grandfather Jacob Bistrong had been a tailor and one of almost 2.5 million Jewish people who emigrated to the United States from Eastern Europe at the start of the twentieth century. After entering the United States at Ellis Island, Jacob began the family company — Strong Uniforms — in a uniform manufacturing factory on 17th Street in lower Manhattan.

Despite three generations before him working in the family tailoring business, Richard had other plans in the mid-1980s. He had completed a master's degree in international relations and intended to become a professor in foreign policy. However, as the eldest son of the Bistrong family, Richard was under intense pressure to continue the family legacy.

Despite some initial reluctance, Richard eventually agreed, and he soon realised working at Strong Uniforms, which was now a body armour company, Point Blank Body Armor, offered him an exciting opportunity. Since its inception the company had been manufacturing fabric uniforms for the police and military. With the invention of Kevlar — a strong, lightweight fibre known for its strength and heat resistance — Strong Uniforms was retired as a brand, and Point Blank Body Armor pivoted and began to manufacture bullet-resistant vests.

Turning out to be a natural at sales, Richard formed strong relationships with his customers. When the family business was sold in the early 1990s, he eventually went to work for a new company called American Body Armor, which would go on to become known as Armor Holdings. It was a fateful decision.

Richard became a rainmaker for his new employer, soon bringing in more revenue than any of his colleagues and earning more in bonuses than the chief executive. He loved the attention and the accolades and became addicted to the feeling of being a corporate hero.

His skills grew exponentially, and his extensive background in the body armour and uniform industry propelled him into leadership roles within the company that demanded quick, decisive action. While his first career chapter with Armor Holdings was focused on the US market, as the vice president of US sales and marketing, in 1997 he took on a new and exciting role as the vice president of international sales and marketing. Richard was excited to combine both his sales experience and foreign policy academic background. But with that experience came a creeping sense of invincibility – what psychologists refer to as the curse of expertise.

'I was considered the go-to guy,' Richard told me during a Zoom call from his New York City home. 'People looked to me for success because I had been doing it for years. But the problem with that is, you stop questioning how you succeed and whether you do so with or without integrity. When I did that, the first person I deceived was myself.'

Richard's vast knowledge of his field made him believe he could operate on autopilot. This sense of mastery fostered a false sense of security – he believed he knew all the risks, knew all the nuances of his business. But his expertise, along with the recognition and accolades he was receiving from his employer, became his blind spot, preventing him from realising when the landscape was shifting or when ethical boundaries were being crossed.

Richard told me about one of the first times he encountered corrupt behaviour: he was at the most southern tip of Argentina, in Tierra del Fuego. A local business partner admitted to Richard he was 'paying tolls' – a euphemism for paying bribes – to win business for his company in selling the company's products. Richard knew there was illegality involved in making payments to public officials to secure deals, but he admits the use of the word 'tolls' instead of 'bribe' or 'kickback' – something that more overtly signalled wrongdoing – led to the first of many blind spots for him, what he called a 'moral fading'. He rationalised these illegal acts, including accepting illegal payments himself and not reporting others for doing the same, as simply part of doing business and chose to believe that no one was being hurt. He thought of it as 'win-win' and was not thinking about the harm he was causing.

Yet corporate corruption like this does have victims: local communities, where even petty corruption undermines good governance, economic development and human rights, as well as innocent employees of companies caught up in reputational harm. Other victims are competitors who struggle to succeed on an uneven playing field; and end users of products and services who may purchase products not because they are needed but because the bribes are easy. As Richard shared with me, 'That capture of state funding (towards unnecessary products and services) results in the diversion of resources from where they are needed, such as education and medical services.'

Richard added, 'Not recognising the victims of corrupt acts was a huge blind spot.'

Over time, Richard went from hearing about other people paying bribes to having his own Swiss bank account where he received kickbacks, commissions and illegal payments. He told me he was thinking, 'I needed to not only keep my corporate hero status but also needed to keep up with a lifestyle that was above my means.' He continued to engage in illegal conduct, even while knowing the activity was unlawful. He had become, in his words, 'an irrational calculator of risk'. His life was going off the rails without him even realising it.

As Richard's career advanced within Armor Holdings, so did his successes as he won larger and more lucrative contracts around the world. But with each victory came an increasing sense of infallibility – the dangerous belief that nothing could go wrong under his leadership.

'Hubris creeps in slowly,' Richard explained. 'You don't wake up one day thinking you're invincible. It's more subtle. You start making decisions without considering all the consequences, because you think your track record will carry you through.' As he shared, 'In my case, success blocked scrutiny, and bad behaviour hid behind great performance, until it was too late for everyone.'

The high-pressure environment of international business and travelling two hundred and fifty days a year overseas without any accountability other than financial performance, fed his sense of control. His leadership instincts, honed over years of experience, told him to press forward without questioning the legitimacy of the deals being made.

'I didn't see myself as doing anything wrong,' Richard said. 'After all, I was closing deals, meeting targets, and the company was thriving. I thought I was untouchable.'

Hubris leads to a disconnect between perception and reality, where people believe they can do no wrong even as the consequences of their actions spiral out of control. For Richard, hubris blinded him to the dangers that were lurking just beneath the surface of his success.

'I was behaving corruptly, thinking corruptly, acting corruptly, and as I was successful in what I was doing, I think that distorted my view to the point where I thought I would never get caught,' Richard admitted.

Ultimately, Richard was caught. He was sentenced to eighteen months in a United States federal prison for violations of the Foreign Corrupt Practices Act, the US anti-bribery law. In the end, he was imprisoned for the supply of pepper spray to the Dutch Police, the sale of fingerprint ink pads to the Nigerian Independent National Electoral Commission and making illegal payments to obtain a United Nations contract for body armour. At the height of his career, Richard earned almost half a million dollars, year after year. While an inmate at Lewisburg federal correctional institution, he was grateful to have a job teaching other inmates for five cents per hour.

Richard's story is a powerful reminder of how the curse of expertise, the pull of hubris and the illusion of knowledge can sabotage leaders. It's also possible to see how blindspotting – being intellectually honest, curious and open to the views and opinions of others, colleagues and mentors included – could have changed his trajectory and saved him from the mistakes that nearly cost him everything. As Richard told me, 'Isolation and not reaching out for support when you need it most is a powerful driver of unethical conduct.'

Looking back, Richard believes that his downfall could have been avoided if he had practised blindspotting.

'If I had been more curious, if I had asked more questions, I think I could have avoided a lot of pain,' Richard said. Instead, he relied on what he thought he knew – and he thought he knew everything. 'If I had just picked up the phone and asked for support, that call could have saved me ten years through the US and UK criminal justice system. But instead, I asked myself the wrong question: "With all these sales and accolades, does the company really want to know what it's like out here?" I decided they didn't, without giving them the chance to respond.

'Leaders have to admit when they're wrong,' he said. 'It's not a weakness; it's a strength.'

Richard's journey from corporate success to federal prison is a powerful reminder of the cognitive traps that can derail even the most accomplished leaders. Hubris, overconfidence, the curse of expertise and the illusion of knowledge are subtle forces that can cloud anyone's judgement and lead to poor decision-making. But through blindspotting – by embracing intellectual honesty, curiosity and flexibility – leaders can avoid these traps and build more resilient organisations.

'I wasn't honest with myself, and I wasn't open to learning,' Richard said, reflecting on his own lack of humility and self-awareness. 'That's what led me down the wrong path. What's really sad, and what I still regret each and every day, is that it was all so avoidable.'

PART 2
THE THREE BLINDSPOTTING MINDSETS

4

BE HONEST

In Part 2 of this book, we'll explore how to unlock the full power of our blindspotting torch through the three essential mindsets: Be Honest, Be Curious, Be Flexible. These mindsets are not just ideas to think about; they are practical tools to help you navigate the complexities of leadership, decision-making and collaboration. Each mindset adds a new level of power to your beam, allowing you to see more of the challenges and opportunities that lie ahead and thus make informed decisions as leader.

The first step to supercharging your blindspotting torch is to be honest. Being intellectually honest is like turning the torch on for the first time – it allows you to see what's directly in front of you. But honesty is more than just seeing clearly; it's about recognising the limits of your own knowledge and understanding. It's about admitting that you might not have all the answers and being open to learning from others.

Once you've embraced honesty and can see what's right in front of you, it's time to widen the beam of your torch by being curious. Curiosity allows you to explore beyond what's immediately visible, to ask questions and seek out new perspectives that might not have been obvious before.

With honesty lighting the path ahead and curiosity widening your view, the final step is to brighten that light with flexibility. Flexibility is about being able to adapt when new information challenges your previous assumptions. It's about staying open to change and being willing to shift your perspective as the situation evolves.

Part 2 will provide everything you need to know about each of the mindsets and the practices within them. We will consider what each practice means, why each practice can be challenging to undertake and when the benefits of each practice emerge.

Let's turn on the torch and get started.

BE HONEST

At the heart of blindspotting is the mindset of honesty. It's not just about being truthful with others, though that is, of course, important. It's also about being radically honest with ourselves: honest about our intellectual limits, about the ways our ego can distort our thinking, and about the biases that cloud our judgement. Honesty isn't easy, especially when we're pressured to be confident, decisive and authoritative. But true honesty, the kind that requires vulnerability and humility, is the foundation of blindspotting. Without it, we cannot fully embrace the other blindspotting mindsets of curiosity and flexibility – all of which are essential for seeing what others might miss.

Leadership isn't about having all the answers – it's about asking the right questions and creating an environment where people feel safe to speak up, where different perspectives are valued, and where learning and growth are prioritised over being right. Leaders who embrace the mindset of honesty model these behaviours for their teams, encouraging the people they lead to also be honest about their own limitations and biases. No matter the size of the organisation or workplace, this creates a culture of openness, curiosity and collaboration, where innovation and creativity can thrive.

> Leadership isn't about having all the answers – it's about asking the right questions and creating an environment where people feel safe to speak up, where different perspectives are valued, and where learning and growth are prioritised over being right.

As you move through this section on honesty, I encourage you to reflect on your own intellectual limits, your relationship with your ego, and the biases that might be influencing your thinking. Ask yourself: How often do I pretend to know more than I do? How does my ego get in the way of my decision-making? What biases might be clouding my judgement?

By answering these questions honestly, you'll be well on your way to developing the mindset of honesty and becoming a more effective, open-minded leader.

Self-awareness is the secret weapon of great leaders. Without it, you're like a captain steering a ship through dense fog – you don't even realise when you're heading toward an iceberg. Blindspotting begins with the simple yet profound act of turning inward, because if you can't see your own habits, tendencies and biases, you'll struggle to understand how they ripple out and affect the people and cultures around you. Leaders who lack self-awareness are often the last to realise their decisions are flawed – while everyone else sees the cracks forming in real time.

Think about a manager or colleague you may have worked with who prides themselves on being a 'strong decision-maker'. You might describe them differently – perhaps as someone who bulldozes through ideas, ignoring better solutions. Why? Because they equate hesitation with weakness and refuse to admit when they don't have all the answers. Their inability to reflect on this tendency blinds them to the real issue: their ego is in the driver's seat, not their judgement. Meanwhile, missed opportunities pile up and team morale suffers.

Now imagine the opposite: a leader you have worked with who openly said, 'I'm not sure I have all the information here. What am I missing?' This single question demonstrates a powerful mix of humility and self-awareness. It acknowledges that they, like everyone else, have limits. It also invites others to contribute, creating a space where perspectives can be shared freely.

When you reflect on your actions and admit what you don't know, you're not just being honest with yourself – you're modelling the kind of vulnerability that encourages others to be honest with you. This is how blindspotting becomes a team sport, and how leaders ensure we're not the bottleneck to better ideas.

To start building this habit, think of a recent decision you made – big or small – and ask yourself: What drove my choices? Were they grounded in evidence and collaboration, or did my assumptions and ego take the wheel? Self-awareness isn't about beating yourself up; it's about spotting patterns and learning from them. The more you flex this muscle, the easier it becomes to recognise your blind spots before they steer you off course. And when you do, you'll discover a kind of clarity that transforms not only your leadership but also the culture and potential of everyone around you.

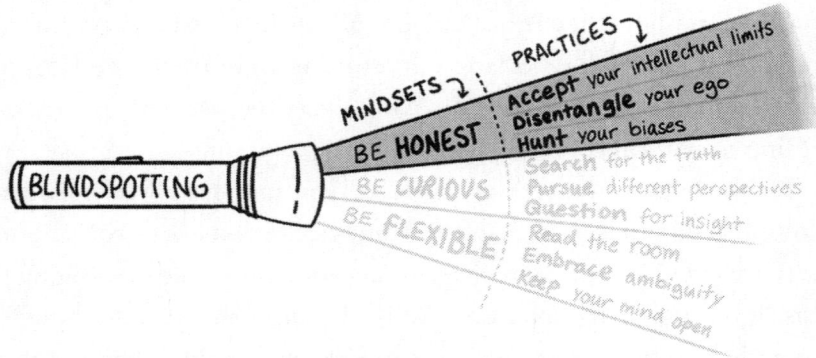

Honesty isn't just a nice-to-have quality – it's the foundation of blindspotting. Without it, we can't fully engage in the other mindsets of curiosity and flexibility. But with it, we can see more clearly, make better decisions and lead with greater confidence and authenticity.

In the context of blindspotting, the mindset of honesty has three key practices:

- **Accept your intellectual limitations.** This practice means acknowledging we don't know everything, and being okay with that. It requires us to have a healthy respect for the boundaries of our knowledge, understanding that what we know is always evolving. By admitting, 'I don't know . . . yet,' we open ourselves to learning and growth. Though it can be daunting to confront the limits of our understanding, this humility isn't a weakness – it's the starting point for gaining deeper insights and expanding our perspective.
- **Disentangle your ego.** This is the practice of separating our self-worth from what we think we know. Often our ego becomes wrapped up in being 'right', making it hard to admit when we're wrong or to learn from others. By shifting our pride away from needing to always have the answers and towards valuing a willingness to learn and evolve, we free ourselves from the need to protect our intellect at all costs. This ultimately allows us to make better decisions without the constraints of ego-driven thinking.
- **Hunt your biases.** Through this practice, we actively seek out the unconscious beliefs and assumptions that cloud our judgement and limit our perspective. Biases can distort the way we interpret information, often without us even realising it. Being honest about the influence of biased thinking allows us to examine our reasoning more critically. While confronting our biases can be uncomfortable, it ultimately sharpens our decision-making and gives us

a clearer, more accurate view of the world. By shining a spotlight on these biases, we open ourselves to seeing what we might otherwise miss.

Let's dive in and begin by considering what it means when we accept our intellectual limits.

PRACTICE 1: ACCEPT YOUR INTELLECTUAL LIMITS
What it means to acknowledge the limits of our understanding
Leaders often feel pressured to have all the answers. But true leadership begins with acknowledging the things we don't know. Blindspotting starts with being aware of our intellectual limits – understanding that we can't know everything, and that is perfectly okay. What matters is recognising our limitations and also embracing them as an opportunity to learn and grow. As individuals, our knowledge will always be incomplete, and accepting this is a crucial part of making better decisions.

Instead of worrying about the gaps in your knowledge, own them. Be prepared to say, 'I don't know . . . yet.' This isn't a sign of weakness or inadequacy. In fact, accepting our intellectual limitations allows us to see more clearly, adapt more quickly and act more effectively when it matters most.

Embracing doubt as a strength
We've all been in situations where we're not the most knowledgeable person in the room, and that can feel uncomfortable. But as French philosopher Voltaire once wrote, 'Doubt is not a pleasant condition, but certainty is absurd.'[1] That sentiment captures a key element of blindspotting: doubt. When embraced honestly, doubt can be a powerful driver of growth. Leaders who constantly project certainty risk being trapped in a single-minded approach and might miss the opportunity to explore new ways of thinking.

Being honest about what we don't know allows us to tap into the insights of others. When we are intellectually honest, we can approach problems with an open mind, and more often than not, this leads to better outcomes. By letting go of the need to appear infallible, we open ourselves to collaboration and shared problem-solving, which benefits everyone involved.

Calibrating confidence

But how do we know when we're overstepping our knowledge? How do we gauge when we are pretending to know something we actually don't? Psychologist Daryl R. Van Tongeren suggests a useful approach: calibrate your confidence. When faced with a challenging situation, ask yourself, 'Given everything I know – and everything I don't know – what's the probability that I'm correct?'[2]

This self-assessment forces you to pause and reflect on the extent of your understanding. For example, imagine you're in a heated conversation with a vaccine expert, an epidemiologist. You've done some online research about vaccine safety and have formed strong opinions, but deep down, you know your knowledge is limited compared to theirs. Calibrating your confidence in this case might reveal that, despite your research, your understanding of vaccine development and safety protocols doesn't quite match that of someone who has spent years studying the topic.

Now consider a workplace scenario. Imagine you're tasked with leading a project that involves integrating complex machine-learning algorithms – something you've never worked with before. As the project unfolds, it hits a snag. Your team comes to you for direction, and you realise you don't have the technical knowledge to solve the problem.

The first mindset of blindspotting would encourage you to be honest. Instead of pretending you know the answer or deflecting the issue, you might say that you don't know but that you're going to work with your team to find out. This small admission allows you to connect with your team, acknowledging the challenge while reinforcing that you will find a solution together. It creates an environment where collaboration can thrive, and your team feels valued rather than dismissed.

More importantly, by admitting your intellectual limits, you empower the people you're leading to bring their expertise to the table. You're not the 'all-knowing' leader who solves every problem, but rather you're a facilitator and role model who enables others to shine. This shift creates a culture of shared ownership and mutual respect, where the best ideas can emerge, and where success becomes a collective achievement.

Finding the sweet spot

Accepting our intellectual limits doesn't mean obsessing over them. The key is to find a balance – a sweet spot – where we're honest about what we don't know but still confident in our ability to learn and lead. On one end of the spectrum are the people who are intellectually servile, constantly doubting themselves and deferring to others. These individuals might struggle with decision-making and feel insecure about their lack of knowledge. On the other end are those who never consider the limits of their understanding – people who, like the classic 'know-it-all', are intellectually arrogant and unaware of their blind spots. As leaders, these people often alienate their teams, stifle innovation and make poor decisions because they refuse to question their assumptions.

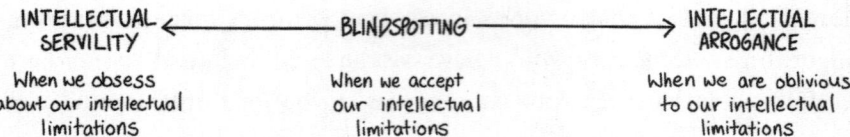

Blindspotting helps us avoid both extremes. It empowers us to admit when we don't know something without losing confidence in our ability to find a solution. This approach fosters a learning culture where intellectual honesty and curiosity go hand in hand. It encourages us to stay flexible, open to new ideas and willing to pivot when necessary.

In the end, accepting our intellectual limits isn't about fixating on our weaknesses – it's about acknowledging the strength that comes from honest self-reflection and the willingness to grow. As leaders, embracing this mindset allows us to make smarter decisions, foster more effective teams and ultimately lead with greater impact.

Why accepting our intellectual limits can be so hard

Admitting we don't know something is often one of the most daunting things we can do, especially in leadership roles. It seems counterintuitive. For decades – perhaps even centuries – we've been conditioned to believe that effective leaders must have all the answers, that competence and knowledge are the bedrock of leadership. The idea of exposing gaps in our understanding feels risky, especially when we worry that admitting what we don't know will undermine our authority or credibility. But here's the reality: the most successful and transformative leaders are those who recognise their intellectual limitations and embrace the opportunity to learn.

We might worry that if we admit we don't know something, others – whether colleagues, clients or those we lead – will perceive us as incompetent. This fear is especially prevalent in workplace cultures where leaders are expected to project confidence and certainty. In high-pressure corporate environments, for example, leaders are often expected to provide instant solutions for complex problems. In traditionally hierarchical organisations such as the military or law enforcement, strict chains of command can discourage leaders from expressing doubt to maintain authority. And the rapid growth and innovation pressure within startup companies often promotes the 'fake it till you make it' mentality. For many, admitting that we have intellectual limitations feels like stepping into a spotlight that exposes every insecurity, every fear of not being good enough.

However, this fear is often misplaced. Research shows that leaders who are honest about their limitations are more trusted and respected by their teams.[3] Transparency doesn't diminish a leader's credibility – it enhances it. When you acknowledge what you don't know, you create space for others to contribute their knowledge and expertise. You signal to your team that collaboration and learning are valued, and that mistakes are part of the journey towards finding the best solution. In fact, when leaders pretend to know everything, we risk alienating our teams and missing out on the collective intelligence that can drive success. We all know when someone is trying to pretend they know something they don't.

> **When you acknowledge what you don't know, you create space for others to contribute their knowledge and expertise.**

As Megan Reitz, an Associate Fellow at Saïd Business School at the University of Oxford, told me, traditional leadership education has long reinforced the idea that leaders must be 'all-knowing and wise'. This mindset, she said, makes it difficult for many leaders to even recognise when they don't know something – let alone admit it. But leaders who can break free from this limiting belief and embrace intellectual honesty will unlock a level of authenticity that can transform their leadership and the culture of their organisations.

The benefits of admitting your intellectual limitations

When we embrace our intellectual limitations, a remarkable transformation takes place. This shift from needing to have all the answers to openly admitting what we don't know brings unexpected advantages, not only to ourselves but also to those we lead. In a world that is evolving faster than ever, the benefits of being honest about the boundaries of our knowledge are more powerful and necessary than ever before. These benefits range from building trust with the people we lead to creating opportunities for growth and innovation within our team and ourselves.

Freedom to learn

Admitting our intellectual limitations frees us from the pressure of needing to know everything. It opens the door to learning and signals to ourselves – and others – that we are committed to continuous growth. This is not about abdicating responsibility or avoiding decision-making, but rather about acknowledging that we don't have all the answers right now.

Even the most talented individuals must acknowledge their intellectual limitations if they want to continue growing and succeeding in new areas. Take the story of Earvin 'Magic' Johnson Junior, the former Los Angeles Lakers basketball legend. Johnson's on-court success was well known, but when he retired from basketball, he recognised that his knowledge in sports did not directly translate to business. He understood he had to start from scratch in his new career.

'My knowledge was in basketball, but I had to transition to the business world,' Johnson told a Las Vegas conference in 2024, where we were both speaking. 'So, I had to gain knowledge on how to run a company, but first, how to even build and start a company.'

Johnson's humility and willingness to admit his knowledge gaps were pivotal to his success. Rather than pretend he had all the answers, he reached out for help. Johnson asked Jerry Buss, the owner of the Lakers, for the phone numbers of all the company presidents and CEOs who were season ticket holders. He then did something few would have the courage to do: 'I called fifty presidents and CEOs,' Johnson said. 'I took them all to lunch and picked their brain.'

One of the CEOs Johnson befriended was Kenneth Chenault, who served as CEO and Chairman of American Express from 2001 to 2018. 'He would call me periodically, ask for advice,' Chenault recalled in a documentary on Johnson's life. 'What [Johnson] said to me was, "There are a set of skills I have to acquire, and I have to take the time and have to demonstrate I can learn those skills."'[4]

By admitting he didn't know everything about business, Johnson gave himself the freedom to learn. This openness allowed him to absorb crucial insights, laying the foundation for what would become a business empire with assets totalling $26 billion in 2023.

Building trust
Another profound benefit of admitting our intellectual limits is that it fosters trust with others. When leaders admit what we don't know, it humanises us in the eyes of our teams and colleagues, and it builds credibility. In today's corporate environment, where authenticity is highly valued, admitting we don't have all the answers can significantly strengthen our leadership.

When leaders are willing to admit we don't know everything, we create an environment where team members feel safe doing the same. This encourages openness and collaboration, as team members realise they don't have to pretend to know more than they do. In turn, it leads to stronger teamwork and a more cohesive workplace culture.

> **When leaders are willing to admit we don't know everything, we create an environment where team members feel safe doing the same.**

Fostering innovation and adaptability
Admitting to our intellectual limitations is also a catalyst for innovation. When we acknowledge that our knowledge is incomplete, we open ourselves – and our teams – up to new ideas and perspectives. This humility fosters an environment where experimentation and creativity thrive.

When we are open about our limitations, we invite new ideas that might not have otherwise surfaced. This adaptability is critical in industries where change happens rapidly and success depends on staying ahead of the curve. Leaders who encourage open dialogue, admit their intellectual gaps and explore different solutions are the ones who create innovative cultures and drive long-term success.

Empowering teams
By recognising we don't have all the answers, we signal to our team that their input is valuable and necessary. Take the approach of Cindy Hook, for example, a leader who knows how to embrace the unknown. With a career that spans nearly four decades, Cindy has worn many hats – none more challenging than her current role as the CEO overseeing the Brisbane 2032 Olympic and Paralympic Games. Having spent thirty-six years climbing the ranks at Deloitte, where she ultimately became the CEO of Deloitte Asia Pacific, Cindy decided to take on a monumental new challenge. She's now at the helm of hosting one of the most complex global sporting events, bringing her expertise from the corporate world into the high-stakes, unpredictable realm of Olympic and Paralympic Games planning.

Known for her ability to navigate ambiguity and adapt quickly to new environments, Cindy isn't afraid to acknowledge when she doesn't have all the answers. Her background in finance and consulting gave her a strong foundation, but her Olympic role requires an entirely different skillset, one that pushes her to lean on her curiosity, flexibility and unwavering honesty. With the Brisbane 2032 Games on the horizon, Cindy is tasked with not just planning a global event, but also leaving a lasting legacy for Australia – and she's tackling that challenge with the same boldness and humility that have defined her entire career.

When Cindy moved on from her long career at Deloitte, she found herself in completely unfamiliar territory. While her experience in business was relevant, the world of sports and the Olympics was entirely new to her. When we met she told me, 'I knew I didn't know a lot about the Olympics yet, but I am a really big reader, I am a researcher.'

Cindy embraced honesty about her knowledge gaps right from the start. Rather than pretending to know it all, she sought out experts who could help her get up to speed. She approached her leadership role with humility, acknowledging things she did not yet understand. She broke the problem into manageable-sized chunks and hired new team members to help reach these goals. Cindy knew she had a lot to learn, and she wasn't shy about seeking out the right people to help her. Instead of sticking to what she knew from her previous role, she dived into unfamiliar territory with enthusiasm.

'I just became a sponge of information,' Cindy said, describing how she actively sought out conversations with counterparts who'd organised earlier Olympic events in the 21st century, such as those in Los Angeles, Paris and London.

This curiosity extended to her team, too. Rather than trying to be the person with all the answers, Cindy focused on tapping into the knowledge and experience of those around her. She constantly asked her team, 'Who's done it before? Who can help us learn?' Through this approach, Cindy was able to accumulate a wide range of perspectives and ideas, helping her make better-informed decisions and avoid potential blind spots.

Cindy's approach exemplified intellectual honesty and ultimately empowered the people around her by signalling to them that their input was valued. This approach encourages a more inclusive leadership style, where different perspectives are considered, and where everyone has a voice. In the end, this leads to better problem-solving, as more ideas and perspectives are brought to the table. In turn, employees are more likely to engage in and take ownership of projects, and contribute to the organisation's or team's success.

Signalling a commitment to growth
Finally, admitting our intellectual limits sends a powerful message about our commitment to growth and self-improvement. Leaders who

are willing to acknowledge what they don't know are leaders who are always striving to improve – not just for their own sake but for the benefit of their teams and organisations.

So, the next time you find yourself in a situation where you don't have all the answers, remember it's okay to say, 'I don't know . . . yet.' By doing so, you open the door to growth, innovation and success – not just for yourself, but for those around you.

PRACTICE 2: DISENTANGLE YOUR EGO
What it means to disentangle our ego

In leadership and decision-making, our sense of self is often closely tied to what we know – or what we believe we know. We all have an innate drive to be perceived positively by others, and our ego is that part of us that needs to be seen in this positive light.[5] Disentangling our ego is about making discussions less personal, not taking offence when our viewpoints are challenged, and focusing more on understanding than on defending our position.

Rather than seeing our beliefs as permanent and unchangeable parts of who we are, disentangling our ego allows us to take pride in our ability to learn and grow.[6] Instead of deriving self-worth solely from what we believe or what we think we know, we learn to value the process of evolving our understanding based on new insights. This creates an environment where we can be honest with ourselves and others, free from the pressure to always be right.

How our ego can limit our perspective

Our ego, if left unchecked, can blind us to alternative ideas or better solutions because it compels us to defend our existing beliefs at all costs. When our ego is tied to our intellectual stance, it becomes difficult to engage openly in discussions, especially when our ideas are questioned. Rather than exploring opposing viewpoints with curiosity, we may feel threatened, defensive and more inclined to double down on our position – whether or not it's correct.

Jim Collins' research on Level 5 leadership, as explored in his book *Good to Great*, demonstrates the power of leaders who can disentangle their ego from their work. Level 5 leaders are distinct from those leaders Collins considers highly capable, productive and skilled (Level 1), a team member who contributes well and supports and enhances the objectives of the team (Level 2), a competent manager who organises people and resources efficiently (Level 3) and an effective leader who can drive commitment and high performance to achieve a clear vision and organisational success (Level 4).

Collins describes Level 5 leaders as those who combine humility with fierce professional will. He writes that these leaders 'channel their ego needs away from themselves and into the larger goal of building a great company'. [7] For them, success is not about being seen as personally brilliant but about achieving something larger than themselves. In Collins' hierarchy of leaders, Level 5 leaders are driven by purpose, not ego, and are able to channel ambition into the success of their organisations rather than working for personal glory. Only Level 5 leaders can take an organisation from good to great.

Why disentangling our ego is so difficult

Most of us don't consciously let our ego drive our decision-making, yet it happens more often than we realise because our sense of self and identity is deeply rooted in the core beliefs we've held about ourselves, often for years. When those core beliefs get challenged, our natural response is to defend them, sometimes without even realising it.

We all have moments where our ego gets in the way, whether it's during a heated conversation or a team meeting. Our ego wants to protect us, making it hard to admit when we don't know something or when we've made a mistake. This defence mechanism can prevent us from growing and learning, and it can ultimately derail our efforts to see things clearly.

Take a moment to reflect on the last time you became defensive. Maybe it was during a meeting where someone questioned an idea you were passionate about. In that moment, it probably felt like more than just your idea was being challenged – you might have felt as though your sense of competence and self-worth were under scrutiny as well. It's natural to feel this way, especially if you've invested a lot of your identity in being someone who always has the right answers. However, that reaction, driven by ego, blocks our ability to engage in open and honest discussions and ultimately holds us back from seeing new perspectives and opportunities.

One of the primary reasons our ego can be so difficult to disentangle is that it is tied to how we want others to perceive us. If our identity is closely linked to being someone who knows all the answers or who has everything under control, admitting any gaps in our knowledge feels like admitting a personal flaw. This is especially true in leadership positions, where we may believe that admitting uncertainty or a lack of expertise be seen as incompetence.

Instead of openly acknowledging areas where we lack expertise, we may feel compelled by our ego to solve problems on our own or brush over critical issues to preserve our self-image. The longer we let our ego dictate our actions, the more likely we are to face negative consequences down the road – whether it's a delayed project, lost credibility or strained relationships with colleagues.

Our ego often prevents us from being vulnerable, even when vulnerability is exactly what's needed to solve a problem. When we fear how others will perceive us, we might avoid asking for help, ignore important feedback or fail to admit when we're wrong. But this defensiveness comes at a high cost, both to us and to the people we lead.

The fighter pilot's lesson

Air Vice Marshal Robert Denney, a two-star general and senior pilot with the RAAF, illustrates this idea powerfully in the high-pressure world of aviation. Fighter pilots, who must often make split-second decisions that could mean life or death, are sometimes perceived as having oversized egos.

'There's a lot of ego,' Robert admitted when we spoke, 'but it's not the kind of ego we see in a Hollywood stereotype of a fighter pilot. In the fast jet world, if you go below the hard deck, like in *Top Gun*, you are dead. The other guy won. There is no more debate about whether you were right or whether it was a good decision. Our ego must be driven by a desire to correctly execute the task, not to prove you were right.'

Robert's insight highlights the importance of separating the ego from decision-making. Ego-driven decisions can lead to dire consequences, especially in high-risk environments. In his world, being right isn't about personal validation; it's about executing the mission correctly for the benefit of the team and the outcome.

'We don't have much tolerance for people like that,' Robert told me, referring to pilots who do let ego get in the way. His Squadron emphasised the importance of being honest about mistakes and limitations in the post-flight debriefs. Pilots must be able to admit their mistakes and learn from them openly – no defensiveness, no blaming. This environment requires them to have an ego that's not invested in protecting their self-worth but focused on improving performance. By keeping ego out of the way, pilots can trust each other, learn from each other and operate more effectively as a team.

Disentangling your ego helps you see more
When we disentangle our ego from our thinking, we open ourselves to deeper understanding, growth and collaboration. This process allows us to take an honest look at ourselves and engage with others without feeling personally attacked or defensive.

Disentangling our ego helps us gain clarity in how we approach problems, decisions and relationships. By turning down the volume on our need to be right, we create space for deeper understanding and collaboration. This doesn't mean we suppress our ego entirely – it's about being aware of its influence and ensuring it doesn't cloud our judgement or close us off from new information.

For leaders, this is a game changer. When our team sees that we are willing to admit what we don't know, to disentangle our ego, they are more likely to do the same. The benefits ripple outwards. Teams become more collaborative, people feel psychologically safe to share ideas and admit mistakes, and overall performance improves. Leaders who can disentangle their ego model the kind of behaviour that fosters innovation, accountability and growth.

Ultimately, disentangling our ego is about showing that leadership isn't about having all the answers. It's about creating an environment where everyone feels comfortable admitting what they don't know, so that collectively, you can find the best path forward. When we let go of the need to be right all the time, we gain the freedom to learn, grow and see the world through a broader, clearer lens.

> **When we let go of the need to be right all the time, we gain the freedom to learn.**

When we disentangle our ego, we free ourselves from the limitations of needing to protect our identity and instead open the door to deeper insight and better leadership. Next time you find yourself feeling defensive or protective of your knowledge, ask yourself: 'Is this my ego speaking?' And if it is, take a moment to let it go.

PRACTICE 3: HUNT YOUR BIASES
What it means to hunt our biases

We all like to believe that we see the world clearly and that our judgements are based on facts and evidence. But the truth is, our brains don't work that way. We all have blind spots, and we all hold cognitive biases – mental shortcuts that can skew our thinking and lead to flawed decisions. When we engage in blindspotting, one of the most critical steps we can take is bias hunting. This means actively seeking out the biases that influence our thoughts and being honest about the ways they distort our judgement. Only when we start hunting our biases can we begin to make better, more informed decisions and see the world with greater clarity.

The reality is, we see far less than we think we do. Our biases are deeply ingrained and often invisible to us, but they influence how we interpret information, how we evaluate situations and how we interact with others. This is why bias hunting is essential. By acknowledging the existence of these subconscious ways of thinking and making a conscious effort to identify them, we can open ourselves up to more nuanced, well-rounded perspectives. Without this awareness, we remain unable to see the bigger picture.

When we hunt our biases, we start to recognise how they might be distorting our perception of situations. It's a critical aspect of blindspotting because if we don't actively challenge our biases, we remain stuck in limited ways of thinking. Bias hunting allows us to pause, reflect and question how our preconceived notions might be impacting our views and decisions. It also encourages us to seek out alternative explanations and viewpoints, ensuring that we consider different angles that might have otherwise been overshadowed by our biases.

Why it's so hard to hunt our biases

Hunting for our biases is not an easy task and requires continuous effort. Our brains are naturally wired to take shortcuts, relying on cognitive biases to save energy and make decisions quickly. This mental efficiency was once crucial for survival – when our ancestors were hunting and gathering for food, they needed to make quick decisions about whether to fight or flee as a predator approached to increase their chances of survival. But in today's complex world, it can lead to flawed thinking and poor decision-making. Even among those with the best intentions, biases infiltrate our thoughts, colouring our judgement without us even realising it. The challenge, then, is not just recognising our biases exist but actively hunting them before they distort our actions and choices.

One reason hunting for biases is so hard is that our brains are designed to conserve energy. When faced with decisions – especially complex ones – our brain looks for the simplest or most familiar option. This mental shortcut allows us to process information quickly, but it also means we're more likely to lean on biases that save us time, rather than taking a moment longer to critically evaluate the situation.

This is where the difficulty lies: once we've made a decision, we naturally look for ways to confirm it. We want to feel good about our choices.[8] So, instead of considering all the evidence, we selectively acknowledge the pieces that support what we already think. This mental shortcut allows us to move forward without the heavy lifting of rethinking our decisions.

Facing the uncomfortable truth
Admitting we hold biases, even ones we try to keep hidden from others, is uncomfortable. No one wants to think their judgement is flawed or unfair. We like to believe we are objective, rational thinkers. However, research shows that most people rate themselves as being less biased than others, a result that is, ironically, a clear indicator of biased thinking.[9]

This cognitive blind spot – our inability to see our own biases – poses a real challenge, especially for those of us who often need to make complicated decisions that influence other people. We can easily spot biased thinking in other people, but we struggle to recognise it in ourselves. The brutal reality is that while we may be blind to our own biases, they are often painfully visible to those around us. These biases seep into our decisions, our behaviours and even our language. One of the biggest mistakes we can make is to deny their existence. The second is failing to hunt for them.

> **The brutal reality is that while we may be blind to our own biases, they are often painfully visible to those around us.**

The feedback gap

Another reason bias hunting is difficult is because we don't always get feedback to help us see where our thinking has gone astray. Feedback is essential in revealing biases that we might not otherwise notice. For many leaders, feedback is often limited or non-existent, either because they don't encourage it, or because the people in their team feel uncomfortable providing it. Let's face it: most of us aren't exactly lining up to critique our boss, challenge a teammate, or even point out a friend's faulty logic. Why? Because feedback is risky – it's uncomfortable to give, and we worry about how it will be received. If you want feedback that's honest and useful, you have to make others feel safe to do so. So, how do you get people to be honest with you about your blind spots?

When we receive feedback, it gives us insight into how others perceive our decision-making processes. It shines a light on biases we might not see on our own. If we're open to hearing it, feedback can become a critical tool in our effort to hunt for biases. Without it, we are left to navigate in the dark, assuming our thinking is flawless when it might be riddled with blind spots.

One way to do this is to invite feedback in a way that makes people feel heard, not judged. Imagine saying to your team, 'I am keen to get better at leading our projects. What's one thing you have observed I do that could be done differently to help us succeed?' Notice how this question doesn't ask for a critique of our personality or performance – it invites collaboration. It shifts the focus from 'what's wrong with me' to 'how can we improve together'. Suddenly, offering feedback feels like contributing to a shared goal, not poking holes in our ego.

Another powerful strategy is to model vulnerability. Share a story with your team about a time when you received tough feedback and how it helped you grow. For example, you might say, 'Last year, someone pointed out that I tend to dominate meetings, and it was hard to hear – but they were right. I've been working on it, and I want to make sure I'm still improving. If you notice me slipping, please let me know. I am eager to do better at it.' By admitting that you've been wrong before, you send a clear signal: it's okay to be imperfect here. You also set the tone for how you'll respond – constructively and without defensiveness – making it easier for others to speak up.

Remember, the key to unlocking honest feedback lies in how you react when it's given. If someone finally builds up the courage to say, 'I think you might be overlooking X,' and your response is to become defensive or shut them down, you have effectively slammed the door on any future feedback conversations. Instead, pause, thank them and reflect – even if it stings. Treat feedback like the gift it is.

The impact of stress and emotion

Bias hunting becomes even harder in moments of stress, multitasking or when we are emotionally invested in a situation. In these scenarios, we are more likely to fall back on our biases because they require less cognitive effort. We cling to familiar thought patterns because they provide comfort in a high-pressure environment.

Think about the last time you had a heated argument. Perhaps it was with a colleague who didn't meet a deadline, or maybe with a loved one over something trivial that spiralled into something bigger. In the heat of the moment, did you catch yourself making assumptions about their intentions? Did you find yourself thinking, *They don't care about this project* or *They always do this to upset me*. These snap judgements feel natural, but they're often driven by biases that flare up when our emotions do. Under stress, our brains seek shortcuts, and biases are the fastest route to what we think of as certainty, even if we are wrong.

Now picture yourself in a stressful meeting where decisions must be made quickly. A colleague presents an idea, and almost reflexively, you dismiss it – not because the idea lacks merit but because of who it's coming from. Maybe they've failed before, or maybe their tone irritates you. Under the pressure to act, your mind draws on past experiences and stereotypes rather than fully processing the new information at hand.

These moments aren't rare – they're human. When the stakes are high, we don't take the time to question our gut reactions. The challenge is that our 'gut' isn't always reliable; it's often a blend of memories, habits and subconscious prejudices. Recognising these patterns takes practice, but the payoff is immense: better decisions, stronger relationships and, most importantly, a clearer sense of how you respond when under pressure. So, next time you're feeling stressed or emotional, ask yourself, 'Am I reacting – or am I relying on my biases to do the thinking for me?'

The benefits of spotlighting our biases

The benefits of hunting for our biases are profound. This practice leads to improved decision-making, better problem-solving, more effective communication and greater trust and credibility as a leader. By actively looking for and uncovering these blind spots, we send a powerful message – not only to ourselves but to those we lead – that we are willing to challenge the way we think in order to get to better outcomes.

> **By actively looking for and uncovering these blind spots, we send a powerful message that we are willing to challenge the way we think in order to get to better outcomes.**

Better decision-making
One of the most significant benefits of spotlighting our biases is enhanced decision-making. When we acknowledge and mitigate our biases before making a decision, we are more likely to evaluate information objectively and consider different angles. It helps us avoid falling into the trap of relying on past experiences or assumptions

when faced with new challenges. Leaders who are aware of their biases can make more balanced assessments of risks, performance and solutions. By hunting for our biases, we reduce the likelihood of making decisions based on incomplete or emotionally influenced judgements, which ultimately leads to better, fairer outcomes and prevents us from making hasty conclusions that could undermine our success.

Leading by example
Leaders who actively hunt for their biases also set a powerful example for those around them. When team members see their leader openly challenge their own assumptions, it creates a ripple effect, encouraging others to do the same. With leaders acting as role models, bias hunting can become a core value within the organisation, where individuals at every level are committed to evaluating their own thought processes and ingrained assumptions. This cultural shift leads to better collaboration and stronger teamwork, as everyone is more open to hearing alternative viewpoints and learning from others. It also helps resolve conflicts more quickly, as people are less likely to be entrenched in their own perspectives and more willing to understand others' views.

The mindset of honesty is key to blindspotting. By acknowledging our intellectual limits, we open ourselves up to the possibility of learning more. Disentangling our ego allows us to be more comfortable with admitting what we don't know, without it threatening our sense of self. And by spotlighting our biases, we improve our ability to think clearly and make sound decisions in complex situations.

Now, as we move forward, we will explore the next essential mindset of blindspotting: curiosity. Building on the foundation of honesty, curiosity encourages us to look outwards and ask the important questions. Let's now dive into how curiosity can help us see what others might miss.

KEY TAKEAWAYS

- **Radical self-honesty is the core of blindspotting.** Blindspotting begins with the mindset of honesty – being truthful to others and also being radically honest with ourselves. This includes recognising our intellectual limits, acknowledging how our ego distorts our thinking, and identifying the biases that cloud our judgement. This form of honesty is crucial for effectively embracing the other two essential mindsets of blindspotting: curiosity and flexibility.
- **Intellectual honesty fosters better leadership.** Great leaders don't need to have all the answers. Instead, they excel at asking the right questions, creating a culture where their teams feel safe to speak up, contribute their perspectives and learn continuously. This honesty and humility at a leadership level encourages openness and collaboration within teams, which ultimately fosters growth, innovation and creativity.
- **Accepting intellectual limits unlocks growth.** Leaders often feel pressured to know everything, but true growth happens when we accept our intellectual limits and admit when we don't know something. This intellectual honesty allows leaders to tap into the knowledge of others, learn from them and collaborate more effectively. The mindset of 'I don't know . . . yet' opens the door for continuous improvement and deeper insights.
- **Disentangling the ego leads to clearer thinking.** One of the essential practices in the honesty mindset is learning to separate our self-worth from the need to be right. Often, our ego becomes wrapped up in being 'correct', which blinds us to learning opportunities. By shifting away from our pride and need to have all the answers and moving towards valuing the ability to learn and evolve, we become

more open to new perspectives, leading to well-informed decisions and clearer thinking.
- **Hunting biases will help you make better decisions.** Cognitive biases can distort our judgement, and many of them operate unconsciously. A critical aspect of blindspotting is actively seeking out biases and recognising their influence on our thinking. By doing so, we can make better, more accurate decisions free from these ingrained assumptions.

FURTHER READING

Mahzarin R. Banaji and Anthony Greenwald, *Blindspot: Hidden biases of good people* (2013).

Christopher Chabris and Daniel Simons, *The Invisible Gorilla: And other ways our intuitions deceive us* (2010).

Jim Collins, *Good to Great* (2001).

Ryan Holiday, *Ego is the Enemy* (2017).

Megan Reitz and John Higgins, *Speak Up: Say what needs to be said and hear what needs to be heard* (2019).

RIPPLE EFFECTS OF TRAGEDY

'You don't really know what your blind spots are until you've messed up.'

David Epstein, investigative journalist and author

In the high-stakes world of journalism, where the demand for content is ever-present and immediate, admitting you've got it wrong can feel like failure. But for David Epstein, it was this very process – rethinking and reworking his original assumptions – that led him to a deeper truth and a better story. His journey from writing a cover story for *Sports Illustrated* to revising the entire thesis behind his bestselling book *The Sports Gene* provides invaluable lessons for anyone navigating the complexities of leadership, whether in business, journalism, sports or any other field.

When David and I first met in early 2024 over brunch in Washington, DC, where he lives with his family, I discovered someone who is committed to the practice of blindspotting. For leaders, people who face the challenge of making decisions based on incomplete or evolving information, David's experience serves as a powerful reminder that intellectual honesty, curiosity and flexibility are the keys to long-term success.

Long before David began writing for *Sports Illustrated* or authoring bestselling books, a tragic event forever changed his relationship with science and journalism – the sudden death of his friend and high school track teammate Kevin Richards at a race in Chicago in 2000.

'Kevin's death was a wake-up call,' David told me. 'It was the first time I realised how little we actually know about our own bodies.'

Kevin had been young, fit and full of promise when he collapsed at the end of a race and died. The newspapers called it a heart attack, but David couldn't accept that explanation. As a sophomore in college, he found himself consumed by questions that no one seemed to be asking: *Why did someone so healthy succumb to a deadly condition? Was there something about Kevin's biology that had made this outcome inevitable?*

This tragedy sparked David's deep interest in the intersection of science and sports. As a runner himself, he had always been fascinated by human physical performance. But now, his curiosity took on a new urgency – he wanted to understand the hidden forces that governed athletic success and failure. This seed of an idea would eventually grow into his work for *Sports Illustrated* and, later, his bestselling book *The Sports Gene*.

Years after Kevin's death, David found a way to combine his interests in sports, science and journalism. After persistent effort to gain interest from publications for his research and writing, he got his first major break: a published article in *Sports Illustrated* about sudden cardiac death in athletes. This was followed by many more, including an article that won a journalism award. The article was on the role of genetics in athletic performance. Its success also provided David with the foundation for a book deal that would allow him to explore the topic further.

But there was a problem.

'When I wrote that article, I came down heavily on downplaying the role of genetics in athleticism,' David explained. 'It was a story that fit the narrative people wanted to hear – that hard work and effort could overcome any biological limitations.'

The article reinforced a common belief in sports and beyond: that genetics play a minimal role in success, and that anyone, with enough grit and determination, can achieve greatness. David himself had grown up believing this message. As a walk-on athlete – someone who joins a college team without being recruited or placed on a scholarship for their athletic abilities – who had risen to hold a university record, David lived the story of hard work overcoming natural disadvantages.

And so, with his book proposal in hand, David began to write *The Sports Gene*. He was confident the data would back up the same position embraced by the *Sports Illustrated* audience.

But as David dug deeper into the science, he learnt he had made a mistake.

'I spent a year really learning about genetics,' he recalled, 'and I realised that most of the things I thought were wrong.'

As David dived into research for his book, he discovered that genetics play a far more significant role in athletic performance than he had initially believed. What he had written in his *Sports Illustrated* article wasn't factually incorrect, but it was conceptually flawed. He had, like many others, allowed his personal biases to shape the story. His personal biases had been reinforced by what scientists were telling him.

'A massive lesson for me was that I can't just take an idea I believe, back it up with statements of brilliant people, and assume I've got it right,' David said. 'It was quite the wake-up call to realise that I need to also try and falsify my own beliefs rather than just hunt to support them; scientists are also human beings with cognitive biases. Who knew?'

This realisation was both a professional and personal challenge. 'It was tough,' David admitted. 'I had sold the book on this idea that was essentially wrong. Not because I was being dishonest, but because I was blind to the other side of the story.'

For many, this would have led to a moment of quiet retreat – an opportunity to double down on the original message and push the book through to meet the deadline. But David did something different. Instead of ignoring the blind spot he had uncovered, he asked his publisher for an extension, threw out his initial proposal and started over.

'It was a hard thing to do,' David told me, 'but I knew it was the right thing. You can't move forward if you're not willing to be intellectually honest with yourself.'

In the business world, and in any type of leadership role, there is often immense pressure to present certainty, even when the facts don't fully align with the desired narrative. But David's decision to rethink his assumptions illustrates the power of intellectual honesty – the ability to admit when you don't know something, or to admit when you've made a mistake.

This kind of humility is often seen as a weakness, especially in environments where confidence and decisiveness are prized. But, as David's story shows, intellectual honesty is a form of strength. It's what allows leaders to pivot, to adapt to new information and to ultimately make better decisions.

David could have continued with his original thesis for *The Sports Gene*, but doing so would have compromised the integrity of his work. Instead, he embraced the process of blindspotting by admitting what he didn't know and adapting his thinking as new information came to light. The end result was a book that offered a more nuanced and scientifically accurate exploration of the role of genetics in athletic performance. Published in 2013, *The Sports Gene* became a *New York Times* bestseller, was named *Runners' World* Book of the Year and was included in the *Washington Post*'s notable nonfiction booklist. Most meaningful for David, however, was that the book was well reviewed by the highly regarded journals *Science* and *Nature*.

'These were people who knew genetics but were not invested in sports,' David told me. 'That is when I felt I had managed to get at least a foot outside my own intellectual bubble.'

When faced with evidence that contradicted his long-held assumptions, David didn't shy away. Instead, he leant into the uncertainty, asking new questions and seeking out experts who could help him understand the complexities of the science – the epitome of embracing blindspotting.

'If you stop asking questions, you stop growing,' David said. 'I thought I knew the story when I started writing the book, but the deeper I went, the more I realised I had to rethink everything.'

Perhaps the most important aspect of David's experience was his ability to be flexible in his thinking. Cognitive flexibility – the capacity to change one's thinking when confronted with new evidence – is a critical skill for leaders in any field. Without it, leaders and their teams become rigid, unable to adapt to changing circumstances or to learn from their mistakes.

David's willingness to throw out his original thesis and start over was an exercise in cognitive flexibility. He didn't cling to his initial assumptions just because they were convenient or aligned with his personal beliefs. Instead, he allowed the data to guide him, even when it led him to a conclusion far more controversial than the one he had originally proposed.

In an increasingly complex and fast-changing world, leaders who practise blindspotting will be the ones who thrive. As David's story shows, the path to success is not always a straight line – it often requires you to rethink, revise and adapt along the way.

5

BE CURIOUS

Most of us appreciate the power of curiosity to drive discovery, spark innovation and compel us to search for answers we didn't know we needed. But what happens when we stop being curious? What happens when we allow our assumptions, beliefs or comfort in what we already know to limit our understanding?

When we stop being curious, it's like walking through our daily routines with a torch whose battery is fading. At work, we might stick to what we know, completing tasks efficiently but never questioning whether there's a better way, a new perspective or an untapped opportunity. We might never ask, 'What if . . .?' The torchlight of curiosity illuminates not just what is, but what could be – the overlooked idea in a meeting, the subtle but telling detail in a colleague's suggestion, or the innovative solution hiding behind a problem we thought we'd already solved. When the light dims, we fall into patterns of sameness, mistaking familiarity for success, while the breakthroughs we long for remain just outside our narrow beam.

> Curiosity illuminates not just what is, but what could be.

In life, too, a lack of curiosity can dim our relationships and experiences. It's like sitting across from someone at dinner and never asking why they seem distant or their laughter quieter than usual. Without curiosity, we see the surface of others, never uncovering the stories, struggles and triumphs that deepen our connections. The torch isn't just a tool: it's a way of seeing the world; a mindset. And when we fail to think curiously, we risk missing the richness, both in ourselves and in the world around us.

The mindset of curiosity is at the heart of blindspotting. Curiosity pushes us beyond our biases, our preconceived notions, and the surface of a problem, enabling us to discover insights that might otherwise have remained hidden. Curiosity is a tool that sharpens our perspective and challenges us to go beyond what's easy, obvious or convenient. It's not about asking questions for the sake of it, but rather actively seeking to understand the full picture.

We often find ourselves relying on what we already know because it's safe. It feels good to be confident in our understanding of things. But that security can blind us to what we might be missing. When we're too comfortable with what we know, we stop looking for new answers. We stop seeking out different perspectives. We stop asking *why*.

Blindspotting asks us to remain curious and refuse to become complacent. It challenges us to question what we think we know and invites us to explore what lies beyond our current understanding. Curiosity, when combined with the two other blindspotting mindsets of honesty and flexibility, becomes a superpower, enabling us to see beyond our blind spots and become better leaders, thinkers and decision-makers.

Curiosity opens the door to new possibilities, not by passively waiting for answers but by actively searching for them. Embracing a curiosity mindset means constantly questioning whether the 'truths' we hold are objective, complete and accurate.

Curiosity is the antidote to stagnation.

A mindset of curiosity is also about embracing the unknown and being willing to admit we don't have all the answers; instead, we understand that the more we explore, the more we realise how much we have yet to discover. When we bring curiosity into our leadership, it becomes our foundation for learning, innovation and adaptability. Leaders who are curious create a culture of inquiry, where questions are not only allowed but encouraged, and where learning is an ongoing process.

> **When we bring curiosity into our leadership, it becomes our foundation for learning, innovation and adaptability.**

As we move forward in this chapter, keep in mind that curiosity is not a passive trait. It is an active pursuit, a relentless drive to understand, explore and discover. It requires effort, energy and a willingness to be vulnerable in the face of what you don't know. But the rewards are immense. When you commit to being curious, you will open yourself to a world of possibilities that can transform not only your understanding but also your leadership practice.

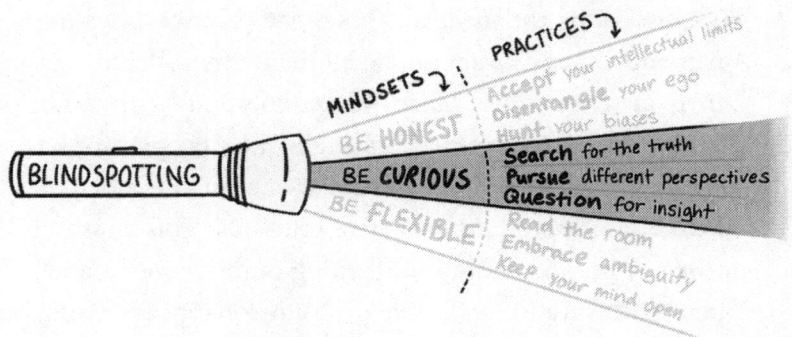

In the context of blindspotting, the mindset of curiosity has three key practices:
- **Search for the truth.** This practice means seeking a deeper understanding of complex issues by moving beyond surface-level explanations. It involves a commitment to uncovering

objective facts – those that exist independently of our personal perceptions or beliefs. Searching for the truth requires us to question our assumptions, to gather evidence from various sources and to remain open to changing our perspective based on what we discover. It's about finding what is *real*, not just what is convenient or what aligns with what we already believe. Searching for the truth means embracing a mindset of intellectual honesty in the pursuit of genuine understanding.

- **Pursue different perspectives.** Through this practice, we actively seek out views that differ from our own, and in doing so we open ourselves to insights we might otherwise miss. Observing things from multiple angles helps us see beyond our blind spots, fostering more informed and balanced decisions. The more perspectives we consider, the closer we get to a well-rounded and complete picture of the truth. Ultimately, we recognise that there's always more than one way to tackle a challenge, and each new viewpoint enhances our understanding.
- **Ask questions for insight.** This is the practice of asking open-ended questions with a genuine desire to learn, not to prove ourselves right. When we ask questions with curiosity, we unlock a deeper understanding of why people think the way they do, fostering greater collaboration and a better likelihood of uncovering creative solutions. This approach moves us beyond simply confirming our own views and opens pathways for collective problem-solving, enriching our perspective through the insights we gain from others.

With that overview in mind, let's explore the first practice of curiosity – searching for the truth – and explore what it means to seek out objective truth in a world filled with complexity, uncertainty and competing information.

PRACTICE 1: SEARCH FOR THE TRUTH
What it means to search for truth

Searching for the truth is no simple task. We often feel certain in our beliefs, confident we know how things stand. As leaders this can be especially true – our confidence has been honed through years of experience and successes. But is this certainty justified? Are we looking beyond the surface to seek a more complex and nuanced understanding of the current issues we're faced with? The truths we hold are often shaped by our experiences, biases and the perspectives we've adopted over time. This can cloud our judgement, making it hard to recognise the objective truth – the truth that exists independently of our beliefs.

What is 'truth' exactly? Most of us go through life believing we are on the side of the truth most of the time.[1] But in an age of information overload, where conflicting reports and opinions flood our screens daily, it can be hard to discern what is true. Misinformation, disinformation and even outright deception blur the lines between reality and fiction. Additionally, truth is often subjective – based on everyone's personal experiences, cultural contexts and ethical standpoints. For example, what one person believes to be true about a political issue may be vastly different from someone on the opposite side of the ideological spectrum. However, beyond these subjective perspectives lies something else: objective truth.

The objective truth exists independently of our personal views or opinions. It is based on facts that can be observed, measured and tested – facts that hold up under scrutiny, regardless of whether we personally agree with them or not. For example, the shape of the Earth is an objective truth. We know it to be a sphere (or more specifically, an oblate spheroid) because of scientific evidence gathered over centuries, including satellite imagery and observations from space. Despite what 'flat-earthers' might claim, their belief is not supported by empirical evidence; it's based on a subjective understanding of the world, influenced by mistrust and other biases.

Most of us accept the objective truth of the Earth's shape without question, but we can easily fall into the trap of accepting subjective truths in other areas of life. When we rely solely on our experiences, intuition or emotions, we might miss the fuller picture. That's why searching for the truth – especially the objective truth – is crucial to improve your decision-making and grow into a more effective leader.

When we search for the truth with a mindset of curiosity, we become more aware of the complexity of the world around us. We realise that the first explanation we encounter is rarely the complete answer. So we dig deeper, gather more data and seek out different viewpoints. In doing so, we come closer and closer to uncovering the objective truth.

Finding the truth is rarely easy, and it's often not black and white. Complex problems demand complex solutions, and truth is often found in the grey areas. But by engaging the mindset of curiosity, we commit to doing the work required to find the objective truth, even when it's inconvenient or challenges our previous opinions.

> **Complex problems demand complex solutions, and truth is often found in the grey areas.**

Imagine you have a colleague who's constantly pushing back on new ideas in meetings. It's tempting to label them as resistant to change or overly negative. But curiosity urges you to look closer. Instead of brushing them off, perhaps ask them: 'What's on your mind when these ideas come up?' Through the conversation, you discover they're not intentionally resistant – they're cautious because they've seen similar initiatives fail before due to poor planning. Their pushback isn't about negativity; it's about protecting the team from repeating past mistakes. By engaging your curiosity, you've turned what seemed like a roadblock into a resource – someone whose insight can strengthen the very ideas you're trying to bring to life.

Now consider a heated family argument. One person storms out, and everyone else quickly labels them 'difficult' or 'oversensitive'.

But curiosity nudges you to pause and wonder: what else might be going on? With a few thoughtful questions, you learn they've been silently dealing with a major stressor — work pressure, health concerns or personal doubt. By seeking the truth beyond the convenient narrative, you not only uncover what's real but also open the door to empathy, understanding and genuine connection. In both cases, curiosity doesn't just find the truth; it makes the complex human, and it makes the grey areas valuable.

Making decisions based on subjective truths can have far-reaching consequences for teams and organisations. By searching for the objective truth, leaders can make more informed, equitable decisions that lead to better outcomes for everyone.

> By searching for the objective truth, leaders can make more informed, equitable decisions that lead to better outcomes for everyone.

Why we cling to our existing beliefs

Searching for the truth can be more challenging than it seems. Instead of being open to different realities and perspectives, many of us tend to hold on to the beliefs we already have. This is not just an emotional reaction — it's rooted in how our brains are wired. Humans are driven by an imperative need to feel correct and secure in their understanding of the world.[2] But this innate desire for certainty can become a barrier, preventing us from seeking or accepting new information that threatens our beliefs. The search for truth, on the other hand, requires curiosity to help us challenge these internal biases and keep our minds open to alternative perspectives.

The illusion of certainty

You may recall a viral sensation from 2015 involving a picture of a dress. The image sparked a worldwide debate about its colour.

To many people, the dress was clearly white and gold. Others were equally adamant that it was blue and black. This single image divided opinion like few topics can. Millions of people weighed in, declaring the dress to be blue and black.[3] Yet, just as many were convinced the dress was white and gold.[4]

How could a simple image cause such a strong divergence in perception? Researchers soon dug into the phenomenon.[5] They interviewed 1,400 people and found that 57 per cent saw the dress as blue and black, while 30 per cent saw it as white and gold. The rest saw varying combinations of colours. The objective truth, verified by the manufacturer, was that the dress was indeed blue and black. But for those who saw it as white and gold, including myself, the visual illusion remained incredibly compelling, even after learning the truth.

This phenomenon reveals a critical insight: what we think we know, what we believe to be true, is not always aligned with the objective reality. Psychologist Daniel Kahneman, a Nobel Prize winner, referred to this as the 'illusion of validity'. Kahneman argued that 'We are prone to think that the world is more regular and predictable than it really is.'[6] Our memory builds a coherent story about what is going on around us, suppressing alternatives to maintain that consistency. This is why we often remain confident in our beliefs, even when presented with evidence that contradicts them.

The need for simplicity in a complex world
Another reason it's so difficult to search for the truth is that we crave simplicity. Our brains are not just wired for certainty; they're wired for efficiency. In a world filled with overwhelming information, it's natural to prefer simple explanations over complex, nuanced realities. When faced with ambiguity or a flood of facts, the simplest explanation often feels like the safest.

But the truth, as we know, is rarely simple. It often exists in a nuanced understanding of a complex set of factors. Recognising this is an essential step in the journey of blindspotting. It requires not only curiosity but also intellectual humility – a willingness to acknowledge that our initial perception might not be correct.

Confirmation bias and the comfort of familiarity

At the heart of our difficulty in searching for the truth is confirmation bias, a cognitive shortcut that leads us to favour information that supports our pre-existing beliefs. This bias shields us from discomfort and reinforces the worldview we've constructed over time. Rather than seeking objective truth, we often seek reassurance that we were right all along.

This cognitive bias, coupled with the comfort of familiarity, makes it difficult for us to confront evidence that contradicts what we 'know'. It's easier, and more appealing, to believe that our understanding of the world is correct.

How searching for the truth transforms our understanding

By engaging in the mindset of curiosity and applying critical thinking skills, we can navigate through complicated issues to ensure the objective truth emerges. This process is far more powerful than simply holding on to our initial beliefs. The objective truth has the capacity to reshape our understanding, elevate our decisions and spark shifts in how we perceive the world.

> **The objective truth has the capacity to reshape our understanding, elevate our decisions and spark shifts in how we perceive the world.**

Chris Havrilla is a visionary leader in the world of human capital management (HCM), known for her ability to solve complex business problems using cutting-edge technology and innovative thinking. As the Vice President of Oracle Cloud HCM Product Strategy, she focuses on shaping the future of talent and workforce experience.

With a rich background that spans from software engineering to HR consulting, Chris has honed her ability to bridge the gap between people and technology. What makes Chris stand out is her relentless curiosity, her willingness to question the status quo, and her talent for uncovering the unseen challenges within an organisation. Her career, built on both technical expertise and human insight, has made her a sought-after leader in navigating the complexities of the modern workplace.

Throughout her career, Chris has been confronted by challenges. 'I am always being given complex problems no one has the answer to and being asked to find a solution,' Chris told me when we spoke in 2024. Her work requires her to step outside the boundaries of subjective truth and seek the objective truth – what is really happening in any given situation.

When people approach Chris with solutions to a problem, they often base their ideas on limited information, shaped by prior experiences and personal biases. Their 'truth' is inherently subjective. Yet Chris remains laser-focused on finding the objective truth. 'We live in a world of probabilities, not certainties,' she explains. 'If I don't understand the problem, I can't help. What is the right solution to the right problem we are trying to solve?'

Chris quickly learnt that delivering exactly what clients asked for wasn't always effective. When she was a software engineer, she would complete the projects as requested, only to find that the solution didn't have the impact they were expecting. Frustrated, she realised she needed to ask a critical question of her clients: 'Why do you want this?' This shift in mindset transformed the way she worked. Instead of taking orders, Chris began probing deeper to understand the real problems clients were facing. This curiosity to ask 'Why?' again and again opened up broader possibilities, helping her devise innovative solutions and helping her clients achieve far better results than they had initially envisioned. By seeking to understand the problem first, Chris was able to offer creative solutions that exceeded expectations.

This mindset exemplifies the transformative power of searching for the objective truth. Chris's ability to approach problems from this curious, truth-seeking perspective not only changed the dynamic of the situation but often sparked curiosity in others. 'The minute they realise there is a different solution to the one they perceived to be true, the value proposition changes immediately,' she noted. The search for the objective truth can shift perspectives and open doors to new possibilities we haven't even considered.

The impact of objective truth

When we commit to searching for the truth, our understanding of the world expands. We are no longer limited by the narrow scope of subjective experiences, opinions or preconceived notions. Instead, we begin making decisions grounded in facts and evidence. This not only leads to more informed choices but also ensures that our decisions are equitable, consistent and clear.

> When we commit to searching for the truth, our understanding of the world expands.

Making decisions grounded in fairness

One of the most valuable outcomes of searching for the truth is that it helps us make fairer decisions. When our actions are rooted in objective reality, we reduce the risk of favouritism, bias or misinformation influencing our choices. This is particularly critical in leadership, where every decision can have a ripple effect on team morale, performance and trust. Fairness is the foundation of trust, and when we prioritise the truth, we demonstrate our commitment to equity, honesty and transparency.

Building trust and credibility

Leaders who consistently search for the truth gain trust and credibility from the people around them. We are drawn to leaders and colleagues who prioritise the truth over convenience or comfort. When others see that we are committed to seeking objective truth – even when it's difficult or uncomfortable – they know they can rely on us to be wholly fair. This builds trust in our leadership, deepens professional relationships and creates a collaborative culture based on mutual respect.

In Chris Havrilla's case, her search for the objective truth in solving problems has earned her a reputation as a go-to leader for complex challenges in the HCM industry. By focusing on the truth, she has cultivated a sense of trust and credibility among her colleagues. They know that when she approaches a problem, she will do so from a place of genuine curiosity and a commitment to finding the best solution, not just the most convenient one.

Leaders like Chris remind us that the pursuit of truth is not about being infallible but about being willing to ask questions, learn and grow. It's about creating an environment where the truth is valued and prioritised, where people are encouraged to bring forth ideas, perspectives and solutions, even if they challenge existing beliefs.

PRACTICE 2: PURSUE DIFFERENT PERSPECTIVES

What it means to embrace different perspectives

When we are blindspotting with a mindset of curiosity, it means we are eagerly pursuing different perspectives, especially those that may challenge our own. By recognising there is more than one way to view any issue or situation, we can expand our understanding and reduce the blind spots we might otherwise miss.

Curiosity propels us to seek new insights, and often that means hearing from people whose experiences or perspectives are unlike our own. By engaging with those unique viewpoints, we ensure our decisions are informed by a fuller picture of reality, rather than relying solely on our individual perspective. This is not just a helpful practice – it's critical to avoid falling into cognitive traps such as confirmation bias, where we only hear what we want to hear.

The key to pursuing different perspectives is to ask for input *and* be willing to learn from it. When we seek out and truly engage with the insights of others, we are much more likely to find innovative and effective solutions to the challenges we face, compared to when we rely solely on our own point of view or past experience.

> **The key to pursuing different perspectives is to ask for input *and* be willing to learn from it.**

That said, pursuing different perspectives doesn't mean blindly accepting every piece of feedback we receive. Critical thinking remains essential: evaluating each perspective to discern its value, considering how it fits into the larger picture, and determining whether it enhances or detracts from the overall goal.

The ability to seek and engage with a wide range of perspectives isn't just a skill – it's a responsibility. Great leaders understand their role isn't to have all the answers but to create an environment where the best ideas can emerge. We actively listen, ask thoughtful questions and encourage input from our teams since we know innovation thrives at the intersection of different viewpoints. At the same time, we act as a filter, using critical thinking to sift through feedback and ensure that what gets implemented aligns with our larger vision. Our strength as a leader lies not in dictating solutions, but in empowering others to contribute, guiding the collective insights towards impactful action. This balance – curiosity with discernment – is what distinguishes a good leader from a great one.

Why we struggle to embrace different perspectives

Think of a time when you were convinced you had made the right call on a decision at work. Perhaps a colleague suggested an alternative course of action, but because it didn't align with what you had already decided, you might have brushed off their suggestion – or worse, you didn't even hear it.

When we are confronted with information that challenges our beliefs, it creates what psychologists refer to as cognitive dissonance – a mental discomfort caused by holding two or more contradictory beliefs at the same time.[7] Cognitive dissonance can feel unsettling, especially when we are deeply invested in our current belief system.

It's innately human to crave familiarity. Our brains are wired to seek patterns, certainty and comfort because, for much of our evolutionary history, sticking with what we knew could mean the difference between life and death. Familiarity kept our ancestors safe – whether it was recognising the path back to camp or avoiding the strange plants that might be poisonous. But the truth is, our ancient survival mechanisms don't always serve us in the modern context. Instead, they can trap us in echo chambers and prevent us from adapting to a rapidly changing world. Growth, innovation and resilience demand we push past the pull of familiarity, embrace discomfort and open ourselves to new perspectives, even when they challenge everything we think we know.

For instance, if you've always believed that your management style is effective, but then you hear from a colleague that your approach is hindering team productivity, it can create an internal clash between how you see yourself and how others see you. To avoid the discomfort of reconciling this contradiction, you might dismiss the feedback or justify why it's not applicable. This avoidance might protect your ego or sense of self in the moment, but ultimately it prevents growth and learning, shutting out the opportunity for you to reflect on how a change in your management style might lead to better outcomes.

The groupthink trap
It's not only individual biases that make it hard to pursue different perspectives. In organisational settings, no matter how big or

small the team or company, groupthink can be a major obstacle. Groupthink occurs when the desire for harmony or conformity in a group leads to poor decision-making, as dissenting voices are suppressed to maintain unity.

In many corporate environments, there's an unspoken pressure to avoid rocking the boat. Team members might hesitate to offer their perspective, especially if it differs from the strong consensus or if leadership appears to favour a particular direction. As a result, organisations can fall into the trap of echo chambers, where only similar viewpoints are heard and alternative perspectives are sidelined.

Investigative journalist Duncan Mavin, whose thoughts on hubris we considered in chapter 3, has written about numerous corporate collapses and often observed this phenomenon in boardrooms. 'It is almost impossible to tell board members apart,' Duncan told me. 'They look the same, went to the same schools, have the same professional background. When everyone thinks alike, there is no one to challenge the status quo. It's a massive blind spot not to understand the value of people who might challenge and disagree with you.'

Duncan's observations highlight the dangers of surrounding ourselves only with like-minded individuals. Without a diverse range of perspectives, any team, organisation or workplace can become stagnant – and in worst-case scenarios, this lack of challenge can lead to significant operational failures.

Imagine you're leading a project and your team unanimously agrees on a strategy right away. No one raises a concern, no one suggests an alternative, and everyone nods along. It feels good, doesn't it? The plan seems airtight, and you forge ahead with confidence. But fast-forward a few months – unexpected problems arise, deadlines are missed, and the results fall short. In hindsight, you realise there were warning signs, questions that weren't asked and crucial perspectives that were missing.

Now, ask yourself: have you ever been in a situation where the ease of agreement felt too good to challenge? Where you dismissed or avoided the discomfort of asking, 'What if we're missing something?'

It's tempting to trust consensus, but real progress comes from the courage to invite dissent, dig deep and look for what others might not see. When was the last time you truly welcomed a perspective that made you uncomfortable?

The benefits of understanding the full story

A mindset of curiosity encourages us to actively seek out different perspectives and viewpoints. It humbles us by making us aware we don't have all the answers and others may offer valuable insights. This pursuit of alternative viewpoints fosters an open and collaborative learning environment, which in turn builds a culture that values diverse experiences and perspectives. When we actively seek out points of view unlike our own, we broaden our intellectual horizons and challenge the limitations of our existing knowledge frameworks. Instead of only reading the same chapter over and over again, we are able to understand the full story.

Challenging assumptions

Pursuing different perspectives is not just about inclusion – it's a powerful tool for both personal and organisational growth. When we encounter ideas unlike our own, we are forced to question our assumptions and face our cognitive biases head-on. These biases, such as the tendency to seek out information that confirms our beliefs or avoid information that challenges them, can limit our ability to see the full picture.

By exposing ourselves to different viewpoints, we challenge these biases and uncover blind spots in our thinking. We begin to realise the world is more complex than we may have once thought, and that our way of seeing things is only one of many possibilities. This realisation leads to growth, as we expand our understanding of the issues we face and open our minds to new ways of thinking.

Sparking innovation and collaboration
One of the most significant benefits of pursuing different perspectives is the innovation and creativity that arise when multiple viewpoints are brought together. When we engage with ideas that differ from our own, we're exposed to new ways of thinking that can spark creative problem-solving and lead to novel solutions.

In a team setting, bringing together a range of unique perspectives allows for a cross-pollination of ideas. If we encourage our team members to share their experiences and insights, we'll create an environment that fosters innovation. Each person's contribution builds on the others, creating a more dynamic and creative problem-solving process.

Not only that, but when team members feel their perspectives are valued and heard, they are more likely to be engaged and motivated to participate in these group settings. This creates a culture of collaboration, where individuals are encouraged to contribute their unique insights and ideas. In turn, this collaborative environment leads to better teamwork, as individuals feel respected and invested in the team's success.

When leaders make a habit of seeking out different perspectives, we also build trust and credibility within our teams and organisations. By showing we are willing to listen to others and value their input, we create an environment where open communication is encouraged. This trust makes it easier to navigate difficult conversations and reduces the likelihood of conflicts arising.

Enhancing decision-making
In addition to fostering creativity and collaboration, pursuing different perspectives also leads to better decision-making. When we seek out multiple viewpoints, we expose ourselves to a wider range of information. This broader perspective allows us to see the potential risks and benefits of various solutions, which enables us to make

more informed and balanced decisions, leading to better choices and outcomes.

Pursuing different perspectives is more than just a beneficial skill – it's a cornerstone of effective leadership. We recognise that our perspective or point of view, no matter how well informed, is just one piece of the puzzle. By seeking out and engaging with a wide range of viewpoints, we gain access to the full picture, uncover blind spots, challenge assumptions and foster innovation. When we embrace this blindspotting practice, we create workplaces where creativity thrives and collaboration deepens, ensuring our teams feel valued and motivated to contribute.

PRACTICE 3: ASK QUESTIONS FOR INSIGHT
What it means to ask questions for insight

Asking questions for insight means our goal is to learn and understand rather than to prove a point or win an argument. It's about seeking deeper knowledge by engaging with other people from a place of a genuine curiosity about their thoughts, experiences and perspectives. To truly gain these insights, we need to reframe how we ask questions. We're not just gathering information – we're embracing an ongoing process of exploration and inquiry. The intent behind our questions is critical. Ask yourself: are you trying to listen and learn, or are you trying to validate your own perspective?

> **Ask yourself: are you trying to listen and learn, or are you trying to validate your own perspective?**

The intent behind the question

The tone and structure of our questions reveal our intent. When we approach someone with a question, they can tell if we are genuinely interested in their perspective or if we are asking simply to affirm our own views. Questions that are designed to trap or corner someone into a specific answer shut down productive dialogue. Conversely, questions that are open-ended and invite exploration will encourage the other person to share more freely.

Framing questions for discovery

Asking questions for insight requires framing your words in ways that welcome discovery rather than dictate answers. Insightful questions are often open-ended, meaning they do not have simple yes or no answers, and they encourage people to think more deeply and express their thoughts in ways they might not have initially considered.

> **Asking questions for insight requires framing your words in ways that welcome discovery rather than dictate answers.**

For example, instead of asking a direct report, 'Why didn't we achieve this result?' – which limits responses to a specific issue – you might ask, 'What are some of the factors that contributed to this outcome, and how can we adjust?' This invites a broader discussion about various influences and encourages the people you lead to reflect on more than just one aspect of the problem.

The beauty of asking questions for insight is that it turns the process into a collective exploration. Both the questioner and the person answering are participating in a search for understanding, which in turn builds a stronger connection between team members and creates an environment where new ideas and solutions can emerge.

Challenging assumptions through questions

Insightful questions force us to confront the biases and beliefs we hold and consider whether they are valid. They prompt us to ask ourselves,

'What don't I know?' or 'What am I missing?' These kinds of questions help uncover potential blind spots and lead to a more thorough understanding of the issue at hand.

Every day, leaders encounter complex problems that don't have clear solutions. In these situations, asking questions for insight is valuable to help identify the root causes of the problem rather than treating the symptoms. It allows us to dig deeper and discover what's truly going on beneath the surface – to challenge any underlying assumptions about the situation.

The power of simple, thoughtful questions
Asking questions for insight doesn't need to be complicated. In fact, some of the most effective questions are simple but thoughtful, such as, 'What do you think?' or 'How do you see this?' These seemingly innocuous queries can help people open up and engage in conversations that lead to powerful insights.

By framing our questions in this way, we are not just gathering information – we are encouraging a deeper level of thinking and engagement. We are creating space for our team to contribute meaningfully and to explore the full scope of the challenges they face.

Why we find it hard to ask questions for insight

We often underestimate the power dynamic at play when it comes to asking these sorts of questions, especially in leadership roles. When leaders ask questions, they do so from a position of authority, and their words carry weight. Team members might not feel comfortable challenging their leader's perspective or even fully engaging with a question if they feel their leader has already decided on an answer.

The nature of a leadership role means our questions come with power, and we may not realise how intimidating we can be. Danish philosopher and technology entrepreneur, Pia Lauritzen, whose life's

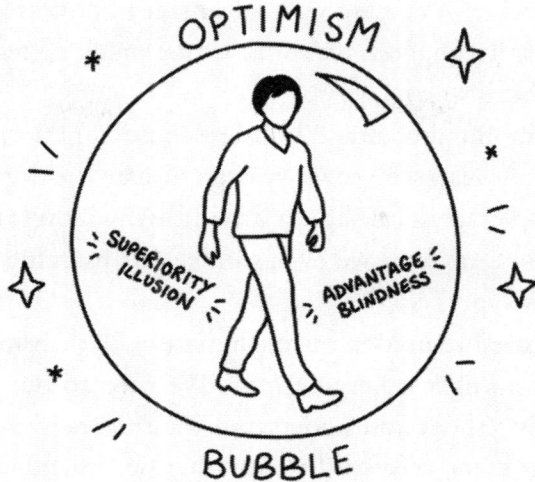

work revolves around the importance of questions, emphasises that 'the questions we ask, and those we fail to ask, determine whether we gain the insight we need to do our jobs'.[8] Pia told me questions are an essential characteristic of being human; they are what distinguishes us from animals. Yet, for many leaders, it is difficult to reflect on whether they are asking the right questions, because they might not be aware of the subtle power dynamic at play in their interactions with the people they lead.

Megan Reitz, an Associate Fellow at Saïd Business School at the University of Oxford, told me leaders must be aware of the 'optimism bubble' in which we often operate.

'The optimism bubble is a combination of advantage blindness and superiority illusion,' said Megan. She went on to tell me about advantage blindness, which is when we have formal titles or labels that mean we are perceived by others as powerful. If we have that power advantage, we've usually had the privilege of being able to speak up and ask questions whenever we need to – and we generalise that personal experience for everyone else, assuming they feel comfortable to speak up and ask questions too.

Often working in tandem with advantage blindness is superiority illusion, a bias that suggests we think we are much better at listening than others think we are.

'If we combine advantage blindness and superiority illusion,' Megan said, 'our research shows we overestimate the degree to which we think people are speaking up around us, we overestimate how approachable we are, and we overestimate our listening skills; these are major blind spots.'

This all proves we need to do much more work than we may realise to see what we might otherwise miss. We need to put ourselves in another person's shoes and understand the titles we hold mean our questions may come across differently than we intend, and that the people we lead might not feel as comfortable answering or asking questions as we do.

When we ask questions from a position of power or authority, people may hesitate to provide honest answers, especially if they believe the question is framed to elicit a particular response. Instead, when we ask questions from a place of genuine curiosity, we create an environment where honest and insightful answers can thrive. Rather than framing questions in a way that feels rhetorical or accusatory, we can focus our questions on being open-ended and non-judgemental. For example, replacing 'Why didn't this work?' with 'What can we could do differently next time?' shifts the tone from blame to collaboration. This simple reframing signals to a team that their perspectives are valued and invites meaningful dialogue, unlocking insights and ideas that might otherwise have gone unheard.

Asking questions to win
Another reason we struggle to ask questions for insight is that we are invested in being right. It feels good to know the answer, to be the expert in the room. However, this desire to be right can hinder our ability to ask genuine questions. Instead of seeking insight, we may

be more focused on defending our knowledge or proving someone else wrong. Questions become weapons used to maintain our intellectual position rather than tools for learning.

When we feel our position, reputation or expertise is at stake, we are more likely to use questions to challenge, trap or undermine others. We might ask, 'Why didn't you follow my instructions?' rather than 'What challenges did you encounter that prevented you from following the plan?' The first question is accusatory and closed, designed – intentionally or not – to assert dominance and put the blame on someone else. The latter is open and seeks understanding, inviting the other person to share their experience.

Pia Lauritzen told me that one of the biggest risks we face is asking questions when we believe we already know the answer. This behaviour shows that we are not prepared to question ourselves, nor do we expect others to question us; we're looking for validation rather than insight. Pia added, 'We might ask lots of questions and be very convincing but may not get to the problem behind the problem . . . because it can be extremely difficult to reflect on whether that is the right question to ask.' Asking the right questions requires two things: being willing to challenge our assumptions; and accepting we may not have all the answers.

> **Asking the right questions requires two things: being willing to challenge our assumptions; and accepting we may not have all the answers.**

When leaders ask questions to win – whether to make a point, prove we are right, or undermine someone else – we erode trust and create a culture of fear and disengagement. The people we lead quickly learn questions are traps and become hesitant to share their thoughts or challenge our ideas. This stifles innovation, creativity and open communication, all of which are critical for a high-performing team.

If we are only asking questions to validate our own perspectives, we will not only harm morale and collaboration within our teams, but also miss opportunities to uncover deeper issues and gain valuable insights. It's through asking the right questions – those designed to gain insight, not win – that we can truly solve problems, learn from others and make informed decisions.

The benefits of using questions to learn

Asking questions can be one of the most powerful tools a leader has, but not all questions are created equal. When used correctly, questions can unlock new ways of thinking, challenge our own and others' assumptions and promote a culture of curiosity. Asking questions for insight becomes a tool for gathering information and driving innovation.

> **Asking questions can be one of the most powerful tools a leader has, but not all questions are created equal.**

Indra Nooyi became the first woman of colour and the first immigrant to the United States to head a Fortune 50 company when she was appointed CEO of PepsiCo in 2006, a role she held until 2018. She has been widely recognised for her leadership, receiving fifteen honorary doctorates, and her portrait hangs in the Smithsonian. Nooyi developed a reputation for her ability to grasp and simplify complex problems so she and others could more easily understand the core issues and make better decisions. When given a complex problem, Nooyi says, 'I become a student. I don't care that I'm CEO, president or CFO. I become a student.'[9]

Nooyi asks many questions to learn and understand complicated issues. Her questions push people to think critically and prompt curiosity within herself and others to ask further questions, leading to even more innovative solutions. Nooyi likens her focus to that of a telephoto lens.

'Any issue I was given to address, I'd zoom out instinctively, hover 15,000 feet above the issue to understand it,' Nooyi says. 'And then I'd dig deep into the issue and understand every nut and bolt and screw of [it].'[10] The questions she would ask to understand a particular problem would also be driven by, in Nooyi's words, the side of the decimal place from which she was thinking. This useful analogy highlights how we can use questions effectively depending on context.

'Zooming out is done to the left of the decimal,' Nooyi told a packed audience at the World of Business Ideas' World Business Forum in Sydney in 2023. She says this is where you make big deals happen or significant transformational moves. But to the right of the decimal place, 'you zoom in, trying to save a penny on a route or half a penny on a bag of crisps . . . money is made in companies working on the right side of the decimal; direction is set working on the left.'[11] Her powerful use of questions allows Nooyi to operate effectively on both sides of the decimal.

Enhancing problem-solving and decision-making
When leaders ask questions from a place of curiosity, we enhance our ability to solve problems effectively. Insightful questions help uncover the root causes of problems, clarify objectives and reveal overlooked information. By asking open-ended questions such as, 'What assumptions are we making about this problem?' or 'What alternative solutions haven't we considered yet?' we can guide our teams through a deeper exploration of an issue.

Encouraging continuous learning
One of the most significant benefits of asking questions for insight is that it promotes continuous learning and development – both for ourselves and our team. Leaders who ask questions to learn are constantly seeking new information, perspectives and ways of thinking. This mindset of lifelong learning sets an example for the entire

organisation, no matter the size, and encourages people around them to adopt a similar approach.

Open-ended questions encourage discussion and can spark new lines of inquiry. Leaders who ask questions such as, 'What additional information do we need to make an informed decision?' or 'What are we missing?' invite the people they lead to contribute their thoughts and ideas. This collaborative approach fosters a sense of ownership and accountability, leading to more innovative and successful outcomes, as well as boosting morale.

The very best ideas often come from collective inquiry, not individual certainty. By asking questions from a place of genuine curiosity – not to assert dominance or validate our own views – we build stronger connections, uncover deeper insights and make more informed decisions. In doing so, we can help transform our teams into dynamic problem-solvers, ready to tackle challenges with creativity and confidence.

> **The very best ideas often come from collective inquiry, not individual certainty.**

Having explored the mindsets of honesty and curiosity, it's time to consider the third and final mindset in the practice of blindspotting: flexibility. In the next chapter, we will dive into how flexibility allows us to adapt our thinking and approach new information, helping us navigate complex challenges and uncertain environments with confidence and agility.

KEY TAKEAWAYS

- **Curiosity drives discovery.** The mindset of curiosity is not about asking questions for the sake of it but rather using questions to understand the full picture. Curiosity pushes us beyond our biases, preconceived notions and surface-level problems, leading to deeper insights that might otherwise remain hidden.
- **Search for the objective truth to counter subjective beliefs.** The concept of searching for the objective truth – truth that exists independently of personal beliefs or biases – is central to the process of blindspotting. Finding the objective truth is often challenging because it requires moving beyond our subjective experiences and biases, which can cloud our judgement.
- **The importance of seeking out other perspectives.** Pursuing different perspectives is crucial in diminishing blind spots. By actively seeking out views that differ from our own, we can arrive at more informed and balanced decisions. The more perspectives we engage with, the more complete our understanding of a situation becomes.
- **The power of asking questions for insight.** Asking open-ended questions with a genuine desire to learn fosters greater collaboration and collective problem-solving. It's about discovering the truth together, not proving oneself right. This approach moves beyond simply confirming our own views and opens pathways for richer insights and stronger leadership.
- **Leaders set the tone with their questions.** The way we ask questions – whether open-ended or accusatory – shapes team dynamics. When questions come from a place of genuine curiosity, they signal trust, value diverse perspectives and encourage a culture of honest dialogue and collaboration.

FURTHER READING

Safi Bahcall, *Loonshots: Nurture the crazy ideas that win wars, cure diseases, and transform industries* (2019).

Brian Grazer and Charles Fishman, *A Curious Mind: The secret to a bigger life* (2015).

Pia Lauritzen, *Questions?* (2023).

Edgar H. Schein, *Humble Inquiry: The gentle art of asking instead of telling* (2013).

Tali Sharot and Cass R. Sunstein, *Look Again: The power of noticing what was always there* (2024).

FROM PHYSICS TO BUSINESS

> 'I get really curious about what doesn't agree with my view of the world.'
>
> Safi Bahcall, physicist, entrepreneur and author

It's not often that you meet someone who seamlessly transitions from theoretical physics to running a biotech company, and then to authoring a bestselling book. But Safi Bahcall is not your typical leader. His career path has been anything but linear, taking sharp turns from academia to consulting, to entrepreneurship, and back into deep research. When I met Safi in the restaurant of the historic Mayflower Hotel in Washington, DC in early 2024, I was immediately fascinated by his story. He is, by any measure, a polymath.

'I really like solving real-world mysteries,' Safi told me. 'I like seeing stuff in the world we don't understand and trying to figure out how it works and why it works that way.'

Blindspotting – acknowledging your intellectual limits, embracing curiosity and staying flexible in your thinking – is core to Safi's success. As he explained to me, 'The first, most important principle that has shaped my career choices over the past thirty years is curiosity.' This principle has led him to explore new fields, rethink accepted ideas and uncover insights that others missed. For leaders, his journey offers essential lessons in how blindspotting can turn challenges into opportunities.

Safi's story begins in the world of theoretical physics, where he pursued his love for exploring the unknown. His parents, both astrophysicists, instilled in him a passion for understanding the universe's most complex systems. But after years of studying, Safi reached a crossroads: 'Physics requires a lot of investment in learning the science before it becomes fun. At a certain point, I felt like it wasn't giving me the answers I was looking for.'

Rather than doubling down on a field that no longer fuelled his passion, in the late 1990s Safi made the bold decision to leave academia. He embraced this moment as a chance to explore something new.

In 1998, Safi joined McKinsey & Company, a business management consultancy, and a world far removed from the scientific research he was used to. 'I didn't know anything about balancing a cheque book,' he told me with a laugh, but said he was eager to learn. This willingness to step outside his field of expertise and ask questions was the beginning of his journey towards understanding the bigger picture.

When Safi was recruited by McKinsey, he was probably one of their only hires who had very little to no idea what they did as a company.

'I really didn't know anyone outside of academic science, and in particular theoretical physics, so I was curious about the majority of the people in the world who worked differently,' Safi said. 'I wondered what people in an office did, and how that world worked. I wondered why they got paid, who paid them and why they were paying them.

'I approached working with McKinsey the same way I had approached science. I approached it with intellectual honesty, in the sense that I knew I had no understanding of their world. I was genuinely curious, and flexible in my thinking, especially when my first, second or third pass views on that world were wrong.'

After a stint at McKinsey, Safi turned entrepreneur and business leader. He became the CEO of a biotech company taking on one of the biggest challenges in medicine: cancer. 'Biotech is a roller coaster,' he explained. 'You go through every up and down imaginable. But what kept me going was the constant learning.'

As he scaled the company, moving from a startup to an initial public offering (IPO), Safi kept asking questions, and the answers came from his scientific background: 'I applied ideas from physics – like how systems change behaviour under different conditions – to business.'

It was curiosity that led Safi to connect the dots between science and business. In corporate environments, where change happens rapidly and unpredictably, curiosity is a critical trait. Leaders who remain curious are the ones who push their organisations to innovate, ask tough questions and explore new solutions. As Safi explained, 'For me, when the learning curve plateaus, I start thinking it's time to look at something else.'

Perhaps one of the most critical skills that Safi developed throughout his career was being able to think flexibly and change direction when necessary. After spending years in biotech, he turned his attention to writing. His bestselling book, *Loonshots: How to nurture the crazy ideas that win wars, cure diseases and transform industries*, explores how organisations can foster innovation and breakthrough ideas. But the transition from business leader to author wasn't easy.

Safi admitted, 'When I started writing, I thought I was a good writer. Then I looked at real writers.' With humility, he took a year to 'unlearn' everything he thought he knew about craft of writing. He studied great authors, reworking their paragraphs and sometimes spending entire evenings on just two sentences. This intense practice helped him become the writer he needed to be.

This kind of flexibility – being willing to 'unlearn' and start from scratch – is rare. Many leaders stick to their established routines and resist change, but as Safi's story shows, flexibility is essential for long-term success. In a world where industries are rapidly evolving, a leader's ability to pivot and adapt is more valuable than ever.

'Blindspotting requires you to approach problems with honesty,' Safi said, speaking to the heart of his success. 'To question everything you think you know and to be flexible when the answers aren't what you expected.'

One of Safi's more recent realisations came when he began applying scientific principles – specifically the behaviour of large systems, such as molecules in water – to the business world. He noticed that in companies, as in nature, systems change behaviour when they hit certain thresholds.

'Why do great leaders who build up a company for decades suddenly start missing big ideas?' he asked. The answer, it turns out, wasn't psychological – it was structural.

Safi deduced that in business, when a company reaches a certain size, the forces driving innovation are often replaced by forces driving politics and personal advancement. 'At some point, people stop focusing on the projects that matter and start focusing on themselves,' he said. But by changing the structural incentives within a company – what he calls 'changing the temperature' – leaders can reignite innovation and prevent stagnation.

One of the most compelling things about Safi is his relentless pursuit of objective truth. He approaches each new field with humility, recognising that his initial understanding is likely incomplete or flawed. 'I thought I understood finance, but when I started reading papers in financial economics, I realised I didn't even understand every third word,' he told me. But again, rather than giving up, Safi dived deeper, learning the language of finance, studying the literature and questioning the assumptions that everyone else seemed to accept.

As he started analysing the behaviour of financial markets, his scientific mind identified a disconnect between economic theory and what was happening in the real world. He began to ask: Why do some assets follow logical, predictable patterns while others behave erratically, such as a Picasso painting being auctioned off at an outrageous price?

And so Safi coined two distinct market types: banana markets and Picasso markets.

A banana market operates on rational decision-making. 'In a banana market,' Safi explained, 'you look at a stock or asset and make a decision based on expected cash flows, risks and rewards. You analyse the future and decide what something is worth.' It's a straightforward process – like buying bananas in a supermarket. You don't care what other shoppers think; you just buy what's right for you.

But then there's the Picasso market. 'This is where it gets interesting,' Safi said. 'The Picasso market is based less on objective analysis and more on what your friends think. A Picasso painting might look like scratches to you, but because everyone around you thinks it's worth a million dollars, suddenly you think maybe it is worth that much.'

The problem is that traditional economic models, such as the banana market, fail to account for the emotional, collective behaviour that drives Picasso-like bubbles. Safi's insight, informed by his background in physics, was that financial markets don't behave as logical systems do – at least not all the time. Instead, they behave more like complex, dynamic systems.

As he explained it, 'You can think of it as a phase transition, like water turning into ice or steam. Once you crank up the interactions between investors – once people start caring more about what others think than about the actual asset – you get a market bubble. The shift from rational to irrational happens quickly, almost like flipping a switch.'

In today's corporate world, where leaders are often expected to have all the answers, Safi's story reminds us that the pursuit of truth requires us to seek out new perspectives, to approach unknown fields of learning with curiosity and to question our assumptions. Leaders who rely solely on their expertise or past success are often blindsided by changes they didn't see coming. But those who continuously search for objective truth, as Safi does, are the ones who can adapt and thrive.

6

BE FLEXIBLE

With honesty showing the path ahead and curiosity lighting up your surroundings, we now need to take the final step to harness our blindspotting torch's full power. Flexibility is like adjusting the beam of a torch as you navigate through darkness. Sometimes you need a wide, diffused light to take in the bigger picture, and other times, a focused beam to zero in on a specific detail. Just as the torch adapts to illuminate what's needed, a flexible mindset allows us to shift perspectives, switch strategies and adapt to whatever challenges come our way.

Flexibility in the way we think is one of the most critical skills we can cultivate in a fast-changing world. It allows us to pivot between concepts, think about multiple issues simultaneously and adapt to unexpected situations. Whether it's responding to shifting deadlines, adjusting to abide by new regulations or navigating a rapidly evolving industry, the ability to be flexible in our thinking helps us manage the complexity and uncertainty we face daily. You may have experienced this mental shift when new information completely upended what you thought was true, making you change course entirely. In these moments, you've engaged your mindset of flexibility.

The more we expose ourselves to new ideas and perspectives, the more we need to be flexible in how we think. Uncovering evidence or viewpoints we haven't considered before might force us to rethink or even completely reframe our initial beliefs. Flexibility helps us engage with these potentially challenging ideas from various angles, and it helps us recognise that multiple solutions can exist for any given problem. It allows us to embrace ambiguity, adjust our attitude and accept that what we think we know might not be the whole picture. This mindset is what keeps us adaptable in the face of change.

We've all encountered people who are rigid in their thinking. No matter what evidence they're faced with, they remain steadfast in their beliefs. While some people are more inclined to think this way, the reality is that on certain topics we all hold positions we are reluctant to change. But when we refuse to be flexible, we close ourselves off to new information and fail to realise our views might need to be adjusted in response to changing circumstances. Ambiguity is uncomfortable, so we cling to long-held beliefs to feel secure and in control.

> **Ambiguity is uncomfortable, so we cling to long-held beliefs to feel secure and in control.**

I'll be the first to admit I have firm beliefs I am unlikely to change, no matter what counterarguments are presented. For instance, I believe everyone has the right to love who they want and marry who they choose; no amount of opposing perspectives will sway me from this view. However, there are other areas where I've realised I need to be more open to new perspectives. For example, I've been an advocate for people working remotely since the COVID-19 pandemic in 2020 reshaped the way we work. I believed all workplaces should offer their employees flexibility centred around individual choice. But more recently I've heard stories from younger workers who miss the spontaneous interactions that come with in-person collaboration, and I've learnt more about the declining culture and engagement scores in some fully remote working environments. As a result, I've had to reconsider my original position. While I haven't completely changed my mind, I'm now more open to the possibility that a one-size-fits-all approach to remote work is not ideal, and I'm willing to re-examine the evidence and think more flexibly about the issue. This is the Be Flexible mindset of blindspotting at work.

> **Flexibility doesn't mean we're constantly changing our minds.**

Flexibility doesn't mean we're constantly changing our minds about everything; rather, it means we're willing to adapt our thoughts and actions based on new information. We can engage with views we disagree with, without feeling the need to adopt them wholesale. We remain open enough to balance different perspectives, allowing us to reach a more nuanced and well-rounded conclusion. This kind of mental agility is key to developing creative solutions to problems and prevents us from becoming too fixated on one approach. Flexibility counteracts stagnation.

The world around us is constantly changing, and what seemed certain yesterday might no longer be true tomorrow. The rise of AI and automation, shifting consumer preferences, economic volatility and evolving workplace expectations all underscore the importance of flexibility and the ability to adapt quickly.

Flexible thinking allows us to keep up with the rapid pace of change in today's world, making us better equipped to handle the uncertainty that comes with it. When we remain open to new ideas, embrace ambiguity and adjust our thinking as we learn, we're able to navigate complexity with greater ease.

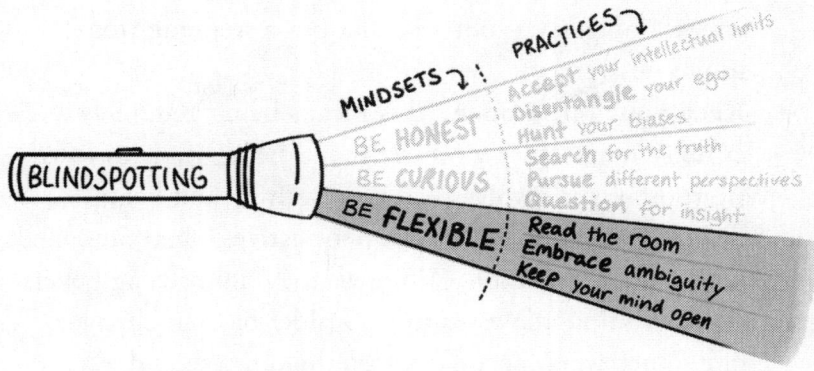

In the context of blindspotting, the mindset of flexibility has three key practices:

- **Read the room.** This means being highly attuned to the ever-changing dynamics of your environment and the people within it. It involves picking up on contextual cues – both verbal and non-verbal – and understanding that the way you lead or approach a situation may need to shift based on those cues. Effective leaders can adapt their thinking and actions to fit the current context, recognising that what worked yesterday may not be appropriate today. This skill enables us to respond flexibly and thoughtfully to the nuances of different situations, ensuring that our decisions and leadership style are aligned with the specific needs of the moment.
- **Embrace ambiguity.** This practice allows us to accept we won't always have all the information or absolute certainty about the future – and that's okay. Rather than fearing the unknown, the most effective leaders view it as an opportunity to experiment, adapt and learn. Flexible thinking encourages us to try new approaches, pivot when necessary and grow from experiences, even if they don't lead to immediate success. By welcoming uncertainty, we

open ourselves to creative solutions and personal growth, where ambiguity is not a barrier but a stepping stone to progress.
- **Keep your mind open.** This means being genuinely curious about other viewpoints and being ready to learn from others. It involves listening actively and being flexible enough to adjust our perspectives when presented with new information. While we may hold strong beliefs, an open mind allows us to reconsider or even change our stance when necessary, fostering growth and a deeper understanding of the issues we're facing. This willingness to rethink our position, even on issues we care deeply about, ensures we remain adaptable and informed leaders.

Let's turn to the first crucial aspect of flexible thinking: the ability to read the room.

PRACTICE 1: READ THE ROOM
What it means to read the room

When we are blindspotting and have a mindset of flexibility, we understand the importance of identifying and responding to the context we are operating in at any given moment. To do this, we can 'read the room' – a simple term for what is quite a complex task. Being able to make sense of what is happening around us means we can understand and assess which blindspotting practices will be most effective in a particular situation. We are alert to possibilities and aware when we need to put in extra effort to ensure we are blindspotting effectively.

Imagine walking into a tense team meeting where a recent project has failed. The atmosphere is heavy with blame and defensiveness. A rigid leader might push ahead with their agenda, demanding explanations or implementing blanket changes without considering the emotional state of the team. However, a leader with a flexible mindset pauses to 'read the room'. They notice the tension, recognise the need to build psychological safety, and adapt their approach.

Instead of diving into problem-solving, they start by acknowledging the team's effort and the difficulty of the situation. They shift the tone of the conversation to a constructive one by asking open-ended questions such as, 'What can we learn from this?' and 'What support do you think would help us move forward?' By tailoring their blindspotting approach to the context – focusing on collaboration and reflection rather than on immediate solutions – they not only address the problem but also rebuild trust and morale within the team.

Context is key
Context is always changing, whether it's the problem you're solving, the conversation you're having, or the people with whom you're interacting. By reading the room, you ensure that you are not rigid in your thinking but adaptable to the evolving nature of your environment. Leaders who excel at reading the room are constantly assessing the situation, interpreting the signals around them and deciding how to respond in the most effective way possible. They know when to ask questions that provoke reflection and when to remain silent. This ability to rapidly adapt ensures that conversations, decisions and actions align with the specific needs and dynamics of the moment.

Knowing when to admit uncertainty
We need to read the room to determine when it's appropriate to admit uncertainty. Saying 'I don't know' can be a powerful statement, but it's essential to understand when it's beneficial and when it's not. In high-pressure situations, such as a courtroom or a surgery, for example, people expect decisive action. Understanding when and how to admit uncertainty is an integral part of reading the room.

Imagine walking into a strategy meeting with your team, discussing plans for entering a new, highly competitive market. Your team looks to you for direction, but instead of pretending to have all the answers, you say, 'I don't know everything about this market yet. What do you think we should consider?'

By admitting uncertainty, you have exhibited a mindset of curiosity and honesty, inviting the team to contribute their insights and expertise. This creates a collaborative environment where team members feel valued and empowered to share ideas. Instead of forcing a potentially flawed top-down decision, you will facilitate a richer, more informed discussion, resulting in a strategy that is stronger and more innovative. Admitting uncertainty in this context builds trust, encourages dialogue and leads to better outcomes.

Saying 'I don't know' at the right moment can enhance your credibility. But saying it in the wrong context – such as when quick, decisive action is needed – can undermine your authority. Reading the room ensures you make these judgement calls effectively as the situation demands it.

How specific is the conversation?
Reading the room helps us gauge the type of conversation and the level of detail needed to engage in blindspotting effectively. Conversations can be understood in layers, beginning with a broad 'domain', which encompasses a wide range of general principles or ideals. As we move within the domain, we find a 'topic' that is more specific and often generates more focus for the conversation. Within those topics, we eventually reach a particular 'issue', the most specific layer, where people tend to hold their firmest opinions.

Let's take the domain of environmental sustainability as an example. This domain is generally accepted as positive; most people agree that taking care of the environment is worthwhile.

However, within this domain, there are specific topics, such as sustainable agriculture, the use of renewable energy and reducing plastic

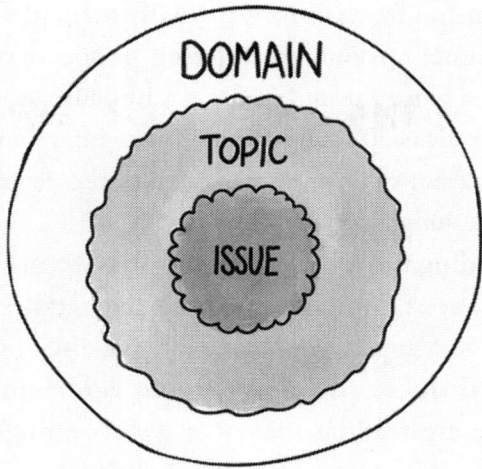

waste. As these topics narrow the focus, opinions begin to solidify. For instance, someone might support the idea of environmental sustainability but have concerns when it comes to the costs associated with renewable energy.

Finally, within the specific topic of renewable energy, we might encounter issues that are even more particular and likely to evoke firm opinions. For example, discussions about installing wind farms in certain communities may prompt heated debates, especially if people feel it could affect local ecosystems or property values.

This is when reading the room becomes vital. We must be aware of when the conversation shifts from broad domains to specific topics and issues, and we need to adjust our blindspotting practices accordingly. As the level of specificity increases, so does the need to be conscious of our biases and to be more intentional in our open-mindedness.

Conversations can shift in tone and focus without warning. Imagine a workplace scenario where your team starts discussing broad goals, such as improving customer satisfaction. The conversation then shifts to specific solutions – revamping the product interface, for example – and suddenly, personal stakes rise. A leader who fails to read the room might push forward with their preferred approach, unaware of subtle tensions or differing perspectives around them. However, if we sense the shift we can can pause, ask questions such as 'What other ideas do we have?' and invite input, ensuring all voices are heard. This not only prevents bias but also fosters collaboration and better decisions.

In life, reading the room is equally vital. Picture a family discussion about finances: it might start with general talk of budgeting but then narrows to a contentious topic like funding a specific expense. The emotional stakes rise, and tensions can simmer beneath the surface. If we are reading the room well, we might acknowledge the shift, saying, 'I sense this is a sensitive topic – how can we approach it in a way that feels fair to everyone?' This awareness defuses conflict and opens space for meaningful dialogue. Whether in work or in life, leaders who can read the room navigate complexity with empathy and precision, building trust and achieving better outcomes.

Why we might resist reading the room
Cognitive rigidity
One of the primary barriers to reading the room effectively is cognitive rigidity. If we are fixed in our thinking, clinging to familiar ideas or past successes, we will naturally resist adapting to new circumstances. When we are entrenched in our own viewpoint, we may struggle to notice the subtle cues that indicate a shift in context. This rigidity is grounded in the comfort that comes with what's known – change is unsettling, and inflexible thinkers tend to avoid it.

Cognitive rigidity can quietly derail even the most well-intentioned of us. Imagine a leader who has always relied on strict deadlines to keep projects on track. Their approach worked flawlessly in the past, so they double down on it – even as their team begins to struggle under the weight of burnout and shifting priorities. Despite the subtle signs of missed deadlines, declining morale and team members expressing they are overwhelmed, their leader insists, 'This has always worked before.' Their inability to adapt blinds them to the reality of the current situation, and the team's productivity suffers.

Now contrast this with a flexible leader who reads the room. When faced with the same signs of burnout, they pause and reassess. They might call a team meeting to ask, 'What's making these deadlines harder to hit, and how can we adjust to make things more achievable?' By being open to change, they identify underlying issues – such as resource constraints or unclear priorities – and collaborate with their team to find solutions, such as reprioritising tasks or changing timelines. Cognitive rigidity might feel like control, but in reality it stifles progress. A mindset of flexibility, on the other hand, builds resilience and keeps the team moving forward.

Cognitive rigidity also limits our ability to grow and evolve. If we only look for information that confirms our beliefs, the room we're reading becomes very small. We trap ourselves in a narrow echo chamber, relying on familiar voices and perspectives that align with our own worldview. In doing so, we miss opportunities to see the bigger picture, understand others' motivations and engage in meaningful dialogue.

> **If we only look for information that confirms our beliefs, the room we're reading becomes very small.**

Biases hinder context recognition

Just as biases affect our ability to hunt for truth or engage with different perspectives, they also prevent us from reading the room effectively. If we are blinded by our preconceived notions, we won't pick up on the changing circumstances around us or be ready to adapt when we should.

Confirmation bias plays a significant role here. If we believe we are right, we are more likely to seek out information that reinforces that belief, while ignoring or downplaying anything that challenges it. Let's say you're a leader in an organisation going through significant changes, such as adopting a new digital-first strategy. If you are convinced that traditional methods have worked in the past and will continue to work, you might overlook signals from your team or the market indicating a need for a shift. Your bias clouds your ability to read the room, and as a result, you miss important contextual clues that should inform your decisions.

Information overload
In our fast-paced lives in the twenty-first century, information overload is a common reason why many of us fail to accurately read the room. We are bombarded with emails, notifications and data streams at every turn – from our computers, to our phones, to the TVs in almost every room. This constant flood of information makes it difficult to discern what is truly relevant and what isn't.

When we are overwhelmed, we might only focus on the tasks directly in front of us, while ignoring the bigger picture. For instance, in a high-pressure work environment, you might be consumed by your to-do list – focused on meeting immediate deadlines, completing essential projects and responding to urgent requests. This tunnel vision can make you miss the underlying shifts occurring around you. You might not notice that a colleague is struggling with burnout or that a project's likelihood of success may have subtly changed based on new market data. When buried in the details, we overlook the evolving context – we fail to read the room.

Moreover, in such overloaded states, we might prioritise efficiency over reflection. In the rush to get things done, we miss subtle cues or changing dynamics in meetings, conversations and relationships. We might opt to rely on past experiences and assume they'll apply in the present situation, rather than taking the time to understand how the context may have shifted this time around. The result is we continue operating based on outdated information, not realising the room we are in has changed entirely.

Failing to prioritise context awareness
Many of us simply don't prioritise reading the room. With so much focus on action and execution – a common expectation for leadership roles – there is little time carved out for reflection or reassessment. However, the cost of not prioritising this practice can be high. When we fail to look up from our immediate tasks and scan our environment, we can miss the crucial opportunities to recalibrate or adjust our strategies.

If you are running a team meeting, for example, you might rush through the agenda without pausing to check in on the team's morale or energy levels. You might stick rigidly to the plan in order to tick the meeting off your list, unaware people are feeling disengaged or burnt out. Everyone returns to their desks exhausted and uninspired, and this lack of morale flows through to the projects they are trying to complete – or worse, they might even be tempted to try to leave the team altogether. By failing to take a moment to assess the room in that meeting, you missed a critical chance to adapt your approach and meet your team's needs more effectively.

The benefits of reading the room
Recognising when blindspotting is most useful
Reading the room gives us the ability to know when the three blindspotting mindsets will be most effective.

For instance, in an emotionally charged conversation, knowing when to be honest about what we don't know, when to be curious about different viewpoints, or when to be flexible in our approach can make a significant difference in the outcome. Sometimes an honest admission is the best strategy; other times an open-ended question could be the most effective course of action.

If we fail to read the room accurately, we might not use blindspotting to its full potential. Understanding the emotional and intellectual climate of a situation helps us navigate it more effectively, allowing us to make better decisions and build stronger relationships with those around us – essential aspects of effective leadership.

By reading the room, we know when it is appropriate to admit uncertainty and when it's necessary to project confidence and authority. An ability to calibrate our response to the situation at hand is essential.

> **By reading the room, we know when it is appropriate to admit uncertainty and when it's necessary to project confidence and authority.**

Better decision-making
Leaders who can read the room are much more likely to make well-informed decisions, because they remain attuned to internal and external signals. Internal signals might include our gut feelings, emotional reactions or observations of team dynamics, such as shifts in morale or engagement. External signals relate to broader organisational or market trends, like changes in customer behaviour, competitor actions or economic conditions. Together, these signals provide critical context, helping us make decisions that are both empathetic and strategically aligned. By staying alert to these cues, we can make decisions that reflect current realities and future trends rather than relying on outdated information or assumptions.

For example, if we notice a drop in team engagement or a rise in competitor activity, we can quickly adjust our strategy or approach to respond to these changes and resolve problems before they arise. This ability to pivot quickly and adapt in real time is critical for staying ahead in today's fast-moving business environment. Reading the room is a vital practice to stay agile, adaptable and responsive to change.

PRACTICE 2: EMBRACE AMBIGUITY
What it means to accept the unknown
When we adopt a mindset of flexibility, we come to terms with the reality that not everything has a clear-cut answer. Life is filled with complexities, uncertainties and situations that resist easy solutions. Embracing ambiguity means accepting that multiple interpretations of a situation can exist. By doing so, we allow ourselves to engage with issues from multiple angles and create space for growth and innovation.

Ambiguity involves accepting that we will rarely have all the information we want. Instead, we must make decisions based on the incomplete data we *do* have, while remaining open to the possibility that new information will inevitably emerge. Flexible thinkers recognise that action is necessary, even with limited facts – the key is to be open to adjusting those actions as circumstances evolve.

Ambiguity often surfaces in the form of complexity. The world is not binary, and many situations don't fall neatly into categories of right or wrong, success or failure. When we embrace ambiguity, we open ourselves up to multiple possibilities and viewpoints, allowing us to navigate complex scenarios more effectively. For many, ambiguity feels uncomfortable because it represents the unknown. But when we embrace ambiguity, we reframe it as an opportunity for growth rather than a threat.

> Embracing ambiguity means accepting that multiple interpretations of a situation can exist.

The challenge of a growth mindset
To effectively embrace ambiguity, we must cultivate a growth mindset. The concept of a growth mindset, coined by psychologist and Stanford professor Carol Dweck, refers to the belief that abilities, intelligence and talents can be developed through effort, learning and perseverance,

as opposed to being fixed traits.[1] Leaders with a growth mindset recognise they don't need to have all the answers upfront. Instead, they view ambiguity as an opportunity to learn and grow, both personally and professionally.

As the world grows increasingly interconnected and complex, embracing ambiguity becomes even more essential. Leaders who can navigate uncertainty are better equipped to guide their teams through rapid change, helping them to become more adaptable and resilient, and to accept ambiguity as a natural part of the human experience. While our instinct may be to seek certainty and clarity, learning to embrace ambiguity opens us up to new possibilities and perspectives. It allows us to approach complex problems with a flexible mindset, adapting our strategies as additional information arises.

Why we find ambiguity so difficult

Researchers have long shown humans crave certainty.[2] Our brains are wired to avoid uncertainty because it triggers discomfort, anxiety and fear. Ambiguity – the unknown – can feel like a threat to our sense of control. As a result, we often gravitate towards simple answers, cling to familiar routines and adopt rigid beliefs. Anything that preserves a sense of stability can feel like a shield against the chaos of the unknown.

Billionaire Howard Marks, co-founder and co-chairman of Oaktree Capital Management, has spoken about this tendency to seek out certainty, even when it is unattainable. Marks has written extensively on the dangers of trying to predict the future. He emphasises that the quest for certainty in an unpredictable world is a flawed pursuit, arguing: 'There's no way a macro-forecaster can produce a forecast that correctly incorporates all the many variables that we know will affect the future as well as the random influences about which little or nothing can be known . . . The only thing worthy of certainty is the conclusion that economists shouldn't be expressing any of it.'[3] His point is clear: certainty is comforting, but it's ultimately an illusion.

This aligns with the views of the late Nobel Prize–winning psychologist Daniel Kahneman, who noted that people gravitate towards those who offer certainty, even if it's misguided, because overconfident individuals 'sincerely believe they have expertise, act as experts and look like experts'.[4] This makes it difficult to question their conclusions, especially in a world where we crave stability.

Embracing ambiguity is essential because overconfidence can be a trap that blinds us to alternative perspectives and better solutions. As Kahneman observed, we are naturally drawn to those who project certainty, even when that certainty is unfounded. This can create a dangerous feedback loop: the more confident we appear, the less likely we are to be challenged, and the more likely we are to miss critical blind spots. In a world full of complexity and rapid change, this rigidity can lead to poor decisions with far-reaching consequences.

Instead, great leaders model open-mindedness. We accept what we don't know, invite alternative viewpoints, and create space for genuine exploration. This doesn't mean abandoning our confidence – it means balancing it with honesty and curiosity. When we embrace ambiguity and admit uncertainty, we signal to our teams that collaboration and learning are valued. This approach not only fosters innovation but also builds trust, empowering teams to navigate complexity with resilience and creativity. Being open-minded isn't a sign of weakness; it's the foundation of adaptive, forward-thinking leadership.

The inherent human need for certainty
The reason we crave certainty is deeply embedded in our psychology. From an evolutionary standpoint, certainty provided our ancestors with a survival advantage. Knowing where food or shelter could be found, or where danger might lurk, allowed early humans to avoid

risk and thrive. Over time, this preference for certainty has translated into modern life, where we still find comfort in the predictable and familiar.

When faced with uncertainty, many people feel vulnerable. It's a space where outcomes are unclear and control seems elusive. Uncertainty can trigger a fear response, leading us to retreat into what we already know, even if that knowledge is incomplete or flawed. This is why people tend to resist ambiguity; they see it as a threat to their personal safety and sense of stability. When our views or beliefs are threatened, we might think in absolutes and be unwilling to recognise that our perspective is only one version of events, or that we might be completely wrong about something.[5]

A need for certainty fertilises our blind spots. It encourages us to hold on to fixed perspectives, even when new evidence suggests we should reconsider our position. The more we try to maintain a sense of certainty, the more our blind spots grow, distorting our understanding of the world. It's only when these blind spots fail us – when reality doesn't align with our rigid beliefs – that we are forced to confront ambiguity.

> **A need for certainty fertilises our blind spots.**

The dangers of forecasting and false certainty
John Kenneth Galbraith, Harvard economist and advisor to President John F. Kennedy, would have agreed with Howard Marks's thoughts on the flaws of economic forecasting. Galbraith was reputed to have said: 'There are two kinds of forecasters: those who don't know, and those who don't know they don't know.'

And yet, despite knowing the inherent fallibility of forecasts, we continue to seek them out, hoping for definitive answers about the future. Will interest rates rise or fall? Will taxes increase? What impact will political decisions have on the global economy? These questions are often posed in a search for certainty, and many experts are happy to provide confident answers, even in the face of undeniable ambiguity.

Mark Lilla, a Columbia University professor, observed this phenomenon in the early months of the COVID-19 pandemic. Writing in the *New York Times* in 2020, Lilla explained how desperate people were for certainty during such uncertain times: 'At some level, people must be thinking that the more they learn about what is predetermined, the more control they will have,' he wrote.[6] But this, he argues, is an illusion. 'Human beings want to feel that they are on a power walk into the future, when in fact we are always just tapping our canes on the pavement in the fog.'[7]

The benefits of getting comfortable with ambiguity
Ambiguity as a source of creativity
By accepting ambiguity, we move away from rigid thinking and towards a mental flexibility that encourages creativity. When we are not bound by a single 'right' answer, we allow our minds to entertain multiple solutions, and this cognitive flexibility is a major source of innovation. For instance, as former professional poker player Annie Duke explains, uncertainty can be a superpower: 'What good poker players and good decision-makers have in common is their comfort with the world being an uncertain and unpredictable place.'[8] In poker, as in leadership, players must make decisions without knowing the outcome. Our ability to embrace this ambiguity allows us to navigate risk and uncertainty with confidence, leading to better decision-making.

Embracing ambiguity makes leaders better decision-makers because it equips us to act confidently in the face of uncertainty. Instead of clinging to a single path or delaying action until every variable is certain – which rarely happens – we evaluate multiple possibilities and weigh risks with clarity. This flexibility allows us to pivot when new information emerges, avoiding the sunk-cost trap of doubling down on a failing strategy. By being comfortable with the unknown, we inspire confidence in our teams and create a culture where experimentation and calculated risks are encouraged. We understand that waiting for absolute certainty often means missing opportunities, and it is our ability to make informed decisions amid uncertainty that helps us see what others might miss.

Fostering humility and open-mindedness
Another key benefit of embracing ambiguity is that it fosters humility. When we acknowledge that the world is full of uncertainties, we become more open to different perspectives. As Duke highlights, good decision makers 'embrace that uncertainty and, instead of focusing on being sure, they try to figure out how unsure they are, making their best guess at the chances that different outcomes will occur.'[9] An acceptance of uncertainty encourages us to hold our beliefs lightly, knowing we might not have all the answers.

> **An acceptance of uncertainty encourages us to hold our beliefs lightly, knowing we might not have all the answers.**

Co-founder of Oaktree Capital, Howard Marks, advocates the same mindset. Marks praises individuals who are comfortable with ambiguity, stating that people who say 'I don't know' or 'I might be wrong' are the ones he prefers to work with.[10] According to Marks, such individuals understand that predicting the future is impossible and instead focus on making the best decisions based on available information. These individuals, comfortable with not knowing everything, create a more honest and collaborative environment where learning and adaptability are prioritised.[11]

PRACTICE 3: KEEP YOUR MIND OPEN
What it means to open our minds

Imagine you're leading a meeting to finalise the strategy for an important project. You've just presented your plan when a team member speaks up with a completely different idea. You can feel the attitude in the room shift – some team members nod in agreement, while others cross their arms, visibly attached to the original approach. What you do next will set the tone for the rest of the discussion. Do you dismiss the new idea to keep things moving, or do you pause and say, 'Let's explore that further – what makes you think this could work better?' By staying open-minded, you not only encourage innovation but signal to your team that all voices matter. Great leaders know progress isn't about clinging to their own perspective – it's about creating space for the best ideas to emerge.

> **Great leaders know progress isn't about clinging to their own perspective – it's about creating space for the best ideas to emerge.**

Holding convictions lightly

One of the key aspects of keeping our minds open is learning to hold our convictions lightly. This doesn't mean abandoning our beliefs or principles but being flexible enough to adjust them when new information or compelling evidence is presented. In the workplace, this translates into being willing to reconsider a project direction, revise a strategy, or listen to a colleague's viewpoint – even if it initially conflicts with what we think is best.

A great leader is someone who is willing to engage with other ideas rather than clinging to their own perspective. Leaders who maintain an open mind will listen to their team, weigh the new evidence and be ready to adjust their initial plan to obtain the best outcome.

Engaging with different opinions
Keeping our minds open requires us to actively engage with opinions that may contradict our own. When someone challenges our view in a meeting or points out a flaw in a proposed plan, our first instinct might be to defend our position. However, keeping an open mind means welcoming these challenges as opportunities to learn and grow. We must listen objectively to the critique or alternative perspective being offered, review the evidence and consider how this information can expand or refine our understanding.

Adjusting to new evidence
A crucial part of keeping our minds open is being prepared to change our stance when new, credible information becomes available. Blindspotting encourages us to balance conviction with flexibility. We can believe something strongly, but as evidence or perspectives emerge that might contradict our beliefs, we need to be willing to adjust our thinking accordingly.

Balancing core beliefs and flexibility
Holding our convictions lightly doesn't mean we abandon our core beliefs or that we shift our stance with every conflicting piece of information we encounter. As Professor Walter Kotschnig once humorously warned, we should keep our minds open 'but not so open that your brains fall out'.[12] The challenge is to remain open to new ideas without becoming so easily swayed by every argument that we lose sight of our core principles. It means we approach situations with intellectual honesty, recognising that our perspective is only one of many. This mindset acknowledges that the evidence we have is often incomplete, and our understanding of a situation can always be deepened or broadened.

In practice, this means striking a balance between standing firm on our values and being open to new approaches. For example, if you strongly believe in diversity and inclusion within the workplace, you'll maintain this belief even if some challenge it – and having conviction is a good thing, especially when it comes to decisive leadership. However, an open mind would allow you to think about fostering diversity and inclusion in ways you hadn't previously considered.

Why we resist changing our mind

In a world full of complexities, having a solid, unwavering belief system provides comfort and security. Kathryn Shulz, Pulitzer Prize–winning writer, explains it well: 'Wrong never feels wrong in the moment. It feels like being right.'[13] This insight into human psychology highlights how being wrong is indistinguishable from being right until we are proven otherwise. The problem is, as long as we feel right, we cling to that belief.

Our brains are wired to prefer stability and predictability. Over time, we build narratives that support our existing beliefs, whether they are about the people we hire, the strategies we employ or the ideologies we hold dear. For example, if you've made a hiring decision, your brain will likely work to reinforce the belief that the candidate you chose is the right one. It's only when the evidence to the contrary becomes overwhelming that this belief might shift. However, until that undeniable moment of contradiction, we feel justified in our decisions, even if they might not be correct.

The human brain has a defence mechanism rooted in evolution. Back in prehistoric times, belonging to a group was crucial for survival. If a belief was tied to our group identity, admitting we were wrong could mean alienation – or worse. That ancient instinct still exists today, particularly when our core beliefs or values are challenged. This is why we often double down on our core beliefs when they are questioned, rather than opening our minds to new perspectives. We instinctively resist anything that threatens our standing in a group, whether that group is a family, a political party or a company. When we feel threatened, we become more closed-minded.[14]

Shulz emphasises that we are often unaware of our own mistakes in the moment. By the time we recognise an error, the damage may already be done, and we are more likely to defend our original position than admit fault.[15] This deeply ingrained resistance to changing our minds is why cognitive dissonance can feel so uncomfortable and why keeping an open mind requires conscious effort.

Admitting we're wrong or that we've changed our mind can sometimes be perceived as a weakness. In the workplace, where there might be a strong emphasis on being right or successful, this can be especially true. We often associate strong leadership with confidence, decisiveness and consistency, and less so with flexibility or uncertainty. Admitting a mistake or revisiting a decision can be seen as a failure, which may undermine a leader's credibility.

The pressure to maintain expertise

In fields that require a high level of expertise, we become so invested in our knowledge and skills that we become resistant to change.[16] The more experience or success we have in a particular domain, the more we build our identity around being right. This is particularly common among professionals with years of experience, who can fall into the trap of assuming they know everything there is to know in their field.

The irony here is that expertise, while valuable, can sometimes be a barrier to open-mindedness. The more we know, the more inflexible we may become in our thinking. Daniel Kahneman argued that experts, while often confident in their views, can become blind to alternative solutions. They rely heavily on their past successes and are less willing to explore new avenues of thinking, which requires them to keep their minds open.[17]

> **The more we know, the more inflexible we may become in our thinking.**

The benefits of open-mindedness
Groundbreaking innovations
Embracing new perspectives and keeping an open mind is not only beneficial, it's essential for real breakthroughs. Consider how many pivotal discoveries in history have only occurred because someone was willing to think differently. This mindset of openness to change allows us to tap into new ideas, solve complex problems and adapt to shifting circumstances with ease.

Some of the most groundbreaking innovations have come from people having an open mind. Scottish scientist Alexander Fleming, for example, discovered penicillin because he noticed that a Petri dish left in his lab was covered in mould – while in other areas, no bacteria grew. Rather than dismissing this as contamination, he kept an open mind and explored why it was happening, leading to the creation of one of the most important drugs in history.

The same can be said for George de Mestral, the Swiss engineer who invented Velcro after noticing how burrs stuck to his clothes and his dog's fur during a walk. Instead of brushing the burrs off as an inconvenience, he saw the potential for something greater. His open mind allowed him to transform a natural annoyance into a useful product now used everyday.

Inspiring creativity
Keeping an open mind does more than just lead to historical inventions – it sparks creativity in everyday life. In any work environment, rigid thinking can trap us and our teams in a cycle of doing things the way they've always been done. This stifles creativity and makes it difficult to adapt to new challenges. In contrast, an open-minded approach fosters a culture of innovation and creativity, where all ideas are welcomed, and team members feel safe to share their unique perspectives.

Working together

An open mind not only improves how we approach challenges but also how we relate to others. When we are willing to listen to other viewpoints – even those that contradict our own – we build trust and mutual respect with the people around us. Showing others that we value their input, even if we don't necessarily agree with them, also fosters empathy, which is essential in any collaborative environment.

Moreover, open-minded individuals are better able to resolve conflicts and find common ground with people. By acknowledging that our beliefs are not always definitive or unchangeable, we create an environment where others feel safe to express their ideas, leading to more productive and meaningful dialogues.

Flexibility is a cornerstone of effective leadership in a world where change is constant and ambiguity is unavoidable. We cannot cling to outdated methods or rigid beliefs; we need to adapt, pivot and remain open to new possibilities. By reading the room, embracing ambiguity and keeping an open mind, we can navigate complexity with confidence and create space for innovation. This flexibility allows us to see beyond our own perspective, challenge assumptions and engage teams in collaborative problem-solving, so we foster a culture where ideas can flourish and solutions can evolve.

> **Flexibility is a cornerstone of effective leadership in a world where change is constant and ambiguity is unavoidable.**

When we embrace flexibility, we model the mindset needed to thrive in uncertain times. We balance conviction with openness, acting decisively while staying receptive to new information. This approach builds trust, empowers teams and unlocks creativity, turning obstacles into opportunities. In a fast-changing world, this mindset will allow us to drive progress and shape the future.

Now that we've explored the benefits of embracing ambiguity, it's time to turn to the practical side of blindspotting. In the next part of the book, we'll dive into how we can incorporate blindspotting into our daily leadership practices, build cultures that encourage it and embed it into our organisation's values.

> **KEY TAKEAWAYS**
> - **The value of flexibility in leadership.** Flexible thinking allows us to adapt to rapidly changing environments. Flexibility isn't about constantly changing your mind but about being open to new information and considering different perspectives, a particularly important skill when navigating complex, fast-changing markets where old approaches may no longer work.
> - **Reading the room is a key skill for flexible leaders.** 'Reading the room' means being aware of the social and environmental cues that help you gauge when to change your approach or strategy. Effective leaders can adjust their communication, decision-making and actions based on the current dynamics in a room or meeting, ensuring their strategies align with the moment.
> - **Embracing ambiguity is essential for change.** Leaders who are comfortable with uncertainty don't rush to find definitive answers, but instead remain open to multiple possibilities. This helps us navigate situations where we might not have all the information, and it helps us make informed decisions as clarity unfolds over time. Embracing ambiguity encourages experimentation, adaptability and personal growth.
> - **Keeping an open mind invites new ideas.** Holding your personal convictions lightly and keeping your mind open fosters innovation, empathy and better decision-making.

Effective leaders don't cling to their beliefs when new evidence or better solutions arise, an essential practice for long-term growth and for cultivating a collaborative and trusting team environment.

- **Flexibility as a corporate culture.** Organisations that promote flexibility in thinking and decision-making are more adaptable to market changes, competitor actions and internal developments. When flexibility is encouraged as part of a corporate culture, employees feel empowered to suggest new ideas and pivot when necessary. This results in more innovative solutions and a competitive edge in the marketplace.

FURTHER READING

Annie Duke, *Thinking in Bets: Making smarter decision when you don't have all the facts* (2018).

Amy Edmondson, *Right Kind of Wrong: Why learning to fail can teach us to thrive* (2023).

Adam Grant, *Think Again: The power of knowing what you don't know* (2023).

Howard Marks, *The Most Important Thing: Uncommon sense for the thoughtful investor* (2011).

Steven Sloman and Philip Fernbach, *The Knowledge Illusion: Why we never think alone* (2017).

THE BEYONCÉ BLIND SPOT

> 'I try to come into every room stupid. Not because I am, but because I want to be open to other people's brilliance.'
>
> Marcus Collins, marketing professor and author

In business, there's often a myth you have to know everything – especially if you're in charge. You walk into a room, give confident orders and people follow. But Marcus Collins, a professor and bestselling author, discovered that the key to effective leadership is not in knowing all the answers but in admitting that you don't. Marcus's journey, from his early career as a songwriter to becoming a digital strategist for Beyoncé's team, proves that blindspotting – the practice of intellectual honesty, curiosity and flexibility – can turn challenges into successes.

I first met Marcus in London in 2023 when we were both honoured and surprised to win awards for our work from Thinkers50. We bonded over our excitement, and I watched in awe as Marcus was sought out for his views on marketing and culture around the world. Some months later we spoke by Zoom, Marcus from his car driving on a US interstate highway, and me on the other side of the world in Australia. I wanted to find out more about his fascinating philosophy and approach.

'I try to come into every room stupid,' Marcus told me. 'Not because I am, but because I want to be open to other people's brilliance.'

This mindset of entering rooms with the intention to learn rather than assert isn't just a personal philosophy for Marcus – it's a survival strategy. For leaders facing an unpredictable world, Marcus's attitude is a reminder that embracing your limitations can be the key to success. His story reveals how we can improve decision-making, adapt more quickly to change, and avoid the blind spots that often lead to failure.

Marcus didn't start his career in marketing; his began with a passion for music. 'When I was younger, I wanted to be Michael Jackson. I sang, played instruments, and music was my life,' Marcus recalled. But like many people in the 1990s who showed promise in maths and science, he was pushed into engineering. He hated it. 'I was just doing what was expected of me, not what I loved.'

It wasn't until he returned to his love of music, working in studios with developing artists, that he found his true calling. But the life of a musician wasn't easy. 'I didn't have any hits. The life I was living felt unproductive,' Marcus admitted. With uncertainty clouding his future, he decided to pivot, going back to school to obtain a Master of Business Administration (MBA) in marketing, while still staying connected to the music industry.

It was this pivot, embracing both his passion and the uncertainty of what came next, that set Marcus on a path to work with Apple, and eventually with international superstar Beyoncé. Yet, throughout these many transitions, Marcus maintained one thing – his curiosity. He never allowed himself to be pigeonholed by his past or blinded by his expertise. Instead, he constantly sought out new perspectives, always willing to rethink what he thought he knew.

As Marcus put it, 'Sometimes, walking into a new room is the best way to discover what's next.'

After completing his MBA, Marcus landed a coveted role at Apple in 2008, where he worked on iTunes during the company's meteoric rise in the music industry. 'I felt like I had reached my Zenith, my apex,' Marcus said. It was a dream come true. But after a year, he faced an unexpected hurdle when he was suddenly reassigned to a role he had no interest in, working on what would become iCloud. Marcus wanted to work in music, not cloud computing.

So, Marcus did something bold – he turned down Apple's offer to stay and he moved to New York City, deep in student debt and with no job prospects or clear path forward. His parents thought he was crazy. But Marcus wasn't looking for the easy way out; he knew that pursuing something he was not passionate about just for a pay cheque would only lead to regret.

After leaving Apple in 2009, an email from Marcus made its way to the record label that managed Beyoncé. The people who received the email told Beyoncé's father, Mathew Knowles, about Marcus's unique background. Marcus recalled this fortuitous moment with a laugh: 'They said, "We need to meet this guy. He's an MBA, an engineer, he started a music company, he worked at iTunes, and he is black. He is a unicorn."' Marcus was offered a role to work with Beyoncé, arguably one of the biggest artists on the planet at the time, as her team's director of digital strategy and new media.

Marcus's new role went well and combined his passion for music with his recently honed skills in marketing. The goal was simple: develop a digital strategy to promote Beyoncé and build her online presence. With Beyoncé's star power, Marcus thought it would be easy to attract followers and build engagement on social-media platforms such as Facebook.

'Beyoncé had a huge following. The thinking was simple – just launch the page, put her name on it, and everyone will come,' Marcus said. But it didn't work. They weren't attracting the engagement or followers they expected – the strategy was failing and the pressure on Marcus was mounting.

So, what went wrong? 'The blind spot really was that I didn't know why people do what they do,' Marcus admitted. 'I thought that if you build it and put a big name on it, people will come. But that's not how it works.'

In marketing, especially in today's digital world, simply having a big name isn't enough. You have to understand your audience – what motivates them, what drives them and how they connect. For Marcus, this failure was an important lesson in reading the room. He had relied on marketing orthodoxy, believing celebrity status would automatically translate into social media engagement. But as he came to realise, people are more complicated than that.

'It was extremely uncomfortable,' Marcus said. 'I thought I was going to get fired. We weren't hitting the numbers we wanted, and everyone was pointing fingers.' But one of the most valuable things Marcus learnt from his time with Beyoncé's team was to embrace ambiguity.

Rather than panic, Marcus leant into the uncertainty and discovered the power of the Beyhive, Beyoncé's fiercely loyal fanbase. The Beyhive had already been operating organically online, creating its own content and driving engagement around Beyoncé without any official involvement from her team. So instead of continuing with a top-down approach, Marcus pivoted. He and his team began working *with* the Beyhive, empowering the community to take an active role in shaping Beyoncé's digital presence.

This pivot wasn't about saving face – it was a masterclass in flexible thinking. Marcus was willing to change his strategy mid-stream because he recognised that sticking to the original plan wasn't working.

Marcus's experience with the Beyhive taught him another critical lesson: always keep an open mind. 'When we first got in touch with members of the Beyhive, I was sceptical,' Marcus admitted to me. 'I didn't know what to make of them at first. But once I opened my mind to what they were doing, I realised that they were the key to our success.'

By embracing the Beyhive, Beyoncé's team didn't only improve their digital strategy – they revolutionised how artists could engage with their fanbase. Instead of relying on traditional marketing tactics, they tapped into the power of community and user-generated content. This shift allowed Beyoncé's label to release her self-titled album in 2013 without a traditional marketing campaign or promotional build-up, relying entirely on the Beyhive to spread the word, a stark departure from the music industry norm at the time. Instead of using radio singles or creating pre-release hype, Beyoncé and her team partnered with Apple iTunes and social-media platforms to create a surprise launch for the album.

The album's digital release at midnight on 13 December 2013, was shared with her fans through a simple post on her Instagram account with the caption: 'Surprise!'[18] This tactic created immense excitement and buzz as fans rushed to download the album and spread the news through social media. This strategy leveraged the strength of the Beyhive, with Beyoncé's loyal online community acting as ambassadors, amplifying the album's reach through their organic engagement on social media. By bypassing traditional media channels and engaging directly with her fans, Beyoncé demonstrated the power of community-driven promotion. The album's success not only disrupted conventional marketing strategies but also showcased the increasing importance of digital platforms and fan communities in the modern music industry.[19]

'One of the biggest lessons I learnt from one of my biggest career failures is that you don't build community, you facilitate it. That provocation is one of the key anchors in the work I now do,' Marcus said of this experience.

Marcus's journey, from music lover to marketer to digital strategist, highlights the power of blindspotting. By embracing intellectual honesty, curiosity and flexibility, Marcus was able to turn failures into successes and navigate the complexities of an ever-changing digital world. His story serves as a reminder that the best leaders aren't the ones who claim to know everything – they're the ones who are willing to admit what they have misunderstood and learn from it.

PART 3

PUTTING BLINDSPOTTING INTO PRACTICE

7

BECOME A BETTER SEEKER

Imagine you're in an important meeting. The stakes are high. Every person in the room holds a wealth of experience, deep-rooted opinions and a desire to come to a solution. Yet the tension is palpable, because beneath those sharp outfits and calm exteriors, there's a battle being fought – between sticking to what they know and opening up to what they don't. The decisions made at this meeting could impact the direction of an entire organisation. But there's one thing that will define success in this moment: whether or not the people in the room can identify and navigate their blind spots.

This scenario captures the essence of what this section of the book aims to tackle – blindspotting as a practice, not just an abstract idea. Blindspotting, which we've explored through the mindsets of honesty, curiosity and flexibility, is more than a theoretical framework. It's an action that requires us to apply these principles daily in our leadership roles, within our teams and across our organisations to foster environments where everyone is actively seeking out what they don't know.

It's not enough to simply acknowledge that we have blind spots; we have to intentionally search for them. To help put this into practice, this chapter will walk you through how to become a better Seeker.

Think of it as a guide to not only identifying your own blind spots but also helping those around you do the same. We'll dig into actionable ways you can build a habit of asking the right questions, listening deeply and adapting quickly when new information surfaces.

BECOMING A BETTER SEEKER

Becoming a Seeker is about embracing an approach to leadership and personal growth that harnesses the blindspotting mindsets of honesty, curiosity and flexibility. As we explored in chapter 2, at its core, being a Seeker means acknowledging you don't have all the answers. It is understanding the best way to grow and make better decisions is by continuously learning, adapting and seeking out new perspectives to help shape your own.

The power of the Seeker mindset comes not from any single quality but from how the three blindspotting mindsets interact to create a holistic approach to problem-solving and decision-making. Each mindset strengthens the others:

- **Be Honest** ensures that curiosity is used not for self-promotion but for genuine exploration. It keeps us grounded in the truth, making sure that our search for answers isn't distorted by ego or bias.
- **Be Curious** fuels flexibility by pushing us to constantly question our assumptions and look for different perspectives. The more curious we are, the more willing we are to adjust our thinking when presented with new information.
- **Be Flexible** allows us to implement what we've learnt through our curiosity. It keeps us agile in our decision-making, able to pivot when the situation requires it, without losing sight of our broader goals.

When used together, these three mindsets enable Seekers to approach even the most complex challenges with confidence. Seekers don't simply react to change – they anticipate it, using honesty to stay grounded, curiosity to explore new possibilities, and flexibility to adapt when needed.

> Seekers don't simply react to change – they anticipate it, using honesty to stay grounded, curiosity to explore new possibilities, and flexibility to adapt when needed.

HOW TO BE HONEST
Calibrate your confidence
To ensure we don't fall into the trap of believing we know more than we do, we need to actively challenge our assumptions. This is particularly important in leadership roles, where overconfidence can lead to misguided decisions that affect many people or an organisation as a whole. Make it a habit to 'disprove yourself': when you're about to make a decision, always consider alternative explanations or outcomes,

to ensure you're choosing the best course of action. This will prevent the illusion of knowledge and promote a more nuanced understanding of the situation.

> To calibrate your confidence before making a decision, ask yourself these questions, and encourage others to do the same:
>
> - What don't I know about this situation?
> - What evidence would genuinely make me change my mind?
> - Am I basing this decision on past experiences or current, relevant evidence?
> - What are the risks if I'm wrong?
> - What perspectives or viewpoints am I missing?
> - What would an outsider think of this decision?
> - Is there another explanation for the data or outcomes I'm seeing?
> - Have I asked enough questions to fully understand the situation?
> - What assumptions am I making that need to be validated or challenged?
> - How would I react if someone presented a strong argument against my decision?
>
> By incorporating these questions into your decision-making process, you can better avoid overconfidence and make more well-rounded, informed decisions.

Get comfortable with admitting what you don't know
Admitting you don't have all the answers is one of the most powerful things you can do as a leader. It signals to your team that their

expertise matters and encourages them to step up, share ideas and work together to tackle complex challenges. This simple act of humility shows that leadership isn't about being infallible – it's about guiding the team toward the best outcome together. When you model this mindset, you create a culture where learning, experimentation and innovation thrive, unlocking solutions you couldn't reach alone. Rather than being a sign of weakness, it's the ultimate strength.

> To practise intellectual honesty, try saying the following:
>
> - 'I don't know . . . yet.'
> - 'I don't have the answer to that right now, but I'm eager to find out.'
> - 'That's a great question. I'll need to look into it further before giving you a solid answer.'
> - 'I'm not sure at the moment, but I'll do some research and come back to you.'
> - 'I don't have all the information on that yet. Let's explore this together and figure it out.'
> - 'I hadn't considered that angle. I need some time to reflect and gather more insights.'
> - 'That's outside my area of expertise, but I'll consult someone who knows more about it.'
> - 'I don't know the answer to that, but I'm confident we can figure it out together.'
> - 'I hadn't thought about it from that perspective, and I don't have an immediate answer. Let me get back to you.'
>
> These statements communicate honesty, humility and a willingness to explore uncertainties, encouraging collaboration and further inquiry.

Foster a growth mindset

As a leader, fostering a growth mindset starts with you. Regularly remind yourself – and your team – that it's okay to not have all the answers. Frame gaps in knowledge as opportunities to learn, adapt and grow together. When you embrace the idea that intelligence and ability aren't fixed but can develop over time, you create an environment where experimentation is celebrated, and failure becomes a stepping stone rather than a roadblock. This mindset is essential in a fast-changing world where the old ways of doing things often fall short. By role-modelling this approach, you send a powerful message: your team doesn't need to be perfect; they need to be willing to evolve, tackle challenges head-on and get better every day. That's what drives progress – not just for your team, but for you as a leader too.

> To show your team it's okay to not have all the answers and to frame knowledge gaps as learning opportunities, try using the following statements:
>
> - 'It's completely normal not to have all the answers. What's important is that we stay curious and open to learning.'
> - 'Our gaps in knowledge are invitations for us to explore new perspectives and solutions.'
> - 'The unknown isn't a weakness, it's an opportunity for us to grow together as a team.'
> - 'If you don't know something, ask. We are all here to learn from each other.'
> - 'Let's focus on what we don't know yet, so we can learn and understand.'
> - 'Every time we encounter an unexpected challenge, it's a chance for us to build new skills and improve.'

> - 'None of us have all the answers, and that's okay. What matters is how we work together to find them.'
> - 'When we don't know the solution, it's the perfect opportunity to brainstorm and innovate.'
> - 'Remember, it's okay to say, "I don't know." That's the first step towards discovering something new.'
> - 'I'm not expecting perfection, just progress. Let's learn from what we don't know yet.'
>
> These types of statements help create a psychologically safe environment where learning and curiosity are encouraged.

Recognise your emotional triggers

Be mindful of your emotional triggers – they're your first clue that your ego might be steering the wheel. When a conversation starts to feel personal, or you catch yourself reacting defensively, pause and ask, 'Am I protecting my ego, or am I focused on finding the best outcome?' Recognising these moments is crucial because unchecked emotions can cloud your judgment and derail productive discussions. By staying aware of your triggers, you create the space to respond thoughtfully rather than react impulsively, keeping your decisions aligned with the bigger picture instead of with your ego. It's not easy, but it's the kind of self-awareness that sets great leaders apart.

> Here are some questions we can ask ourselves to help recognise our emotional triggers:
>
> - How do I usually react when someone challenges my ideas or decisions? Do I feel defensive?
> - What specific topics or situations trigger a strong emotional response in me?

- When I feel angry, frustrated or anxious during a discussion, do I take a moment to understand why?
- In tense conversations, do I tend to listen carefully, or do I focus more on protecting my viewpoint?
- Do I find myself getting defensive when feedback touches on areas I feel strongly about?
- When I feel my emotions rising, do I pause to reflect on whether my ego is influencing my reaction?
- Can I separate my sense of self-worth from the feedback or criticism I receive?
- When someone disagrees with me, do I view it as a personal attack or as an opportunity to learn?
- Have there been moments when I've regretted how I reacted to a situation because my emotions got the better of me?
- Do I ever catch myself trying to win an argument instead of focusing on finding the best solution?

These questions can help us become more aware of our emotional triggers and how to manage them effectively in conversations, especially when facing criticism or disagreement.

Admit mistakes freely

Normalise making mistakes and being wrong. Although it can be hard to accept, admitting mistakes doesn't make you weak; in fact, it often increases trust and respect among colleagues. If a project didn't go as planned, admit your mistake and ask your team for ideas on how to course-correct. This will build trust and encourage collaboration and creative problem-solving.

Here are statements we can make to encourage the people we lead to admit mistakes freely:

- 'I made a mistake in how we approached this project, and I'd like us to work together to find a better way forward.'
- 'Looking back, I realise I didn't consider all the options. I'd love to hear your ideas on how we can improve.'
- 'I've realised my initial decision may not have been the best one. What changes do you think we should make?'
- 'I missed something important in my analysis, and that's on me. I'd love to hear your suggestions on how we can address it.'
- 'I overestimated how smoothly this would go, and that's caused some issues. How can we fix this together?'
- 'It's clear I misjudged this situation, and I appreciate your patience. Let's come up with a solution as a team.'
- 'I didn't get this right, but I'm here to own it. What can we do to get back on track?'
- 'I was wrong about our approach, and I'm not afraid to admit it. Let's focus on how we can improve from here.'
- 'I've learnt something valuable from this mistake, and I'm open to hearing what you think we could have done differently.'

These statements show humility and create a safe space for the team to admit their own mistakes, fostering a culture of continuous improvement and collaboration.

Use self-distancing techniques

When you feel defensive or emotionally triggered, try to see the situation from a more distant perspective. Self-distancing allows us to transcend our egos and see the bigger picture.[1] Imagine yourself as an outside observer watching the interaction and remove the emotional charge from the conversation to make a more objective judgement.[2]

> Here are questions we can ask ourselves to self-distance during a challenging situation, especially when we start to feel defensive:
>
> - How would I view this situation if I were an outsider looking in?
> - If a friend came to me with this problem, what advice would I give them?
> - What is the most objective way to look at what's happening right now?
> - Am I reacting based on emotions or the facts of the situation?
> - How will I feel about this situation in a week, a month, or a year?
> - If I were to explain this situation to someone neutral, how would I describe it?
> - What is the other person's perspective, and how might they see this differently?
> - Am I taking this too personally, or is there a bigger picture I'm not seeing?
> - What is the key issue here, and how can I focus on resolving it rather than getting caught up in emotions?
> - What would I want someone else to do if they were in my shoes right now?
>
> These questions help shift the perspective from a personal, emotional reaction to a more balanced, thoughtful approach, leading to better problem-solving and emotional regulation.

Reflect on your biases

Regularly check your biases, and especially before making a significant decision. 'Few leaders pause and notice what is going on in their head in these difficult conversations,' Megan Reitz, Associate Fellow at Saïd Business School at the University of Oxford, told me. 'I always ask people to pause and notice everything that is going on – how do they feel about what is about to be discussed? What is going on in your physical body?'

It is important, says Megan, for leaders to pause and acknowledge the baggage they bring– their biases, their existing beliefs, their experiences – since it will influence their choices, decisions and responses. 'We need leaders to hold the space, not take the space,' Megan told me, 'for people to collectively collaborate and come to decisions.'

> Here are questions we can ask ourselves before making a significant decision to reflect on potential conscious or unconscious biases:
>
> - Am I favouring an option because it aligns with my personal preferences, or is it truly the best choice?
> - Have I considered all relevant perspectives, or am I dismissing ideas because they challenge my beliefs?
> - Am I relying on past experiences too much, assuming that what worked before will work again?
> - Is there any evidence that contradicts my current viewpoint, and have I given it proper consideration?
> - Am I being influenced by the opinions of others because of their status, rather than the strength of their ideas?
> - Have I given fair consideration to ideas from team members who typically think differently from me?
> - Am I unconsciously leaning towards a solution that is more familiar or comfortable?

- Could any stereotypes or assumptions about individuals or groups be influencing my thinking?
- Am I paying more attention to recent information rather than to the overall picture?
- Am I overestimating the likelihood of a positive outcome because I am being overly optimistic? Am I overlooking risks?

These questions help us become more mindful of our biases, ensuring we approach decision-making with greater self-awareness and fairness.

Challenge stereotypes

Actively combat stereotypes in your thinking. This involves going beyond the obvious and questioning deeply ingrained cultural narratives that may be influencing your decisions. For example, if you find yourself automatically assuming a team member is less capable because of their age, ask yourself why you hold that belief. Then, look for evidence that contradicts it.

Here are questions we can ask ourselves to uncover stereotypes or biases influencing our thinking:

- What evidence do I have to support my belief about this person's capabilities, and is it based on facts or stereotypes?
- Have I unconsciously categorised someone based on a single characteristic, such as their gender, age, ethnicity, disability, sexuality or appearance, rather than their actual performance?
- Am I allowing societal or cultural narratives to influence my judgement about this person's potential?

- Could I be overvaluing or undervaluing someone's contribution based on how I perceive they 'fit' traditional roles or expectations?
- Have I taken the time to get to know this individual's skills and strengths, or am I relying on assumptions?
- Am I judging this person more harshly or leniently than others because of preconceived notions?
- What would my decision look like if I removed any stereotypical thinking from the equation?
- Am I confusing someone's communication style or personality with their ability to perform in their role?
- Could I be holding back someone's growth or opportunity because of unconscious biases about their background or experience level?

These questions can help leaders become more aware of potential stereotypes in their thinking and help challenge those assumptions to make fairer and more objective decisions.

HOW TO BE CURIOUS
Think like a journalist

To find the objective truth, you need to adopt the mindset of a journalist. A key difference between humans and machines is our natural curiosity, and we must harness this trait to dig deeper into the issues and situations we're facing. Simply reviewing others' opinions or secondary sources isn't enough – we need to challenge ourselves to think critically and ask, 'What's really going on here?'

Leaders should recognise that, most of the time, what we call 'research' is generally reviewing interpretations of other people's work. To think more critically, we need to approach problems like journalists do: examine multiple sources, make creative connections, assess data

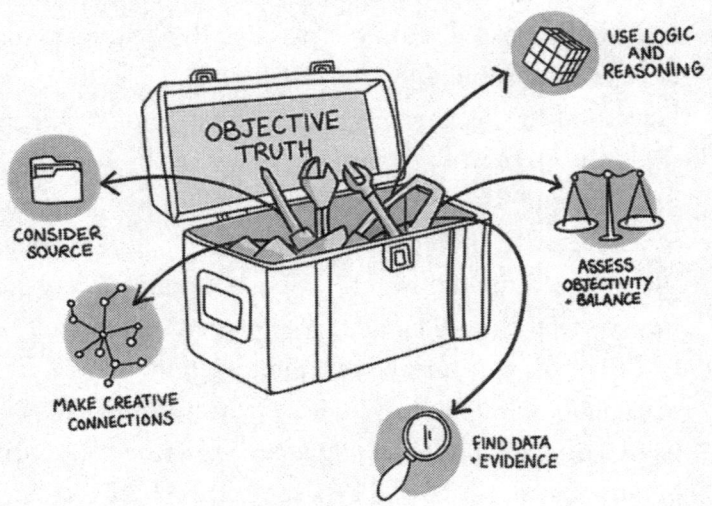

and evidence, and use logic and reasoning to formulate our opinion. It's essential to consider whether there are hidden motivations or biases behind any given viewpoint and to understand the methods we might have used to arrive at our conclusions.

> Here's a range of questions we can ask ourselves and others to find the objective truth:
>
> *Use logic and reasoning*
> - Does this argument or explanation make sense logically? Are there any gaps in the reasoning?
> - What assumptions are being made here? Are they valid or do they need further examination?
> - Is our conclusion based on sound logic, or does it seem like a leap based on the evidence presented?
> - Does our argument align or conflict with other known facts?
> - What's the underlying reasoning behind this conclusion, and does it follow a coherent pattern?

- Are opposing viewpoints being considered and presented fairly, or are they being dismissed or ignored?
- What perspectives or angles might be missing from this analysis? Am I getting the full picture?
- How could personal biases affect how I interpret this information?

Consider data and evidence
- Is there concrete evidence supporting this claim, or is it based on opinion or speculation?
- Where did the data come from, and how was it gathered?
- Is the data being presented in a way that's accurate, and not distorted or framed to mislead?
- Are there any potential errors in the data interpretation or analysis that I should be aware of?
- What further evidence could I seek out to confirm or refute this claim?

Make creative connections
- How does this information connect to other insights or knowledge I already have?
- Can I draw parallels between this situation and previous experiences or decisions?
- Is there an unconventional angle or approach that we haven't yet considered?
- How could combining this information with ideas from a completely different field create new insights?
- What are the potential long-term implications of this information, and how might it shape future decisions?

Consider the source
- Is this source credible and trustworthy? What's their background or expertise on this topic?

- Has this source been accurate or reliable in the past, or have they made questionable claims before?
- Does this source have any affiliations, biases or conflicts of interest that could be affecting their perspective?
- How does this source compare to others in terms of credibility, objectivity and thoroughness?
- If I were to seek information from a different type of source – industry expert, competitor, etc. – would I draw a similar or different conclusion?

Use questions to gain insight

Be aware of how questions are received and ensure they are purposeful and genuine, not just performative. One effective method is to explain the reason behind a question – linking it to a specific goal or outcome. This way, your team understands that the questions you're asking are meant to push the discussion forward, not slow it down.

Open-ended questions can unlock new perspectives, help uncover blind spots and invite creativity. Here are some examples of open-ended questions a leader can ask their team:

- 'What are we not considering that could impact this decision?'
- 'How can we approach this challenge differently to find new opportunities?'
- 'What potential obstacles do you foresee, and how might we overcome them?'
- 'What do you think is the biggest risk if we move forward with this plan?'
- 'What will success look like for us, and how will we know if we've achieved it?'

> - 'How can we improve our current process to be more efficient or effective?'
> - 'What's the most important thing we should focus on to make this project a success?'
> - 'How do you think our customers or stakeholders will respond to this idea?'
> - 'What assumptions are we making, and how might we test or challenge them?'
> - 'What's something we haven't explored yet that could make a big difference in our approach?'

Don't ask too many questions

While questions are essential for gaining insight, asking too many can lead to negative perceptions of you as a leader, making you seem unsure or overly controlling.

In his *Harvard Business Review* article 'When asking too many questions undermines your leadership' Luis Velasquez acknowledges asking questions as one of the most valuable strengths of a leader but also recommends leaders balance their questions with decisive action to avoid looking like they lack understanding or credibility.[3] It is also important to provide context for your questions – explain why you are asking them and what you hope to achieve, and link your questions to achieving results or to a purpose relevant to the people you are addressing.[4]

To truly harness the power of questions, striking a balance is key for leaders. Thoughtful, well-timed questions can inspire creative thinking, reveal hidden insights and foster collaboration. But too many questions, or those lacking context or purpose, can derail progress and erode trust. Link questions to specific outcomes, practise restraint and always aim to add value with what you're asking.

Expand your worldview

By actively expanding our worldview, we can respect different perspectives. Research studies have shown that reading fiction, watching television programs with diverse characters and hearing personal stories from all walks of life can help us open our minds to experiences, opinions and information different from our own.[5] Travelling widely and engaging in respectful and open conversations with people different from ourselves is another powerful way to reframe and reconsider what we think we know.

Imani Perry, a professor of African American culture, wrote in *The Atlantic* about an encounter she had while in Nashville, where she had been invited to speak on a panel for the Southern Festival of Books. The topic being discussed was the study of lynching, particularly the role of legal institutions in sustaining, extending and legitimising this form of violence.

The driver of her car, a '40-year-old, tattooed white man', told Perry he had been raised by 'regular Christian folks' in rural Tennessee.[6] He had served in the Navy, and during his service, particularly travelling across the Middle East, he started questioning his assumptions about other people. The driver told Perry, 'They say Jesus was from [the Middle East]. Well, I met a lot of Arabic folks, and ain't none of them named Matthew, Mark, Luke and John. Somebody lied.'[7] He followed up thoughtfully and said, 'So I realised after I seen so much, I never seen before that you gotta read books. But you can't just read one book. None of them tell the whole story.'[8]

Experiencing other cultures sparked a mindset of curiosity for this traveller, causing him to be open to different perspectives and ways of seeing the world. A mindset of flexibility allowed him to hold his convictions lightly and rethink the beliefs he once held to be true. As Mark Twain famously wrote, 'Travel is fatal to prejudice, bigotry and narrowmindedness.'[9]

Nurture crazy ideas

Safi Bahcall, physicist, entrepreneur and author of *Loonshots: How to nurture the crazy ideas that win wars*, has spent years consulting with CEOs and leaders on how to embrace seemingly crazy ideas. In his book, Bahcall argues that the higher up leaders go, the harder it becomes to stay curious, because they've spent years honing their instincts. They think they know what works – but when a young person comes forward with a wild, untested idea, it's easy to dismiss it.[10]

To be a leader that embraces curiosity, create a culture where crazy ideas are welcomed, not dismissed. Give your team the space to explore their passions and take risks without fear of failure.

> Here are questions we can ask ourselves to determine whether we are encouraging a nurturing environment for crazy ideas:
>
> - Do I actively encourage my team to share unconventional or bold ideas, even if they seem risky?
> - How do I respond when someone suggests an idea that challenges the status quo?
> - Do I create an environment where unsuccessful experimentation is seen as a learning opportunity rather than a failure?
> - Am I open to new ideas that come from all levels of the organisation, not just senior leadership?
> - How do I make space in meetings or discussions for out-of-the-box thinking?
> - When was the last time I pursued or supported a 'crazy' idea from a team member?
> - Do I reward creativity and innovation, even if the outcome is uncertain or untested?

> - Have I built a team culture where challenging assumptions is valued?
> - How do I balance my instincts and experience with the need to stay curious and open to new ideas?
> - Am I fostering psychological safety so my team feels comfortable taking risks without fear of repercussions?
>
> These questions help us assess whether we are fostering a culture that promotes creativity, risk-taking and an openness to ideas that may seem unconventional at first glance.

HOW TO BE FLEXIBLE
Learn to read the room

Reading the room isn't just about gauging what's happening in a literal meeting or discussion; it's about sensing the broader context in which you lead – your organisation's culture, the dynamics of your industry, and even societal trends. Great leaders have an innate ability to tune into these larger environments, understanding not only the immediate signals from their teams but also the underlying forces shaping their industries and organisational culture. By doing so, they can anticipate challenges, identify blind spots and steer their teams towards meaningful solutions.

Understand organisational culture

The culture of your organisation is the foundation that influences how decisions are made, how teams operate and how success is defined. Leaders need to develop an understanding of this culture by asking:
- What values and behaviours are truly rewarded here, beyond what's written in company policies?
- What are the unspoken rules that shape how people work and collaborate?

- How does the culture of this organisation drive or hinder innovation and risk-taking?

By understanding the underlying culture, you can identify blind spots where the organisation may be stifling creativity or overlooking the need for change.

Monitor industry and market trends
All industries are constantly evolving, with new technologies, competitors and market forces emerging at rapid rates. The most effective leaders stay informed about these shifts by:
- Regularly reviewing industry reports and economic forecasts
- Staying connected with peers in the industry to exchange insights and trends
- Identifying the disruptors – the new players changing the game – and how to adapt to them.

Reading the room at this level allows leaders to anticipate shifts and position their organisations to take advantage of new opportunities while minimising risks.

Recognise external forces and societal changes
Societal changes, whether political, environmental, economic or cultural, can have a profound impact on organisations. Leaders would do well to keep their fingers on the pulse of these shifts, asking:
- How do global or local political developments influence our business or our workforce?
- What societal trends are gaining traction, and how can we align with them authentically?
- How are changing customer expectations influencing our brand, products or services?

By recognising these broader forces, leaders can adjust their strategies to ensure long-term relevance and avoid being blindsided by larger transformational trends.

Foster open dialogue across all levels
We often lose touch with broader organisational dynamics when we are surrounded by like-minded peers or insulated at the top of the company hierarchy. Breaking through these silos involves fostering dialogue across all levels of the organisation, by:
- Making a habit of seeking feedback from frontline employees, middle managers and senior leaders to get a full picture of how the organisation functions
- Creating opportunities for dissent and diversity of thought in meetings, welcoming the devil's advocate and encouraging team members to challenge the status quo
- Keeping communication channels open and accessible, ensuring you can get direct insights from those closest to the operational realities.

This approach helps leaders understand the unvarnished truth of how things are going within the organisation at all levels, highlighting blind spots they might not otherwise see.

Stay attuned to emotional and relational dynamics
Just as it's essential to read the room in a meeting, it's also vital to read the emotional and relational dynamics across the organisation. Leaders can do so by:
- Paying attention to morale, burnout signals and engagement levels. Are people feeling motivated and supported, or are they stretched too thin?
- Observing how team members communicate with each other. Are there unresolved tensions or hidden conflicts that could disrupt progress?

- Regularly assess the level of trust within teams. Are people collaborating or working in silos?

These emotional undercurrents can indicate where blind spots might exist, allowing leaders to proactively address challenges before they escalate.

> Consider how well you can read the room by asking yourself these self-reflective questions:
>
> - Am I fully aware of the unspoken cultural norms and values that drive my organisation's behaviour?
> - How well am I staying informed about trends and disruptions in my industry, and how might these changes affect our organisation?
> - Do I regularly seek out different opinions and feedback across all levels of the organisation, or am I only hearing from a select group?
> - How does our organisational culture impact innovation? Are we fostering creativity, or are we too risk-averse?
> - Am I paying attention to the emotional dynamics within my organisation, and do I have a good sense of my team's overall morale?
> - Have I created an environment where my team feels safe to speak up, challenge assumptions and bring my attention to any blind spots?
> - Do I take time to reflect on my own biases and assumptions, and how might these be impacting my ability to see the full picture?
> - Am I being intentional about creating a future-ready organisation, or am I primarily focused on reacting to immediate challenges?

Change your mind with confidence

Nobel laureate Daniel Kahneman was famous for changing his mind, often rethinking decisions and going back to ideas he had previously dismissed. For Kahneman, the ease with which he could change his mind became one of his superpowers.[11] Kahneman's process shows that changing your mind isn't a weakness – it's a sign of intellectual strength and adaptability. Admitting when you're wrong or when the evidence causes you to change your mind will build trust with the people you lead, and it sets an example for your team that flexibility and open-mindedness are valued.

> Ask yourself how willing you are to change your mind through these questions designed to prompt reflection:
>
> - When was the last time I changed my mind based on new information or insights?
> - Do I regularly seek out opinions and ideas that challenge my own?
> - How do I react when someone disagrees with my viewpoint?
> - Am I willing to admit when I've made a mistake or when someone else's idea is better?
> - Do I encourage my team to challenge assumptions, including my own?
> - How do I incorporate feedback, especially when it conflicts with my current thinking?
> - Am I willing to revisit decisions I've already made to ensure they still hold up under scrutiny?
> - Do I actively look for blind spots in my thinking, or areas where I might be wrong?
> - How often do I seek out new learning opportunities, even in areas outside my expertise?

> - Am I comfortable with ambiguity and uncertainty, or do I always seek definitive answers?
>
> These questions encourage self-reflection and help leaders assess whether they are fostering a mindset of intellectual flexibility, adaptability and continuous learning.

Hold your convictions lightly

Marlene Poynder is the kind of leader who defies expectations and rewrites the rules of success. Without the advantage of a formal tertiary education, Marlene rose through the ranks to become a highly respected general manager in the luxury hotel industry, proving that talent and perseverance can trump educational qualifications. Known for her dynamic leadership style, Marlene has turned struggling properties into top-performing hotels, earning a reputation for her ability to balance the needs of guests, staff and stakeholders with grace and precision.

Currently, Marlene is the managing director of one of the world's most iconic hotels, the Carlyle Hotel in New York, a role that demands both vision and flexibility. With a career built on navigating the complex world of hospitality, she has a knack for identifying blind spots others overlook, turning challenges into opportunities. Whether it's winning over long-time local patrons resistant to change or building trust with her team, Marlene's honesty, curiosity and flexibility make her a standout leader in an industry where customer expectations are constantly shifting. She's proof that the most effective leaders aren't those who follow a set path, but those who carve out their own.

In her industry, where guest experiences are paramount, Marlene focuses on making things right for customers, even when it means changing her stance on a situation. Rather than becoming defensive, she embraces the challenge of turning unhappy guests into satisfied ones, showing that listening and adapting are core traits of an effective leader. Marlene admitted to me she used to avoid confrontation and tried to be empathetic in such situations, but she realised that treating every complaint as a challenge is much more effective. She shifted her perspective, becoming more direct in her interactions with guests, and as a result, she noticed a significant improvement in customer satisfaction and team feedback. This shift in mindset is an example of Marlene's curiosity and willingness to adopt new approaches.

As a leader, holding your convictions lightly means being able to change course when necessary, without ego or defensiveness. It's about keeping the bigger picture in mind and being willing to be flexible in order to achieve the best outcomes.

> Use these questions to reflect on how well you keep an open mind. Ask yourself:
>
> - When was the last time I changed my mind based on new information?
> - Am I actively seeking out perspectives that challenge my current way of thinking?
> - How often do I ask, 'What if?' to explore alternative solutions or possibilities?
> - Am I too attached to my instincts, or do I allow for the possibility that someone else might have a better idea?
> - How do I respond when someone presents a 'crazy' or unconventional idea – do I dismiss it, or do I encourage exploration?
> - Have I created an environment where my team feels safe to challenge assumptions and offer new ideas?
> - When faced with a problem, do I consider multiple perspectives before deciding on a course of action?

- Do I hold my convictions lightly, or do I become defensive when my ideas are questioned?
- Am I fostering curiosity within my team, encouraging them to ask, 'What if?' regularly?
- How can I ensure that I'm constantly learning and evolving, rather than becoming set in my ways?

MEASURE YOUR BLINDSPOTTING

To accompany this book, I have developed the Blindspotting Self-Assessment Tool, which measures your perception of how well you engage in the three blindspotting mindsets and the practices within them. It also compares your results to other leaders. You can complete the Blindspotting Self-Assessment Tool for free by visiting blindspotting.com.au. For more information about how the Blindspotting Self-Assessment Tool was developed, please refer to the appendix on page 280.

It only takes a few minutes to complete the self-assessment and receive your personalised results. This will help you to understand where to focus your efforts.

As we conclude our exploration of how to become a better Seeker, it's clear the journey towards deeper understanding begins with individual mindset shifts. While becoming a better Seeker can lead to powerful personal growth for you as a leader, it's even more impactful when this behaviour is incorporated into your team. In the next chapter, we'll dive into how to build teams of Seekers – teams that foster open dialogue, thrive on uncovering different perspectives, and innovate by embracing curiosity as a collective strength. Let's explore how you can create a culture that encourages everyone to seek, question and grow together.

KEY TAKEAWAYS
- **Calibrate your confidence.** We should regularly challenge our assumptions to avoid overconfidence. By asking reflective questions, such as 'What don't I know?' or 'What evidence would make me change my mind?', we can approach decisions with a more nuanced understanding, preventing blind spots and ensuring more well-rounded decision-making.
- **Admit what you don't know.** Acknowledging uncertainty builds trust and opens the door for collaboration. We should make a habit of freely admitting when we don't have the answers and encourage our teams to do the same. Statements such as 'I don't know . . . yet' foster an open and transparent work culture.
- **Embrace being wrong as a learning opportunity.** Effective leaders detach their egos from the need to be right. Mistakes should be viewed as feedback for future growth. Encouraging team members to share lessons learnt from failures normalises being wrong and helps build a resilient, forward-thinking team.
- **Challenge stereotypes and biases.** Regularly reflect on biases and assumptions to ensure fair decision-making. Asking questions such as, 'Am I judging this person based on facts or stereotypes?' can help us avoid unconscious bias, ensuring our decisions are made based on merit and not preconceived notions.
- **Ask effective, open-ended questions.** We can gain deeper insights by asking powerful, open-ended questions that invite new ideas and uncover blind spots. Questions such as 'What might we be overlooking?' or 'Whose perspective have we not yet considered?' drive creativity and encourage informed decisions.

FURTHER READING

Tomas Chamorro-Premuzic, *AI, Automation and the quest to reclaim what makes us unique* (2023).

Amy Edmondson, *The Fearless Organization: Creating psychological safety in the workplace for learning, innovation, and growth* (2019).

Amy Gallo, *Getting Along: How to work with anyone (even difficult people)* (2022).

Adam Grant, *Hidden Potential: The science of achieving great things* (2023).

Edgar Schein, *Humble Inquiry: The gentle art of asking not telling* (2013).

TAKING ON A TYCOON

'I have found over time that it is people who are curious who do well; curiosity makes the difference.'

Julie Inman Grant, eSafety Commissioner, Australia

Julie Inman Grant had faced many challenges in her career, but nothing quite prepared her for going head to head with one of the world's most powerful and controversial figures: Elon Musk. As Australia's eSafety Commissioner, Julie is tasked with ensuring that tech giants comply with laws designed to protect online users, particularly the most vulnerable, children. When Musk acquired Twitter, now known as X, in 2022 and harmful content began proliferating on the social-media platform, Julie had a monumental fight on her hands.

I watched with awe and followed the daily headlines from afar as Julie took legal action against one of the most powerful men in the world in the face of immense pressure from Musk and his millions of online supporters. After the dust had settled, we discussed the experience later in 2024. Julie spoke to me from her home in Sydney, Australia; I was on the other end of the Zoom call, on the Sunshine Coast in Queensland.

The story began when traumatic footage went viral on X, which Musk had championed as the ultimate forum for free speech. In a span of just three days, two horrifying public security incidents shook Australia to its core and set the stage for this high-stakes legal battle.

On Saturday 13 April 2024, chaos erupted at a busy shopping mall near Bondi Beach in Sydney, when a man fatally stabbed six people before being shot dead by police. Just seventy-two hours later, on the night of 15 April, a teenager stormed into Christ the Good Shepherd Church in Wakeley, Sydney, and violently stabbed a bishop during a live-streamed service. The attack, which left the bishop gravely injured, along with two others, was quickly classified as a terrorist act.

Julie was on a tropical island getaway celebrating her twentieth wedding anniversary when news of the attacks broke. Opening her social media apps, she was met with a wave of graphic, violent footage. The first thing she saw on her X newsfeed was the harrowing video of the church stabbing. It wasn't just disturbing content – it was dangerous. Such footage can potentially cause psychological and emotional harm to those who see it, and it can amplify fear and division within the community. More dangerously, it could even encourage copy-cat attacks.

In the aftermath of such incidents, Julie as the eSafety Commissioner works together with Australia's Department of Home Affairs to identify harmful content circulating online. Under Australian law, social-media platforms can be directed to remove this kind of material, and in extreme cases, internet service providers can be compelled to block certain sites. But compliance isn't guaranteed.

Julie, who had spent decades navigating the complexities of tech regulation and online safety, issued a formal removal notice to X. The content in question violated clear safety standards, and it was Julie's job to enforce those rules.

'By any objective measure, the content on X should have been removed, even under [their] own violent content policy,' Julie explained. 'But instead of taking the responsible route, X went all in.'

X's refusal to remove the video of the church stabbing and the ensuing legal battle set the stage for a pivotal clash between two vastly different approaches. Musk, on the one hand, is a firm believer in free speech and adopted a libertarian approach to online content, while Julie is a regulator focused on minimising the harm online content can cause.

'When X said, "Screw you, we're taking you to court," I knew this was going to be a different kind of fight,' Julie reflected. This wasn't just about enforcing child safety policies. It was about power, public perception and standing firm against a billionaire known for using his vast resources to intimidate his opponents.

Throughout her career, Julie has honed a Seeker mindset – a leadership style defined by intellectual honesty, openness to change, and a commitment to curiosity and learning. Her career has been defined by her ability to challenge entrenched systems while advocating for the protection of vulnerable communities. Her journey began in Washington, DC, where she worked on a range of social issues as a legislative assistant before accepting a role at Microsoft, where she became one of their first lobbyists in 1995 and later shaped critical tech policies, including the Communications Decency Act. She then moved on to Twitter, as it was still known when she joined in 2014, and advocated for user safety during a time when online abuse was rampant.

Julie's efforts to embed safety into digital spaces didn't come easily. At Microsoft, she fought to push 'safety by design', a forward-thinking concept at the time that aimed to build user-safety features into tech products from the outset. However, as she recalled, she often faced resistance – many colleagues rolled their eyes at her concerns. Despite these challenges, Julie remained committed to her vision, continuously adapting her approach and seeking ways to bring people onside in her mission to make the internet safer.

It was this same commitment that brought her to Musk's figurative doorstep in 2024. As Australia's eSafety Commissioner, Julie had already made waves by championing laws that held tech companies accountable for enabling the distribution of harmful content on their platforms. When she issued the removal notice to X in the wake of the two attacks in Sydney, Musk seemingly viewed her actions as an assault on his vision for the platform as a haven for free speech. Instead of complying with the removal notice, Musk deployed his legal team and began what Julie described as 'lawfare' – using lawsuits to wear down his opponent.

Musk framed this legal action as a fight for free speech, going so far as to describe Julie as the 'Australian censorship commissar' and accusing her of trying to globally censor the internet.[1]

Despite this antagonism, Julie approached the conflict with the Seeker mindset she had cultivated throughout her career. As Julie explained, she wasn't trying to censor X; she was upholding her responsibility as a regulator to protect users from harmful content. Despite Musk's online attacks and the immense resources he threw at the case, she remained focused on the core issue – online safety – and refused to be bullied out of her role.

The courtroom battle was fierce. Julie's team, though significantly outgunned, won early victories. But Musk, true to form, doubled down, hiring a high-powered legal team. For Julie, it wasn't only about the courtroom fight. She had seen firsthand the damage that could be done when platforms prioritised profit over protection, and she wasn't about to let Musk's free speech absolutism trample over the safety of millions of online users. Julie was forced to withdraw the court case against X when the prospect of winning seemed unachievable.

Julie's career had prepared her for this moment. From her early days in Washington to her leadership roles at Microsoft, Twitter and Adobe, she always approached her work with curiosity and a Seeker mindset, asking the tough questions and challenging long-held assumptions. Although Julie had to drop her first case against X, she did succeed in a second battle waged after the Bondi Beach and Wakeley Church stabbings. In October 2024, Musk's X lost their bid to avoid paying fines issued by Julie for failing to adequately respond to questions about child sexual abuse content on their platform. Julie's eventual success lay in her ability to blend boldness with intellectual honesty, a combination that allowed her to see blind spots and address them head on.

'Having the mindsets of intellectual honesty, curiosity and flexibility is key to success in the fast-moving world of technology regulation,' Julie said to me. 'It greatly assists us to spur innovation in how we approach challenges, helps us see around corners, and allows us to anticipate risks rather than solely reacting to harms.'

Even while being pressured by some of the most powerful people in the world, Julie has shown the combined power of the three mindsets of blindspotting.

8

BUILD TEAMS OF SEEKERS

While personal transformation is key, none of us lead in isolation. This chapter will explore how to create a work culture where blindspotting is encouraged and ingrained in the way our teams operate. We'll look at how to help Seekers thrive, reward Seeker behaviours and hire more Seekers. Teams that excel in blindspotting are more innovative, collaborative and adaptable to change because they aren't limited by the same cognitive traps that hold back traditional teams.

If we all adopt the mindset of a Seeker, it can fundamentally transform an organisation. Blindspotting becomes second nature when the right environment is fostered, where individuals and teams are encouraged and rewarded for making decisions using the mindsets of honesty, curiosity and flexibility. When we practise the blindspotting mindsets ourselves and also actively cultivate a blindspotting culture, the benefits will ripple throughout our organisations, improving collaboration, innovation and team dynamics.

> When we practise the blindspotting mindsets ourselves and actively cultivate a blindspotting culture, the benefits will ripple throughout our organisations.

Blindspotting isn't just for boardrooms or billion-dollar enterprises – it's a game-changer for all types of workplaces. Whether it's a local community sports club working towards better teamwork, a brand-new startup navigating uncharted territory, or a multinational giant driving global impact, the mindsets of honesty, curiosity and flexibility elevate performance at every level. By building teams of Seekers and fostering a blindspotting culture, we can empower everyone to collaborate more effectively, innovate fearlessly and adapt to any challenge – no matter the size or scale of the organisation.

The more Seekers on a team, the greater the team's collective power. While there are times when being a Knower is called for, as we discovered in chapter 2, a team filled with Seekers fosters an environment where everyone is prepared to listen and adjust their views. This leads to richer discussions, stronger collaboration and more robust decision-making. As CEO Satya Nadella demonstrated at Microsoft, shifting from a 'know-it-all' culture to one of growth mindset enhances individual contributions and ignites a company-wide evolution.[1] Nadella's focus on open dialogue and prioritising collaboration over individual ego underscores the value of leaders embracing honesty, curiosity and flexibility.

> The more Seekers on a team, the greater the team's collective power.

Seekers don't just make collaboration easier – they revolutionise it. Team members feel safe to admit their limitations and ask for help, leading to more innovative solutions and learning opportunities. The freedom to express uncertainty opens the door to creative ideas that might otherwise be left unexplored. When feedback and opposing views are received without defensiveness, a team's ability to incorporate new insights and perspectives is significantly improved.

While disagreements are inevitable in any team, a Seeker welcomes the possibility that they might be wrong, using these instances as opportunities to re-examine their perspectives. Instead of defending a position out of ego, they remain open to new ideas, prioritising the relationship and the team's success over their individual need to be right. Seekers are more likely to help resolve disputes constructively, without ego or emotional baggage, fostering a healthier, more productive working environment for the whole team.

HOW TO ATTRACT AND RETAIN SEEKERS

Blindspotting cultures are created in organisations where Seekers are recognised, rewarded, recruited and promoted. By doing so, we can attract team members who are open-minded, adaptable and eager to learn – attitudes that can ultimately guide the team to success. Such a culture will help us retain top talent and ensure that the most desirable candidates gravitate towards our organisations.

> **Blindspotting cultures are created in organisations where Seekers are recognised, rewarded, recruited and promoted.**

When every member of a team trusts one another and feels valued, they will also become less defensive and more open to different perspectives. If a leader can foster productive, collaborative and respectful interpersonal relationships between the people they lead, it will enhance their team's cohesion, creativity and overall performance. Research shows that when people feel accepted and secure, they are less likely to cling to their own opinions, becoming more open to exploring others' viewpoints.[2] This openness directly supports a culture of blindspotting, where honest reflection and constructive feedback are not just encouraged but celebrated.

When individuals prioritise collaboration over competition, they are more likely to share ideas freely, leading to better solutions.[3] Teams that encourage open-minded discussions and constructive feedback thrive in environments of uncertainty and rapid change. When team members feel safe to contribute their perspectives without fear of judgement, innovation flourishes.

Creating a blindspotting culture flattens hierarchies by distributing influence equally across the team. Decision-making becomes a collective, collaborative process, with everyone contributing meaningfully and being less concerned about comparisons or power dynamics. Instead, we focus on finding the best solutions, creating a team environment rooted in empathy, trust and mutual respect, all of which will help ensure an organisation's success.

Help Seekers thrive
Create a psychologically safe team
Psychological safety is present in our teams when we trust and respect the people we work with and when we feel able, or even obligated, to be candid.[4] As a leader, you can encourage open dialogue by reminding your team that saying, 'I don't know . . . yet' is a strength, not a weakness. Lead by example. In team meetings, openly admit when you don't know something. And if a team member admits to a knowledge gap, acknowledge their vulnerability and thank them for their honesty. This builds a culture where transparency and collaboration thrive.

Here are some questions you can ask your team to assess whether people feel psychologically safe to admit their intellectual limits:

- 'Do you feel supported when you express uncertainty or need help with something?'
- 'What can we do to create an environment where everyone feels safe to share what they don't know?'
- 'When someone admits they don't have an answer, how do we respond as a group?'
- 'Are there moments where you felt hesitant to ask a question because you didn't want to appear uninformed?'
- 'How often do we celebrate learning from mistakes or being honest about not knowing something?'
- 'Are there specific situations where you feel more comfortable being candid about gaps in your knowledge? What makes those moments different?'
- 'When was the last time you felt confident admitting you didn't know something? What helped you feel that way?'
- 'What barriers, if any, prevent you from speaking up when you are unsure about something?'
- 'How can I, as a leader, better model the behaviour of admitting when I don't know something?'
- 'Do you think our team encourages intellectual curiosity and the idea that we are all here to learn?'

These questions can help uncover whether the culture fosters openness and psychological safety, allowing people to feel secure in admitting intellectual limits.

Encourage teams to hunt their biases
As we explored in chapter 4, hunting out biases is one of the most powerful ways to improve decision-making and foster growth. As leaders, it's important to regularly challenge our assumptions by seeking out opposing views, and create an environment where it's safe for team members to respectfully call out potential blind spots. Establish regular feedback loops so your team feels empowered to flag when bias might have influenced decisions – yours or their own. Frame this as an opportunity to improve, not a critique.

Want to take it a step further? Try a 'red team' exercise – a strategy borrowed from military and intelligence communities. A red team's job is to intentionally poke holes in a plan and simulate alternative perspectives. This approach doesn't just identify blind spots; it builds resilience and sharpens strategies, ensuring your team makes smarter, more balanced decisions. By normalising this kind of constructive dissent, you'll cultivate a culture where critical thinking and innovation thrive.

> Ask your team these questions to help them adopt a bias-hunting mindset:
>
> - 'What assumptions are we making that we haven't questioned yet?'
> - 'Are there any perspectives or viewpoints we might be overlooking in this discussion?'
> - 'Could there be any biases influencing our decision that we're not fully aware of?'
> - 'Who might disagree with this approach, and why? How can we consider their perspective?'
> - 'What evidence exists that contradicts our current thinking, and have we explored it thoroughly?'
> - 'Are we gravitating towards a solution because it feels familiar or comfortable, rather than because it's the best option?'

- 'If we were an outsider looking at this plan, what potential flaws or biases would we see?'
- 'Have we considered all sides of the argument, or are we focusing more on what supports our existing views?'
- 'How can we ensure we're giving equal weight to diverse perspectives and not just following the loudest or most confident voice?'
- 'If we were running a "red team" exercise to challenge this plan, what weaknesses or blind spots would we uncover?'

These questions encourage teams to actively seek out biases, challenge their thinking and create a more rigorous, objective decision-making process.

Identify known unknowns

Encourage your team to try to list everything they don't know about the topic at hand before making an important decision. Identifying and confronting these 'known' unknowns will help highlight where your team might need more information and prevent blind spots in your collective thinking.

Here are some questions we can ask ourselves and our team to help identify known unknowns before making important decisions:

- 'What assumptions are we making about this decision that we haven't yet tested?'
- 'What aspects of the situation are we unsure about?'
- 'What key information do we not yet have, and how might it affect the outcome?'
- 'What are the potential risks or obstacles that we haven't fully explored?'

> - 'Are there any market trends or competitor activities that we don't have clarity on?'
> - 'What data or research do we need to better understand the situation?'
> - 'What areas are we currently unsure about, and how might those uncertainties impact our decision?'
> - 'What are potential customer reactions we might not have considered?'
> - 'What are the most likely external factors (for example, new regulations or economic changes) that could disrupt our plans?'
> - 'What blind spots might exist in our current approach, and how can we uncover them?'
> - 'Who else could provide insight or expertise on the areas where we feel less confident?'
>
> These questions help ensure that we thoroughly examine and seek to address areas where there may be gaps in knowledge before proceeding with major decisions.

Reward Seeker behaviours
Acknowledge Seeker behaviours publicly
When a team member displays Seeker behaviours, such as admitting they don't know something, being open to feedback or changing their viewpoint based on new evidence they uncovered, recognise it publicly. This not only reinforces the behaviour for that individual but also signals to the entire team that blindspotting is something to be celebrated. A simple, well-timed comment such as, 'I really appreciate your honesty in identifying what we might be missing here – let's explore this further,' can make a significant impact on the broader team culture.

Here are statements you can make as a leader to publicly recognise Seeker behaviours when you see them:

- 'I really appreciate how you openly admitted that you didn't have all the answers – it's a great example of intellectual honesty.'
- 'Your willingness to rethink your perspective shows real courage and growth. That's exactly the kind of mindset we need.'
- 'Thank you for seeking out feedback and using it to improve. It takes humility to do that, and it makes us all better.'
- 'I love how you questioned our initial assumptions. It's that kind of curiosity that drives innovation.'
- 'Your openness to considering different viewpoints is exactly what helps us avoid blind spots and make smarter decisions.'
- 'I really respect how you challenged our thinking today. It shows that you're committed to finding the best solutions, not just sticking to what's comfortable.'
- 'Your thoughtful questions are helping us see this issue from a completely new angle – thank you for driving deeper exploration.'
- 'It's great to see how you embraced this feedback and adjusted your approach. That kind of flexibility is a strength.'
- 'Your curiosity is contagious – thanks for encouraging the team to think more critically and creatively.'
- 'The fact that you're comfortable saying "I don't know" is a powerful leadership quality. It opens the door for us to find better answers together.'

These sorts of statements reinforce the value of Seeker behaviours and encourage others to implement them, promoting a culture of learning, curiosity and adaptability within the team.

Coach Knowers, don't punish them

Just as important as rewarding Seekers is addressing Knower behaviours – where individuals might cling steadfastly to their own views or resist feedback and change. Instead of reprimanding people for these behaviours, which could cause them to become defensive, we can coach these individuals to reframe their thinking. Provide constructive feedback, highlighting the importance of remaining open-minded and flexible.

> Here are some statements you can use as a leader to help coach a Knower when needed:
>
> - 'I appreciate your confidence in your viewpoint, but let's take a moment to explore other perspectives – there might be something valuable we're missing.'
> - 'It's great that you're passionate about this, although sometimes stepping back and asking new questions can help us see the bigger picture.'
> - 'I understand why you feel strongly about this, but let's remain flexible in our thinking so we can open doors to new opportunities.'
> - 'I value your input, and I think we can make it even stronger by inviting other viewpoints into the conversation.'
> - 'Let's work on balancing confidence with curiosity; it's okay not to have all the answers, and sometimes the best ideas come from collaboration.'
> - 'Your ideas have been really helpful so far, so let's challenge ourselves to look at this issue from different angles to ensure we haven't missed anything.'
> - 'You've clearly thought about this carefully; now let's see what happens when we integrate a few different perspectives to refine our approach.'

> These statements focus on encouraging open-mindedness, flexibility and collaboration, helping Knowers become more receptive to feedback without becoming defensive or feeling like they're being punished.

Encourage different perspectives
Building a team of Seekers is about encouraging a wide range of viewpoints, not confirming what the team already believes. When different perspectives and opinions are raised, celebrate the fact that your team is thinking critically and creatively. If a team member challenges a popular idea, thank them for their courage.

> Try using any of these statements to encourage your team to embrace different perspectives:
>
> - 'I really appreciate you bringing a different viewpoint to the table – it's exactly what we need to see the full picture.'
> - 'Thank you for challenging the status quo. It's through these discussions that we find the best solutions.'
> - 'I want to hear from everyone: what are we missing that we haven't considered yet?'
> - 'Your perspective offers a fresh angle that we hadn't explored yet. Let's dive into that further.'
> - 'It's important that all voices are heard. Does anyone have an alternative view or a concern we should discuss?'
> - 'I value how you're thinking about this differently from the rest of us. Keep pushing us to explore new possibilities.'
> - 'This team thrives when we hear from all sides. Who else has a different take?'

> - 'Great point! Your insight has helped us consider something we hadn't before; this is exactly why different perspectives matter.'
> - 'Don't hesitate to speak up if you disagree with the majority – I want us to feel safe exploring all angles.'
> - 'What other perspectives should we bring into this conversation to make sure we're not missing anything?'
>
> These statements help create a culture where different perspectives are welcomed and valued, promoting critical thinking, open-mindedness and innovation within the team.

Reward the process, not just the outcome

To truly embed the Seeker mindset within a team's or organisation's culture, reward the process – not just the result. Expand your performance scorecards to include metrics around *how* decisions were made. Did the team engage in open dialogue? Were a range of perspectives considered? Were individuals honest about their knowledge gaps? Recognising these Seeker behaviours will encourage a long-term culture shift rather than merely short-term performance boosts.

> Here are reflective questions you can ask yourself to prompt you to think about the process as a whole, not just the result:
>
> - Did we engage in open and honest dialogue during the decision-making process?
> - Were different perspectives actively sought out and considered before arriving at a decision?

- How well did we handle uncertainty and knowledge gaps throughout the process?
- Did we approach this project with curiosity and a willingness to challenge assumptions?
- How did we collaborate and share ideas to build on each other's strengths?
- Was feedback encouraged and embraced, even when it was constructively critical?
- How adaptable were we in the face of new information or changing circumstances?
- Did we make space for creative thinking and innovation, even if it meant taking risks?
- Were mistakes treated as learning opportunities, and did we capture those lessons for future improvement?
- How did we handle differing opinions, and was there a genuine effort to understand opposing viewpoints?

These questions will help shift the focus towards fostering a healthy, collaborative process that encourages learning and adaptability, rather than only emphasising the final outcomes.

Hire Seekers

If you want to create a culture that values honesty, curiosity and flexibility, it begins with how and who you hire. Hiring people with Seeker qualities ensures that you build a team that is not only skilled but also prepared to thrive in uncertainty and drive innovation.

Laszlo Bock, former Senior Vice President of People Operations at Google, wisely said, 'without humility, you are unable to learn'.[5] Bock identified that the most successful people at Google were those who argued fiercely for their position but were flexible when presented with new, relevant facts. They would say, 'Oh, well, that changes things; you're right.'[6] These people are Seekers, and it's critical to identify them during the interview process so you can add them to your team.

To recruit Seekers, design your hiring practices to assess people's adaptability, intellectual humility and openness to learning.

Ask questions that reveal self-awareness and adaptability
Structured interview questions can help you assess how open candidates are to changing their views and learning from others. Use questions that dig into their past experiences of personal growth, adaptation and learning.

> Here are interview questions that can help you assess whether a candidate has a Seeker mindset:
>
> - 'Can you give an example of a time you had to change your mind about something you strongly believed? What led to that change, and how did it impact your thinking?'
> - 'Describe a situation where you actively sought feedback or a different perspective. How did that feedback influence your approach or decision?'
> - 'Tell me about a time when you had to make a decision with incomplete information. How did you handle the uncertainty?'
> - 'Can you share an experience where you were challenged by someone else's opinion? How did you navigate that disagreement?'
> - 'What's an example of a situation where you had to admit you didn't know something? How did you go about finding the answer?'

- 'Describe a time when you worked hard to prove yourself wrong. How did that influence the outcome of the project or task?'
- 'Can you give an example of when you changed your opinion after learning something new or being presented with new data?'
- 'When was the last time you asked for help or advice on something? What did you learn from that experience?'
- 'Tell me about a time when you encountered a perspective you hadn't considered before. How did you integrate that into your thinking or decision-making process?'
- 'Can you describe a moment when you had to question your assumptions or deeply held beliefs to get to a better solution?'

These questions will help uncover a candidate's openness to learning, flexibility in thinking and ability to seek out and embrace different perspectives – all core traits of a Seeker.

Test for passion and intellectual honesty

Jensen Huang, co-founder and CEO of technology giant NVIDIA, has made intellectual honesty a core value of the company. When hiring, he looks for three key characteristics in candidates that align with this mindset: the ability to fall in love with something and be passionate about it, the capacity to handle change and mistakes, and the ability to see the world with a child's curiosity.[7] Huang says he goes so far as to ask the candidate to teach him something in an interview. As they explain, he will ask them 'What if . . .?' and pose a new idea, because he likes to gauge someone's openness to feedback and how curious they are about alternative solutions.[8]

Dwight Diercks, vice president of software engineering at NVIDIA, says, 'You can see right away who is going to last here and who is not. If someone starts getting defensive, I know they're not going to make it.'[9] Candidates who are quick to become defensive or protective of their ideas are unlikely to embody the Seeker mindset. Look for people who welcome challenges, seek feedback and remain open to different opinions.

> Here are interview questions to test candidates for their passion, curiosity, intellectual honesty and adaptability to change:
>
> - 'What's something you've become really passionate about in your career? How did that passion influence your work?'
> - 'Describe a time when you made a mistake. How did you become aware of it, and what did you learn from the experience?'
> - 'Can you think of a time when you had to adapt to a major change at work? How did you approach the situation, and what was the outcome?'
> - 'Tell me about a time when you received critical feedback. How did you react, and how did you use it to improve?'
> - 'What's something new you've recently learnt that you found exciting? How has it impacted the way you work or think?'
> - 'Can you give an example of when you had to completely rethink an idea or project after someone challenged your approach?'
> - 'How do you stay curious in your work? Can you describe a recent instance where your curiosity led you to a new discovery?'

> - 'Tell me about a time when you pursued something you were passionate about, even when others were sceptical. How did you handle the challenges?'
> - 'What do you do when you encounter an obstacle or failure? Can you give an example of how you turned a setback into an opportunity?'
> - 'When was the last time you questioned something you initially thought was right? How did that process help you grow?'
>
> These questions will help assess whether candidates exhibit adaptability, a passion for learning, intellectual honesty and openness to feedback – key traits that align with the Seeker mindset.

With the right people in place within the team you lead, the next critical step is to scale this Seeker mindset across the entire organisation. To truly embed blindspotting into your company's DNA, we will explore how to create a culture that values and rewards these behaviours at every level. In the next chapter, we will discuss how to build and sustain a blindspotting culture, supported by values that foster openness, reflection and continuous learning, throughout your organisation.

> **KEY TAKEAWAYS**
> - **A Seeker mindset is powerful.** Building teams of Seekers, people who embrace honesty, curiosity and flexibility, can fundamentally transform organisations. These individuals contribute to a culture where blindspotting – recognising gaps in knowledge – becomes second nature. This fosters an environment of collaboration, innovation and stronger

decision-making, enabling teams to thrive in dynamic and complex situations.
- **Collaborate without ego.** Seekers revolutionise team dynamics by removing ego from collaboration. They create an atmosphere where all team members feel safe to admit limitations and seek help, leading to more creative solutions. Feedback and opposing views are welcomed without defensiveness, encouraging richer discussions and helping teams innovate by incorporating a range of different perspectives.
- **Blindspotting cultures reward process over outcome.** To create a long-term culture shift, we should reward the entire decision-making process – including our team's intellectual honesty, openness to feedback and willingness to embrace different perspectives – not just tangible results.
- **Create a Seeker-attracting culture.** Organisations that recognise, reward and promote Seekers will attract top talent and foster a culture of openness and adaptability. In this environment, mutual trust and respect will enable team members to feel valued, reducing defensiveness and increasing receptiveness to different perspectives. This supports more innovative problem-solving and strengthens overall team cohesion.
- **Create psychological safety and encourage bias hunting.** Psychological safety is essential for blindspotting to thrive. When individuals feel secure admitting their knowledge gaps and biases, teams are better equipped to challenge assumptions and consider alternative viewpoints. We can enhance this by fostering open dialogue, encouraging people to hunt their biases, and ensuring team members feel comfortable admitting when they don't know something.

FURTHER READING

Safi Bahcall, *Loonshots: Nurture the crazy ideas that win wars, cure diseases, and transform industries* (2019).

Amy Edmondson, *The Fearless Organization: Creating psychological safety in the workplace for learning, innovation, and growth* (2019).

Megan Reitz and John Higgins, *Speak Up: Say what needs to be said and hear what needs to be heard* (2019).

Shane Snow, *Dream Teams: Working together without falling apart* (2018).

Liz Wiseman, *Multipliers: How the best leaders make everyone smarter* (2017).

ONE SHOT TO TRANSFORM

'I have never been comfortable pretending to have skills that I didn't.'

Meg Bear, former President and Chief Product Officer,
SAP SuccessFactors

When Meg Bear was the President and Chief Product Officer of technology company SAP SuccessFactors, she and her team faced a daunting and unprecedented challenge: transitioning 7,000 customers, 2,000 payroll systems, and 150,000 data-centre tenants across five continents from decades-old legacy data centres to a new cloud infrastructure. This task, internally dubbed Project One Strike, was unlike any other the team had ever encountered. The name itself captured the gravity of the situation – they had only one chance to get it right. I spoke with Meg via Zoom in 2024 to understand how she did it.

The stakes for Project One Strike were incredibly high. The upcoming transition had already been publicly announced, setting a two-year deadline with a fixed budget. There was no room for error, no chance to delay, and no opportunity for a redo. The project required a complete overhaul of systems that had been in place for decades, making the transformation both technically complex and organisationally challenging. The pressure on Meg and her team was immense; failure would mean not only significant financial loss for the company but also potentially damaging SAP SuccessFactors' reputation in the competitive tech industry.

When Meg asked her engineers how they planned to tackle the challenge, their initial suggestion was to migrate one customer at a time – a cautious approach that would have taken fifteen years and a billion dollars to complete. Realising this was not a viable option given their two-year timeframe, Meg knew they needed a different strategy. But she didn't have all the answers, and she wasn't afraid to admit it. Instead, she led with honesty and curiosity, openly acknowledging her uncertainty and encouraging her team to think creatively and collaboratively.

Meg asked tough, probing questions of her team: 'What won't work with this plan? What data are we missing? What expertise are we lacking? What risks don't we have the right expertise to see? Whose perspectives are missing?' Instead of defaulting to a safe but impractical solution, she pushed her team to rethink their initial idea and find a more innovative path forward.

Her leadership resulted in a unique solution that allowed the transition to be completed on time and within budget. It was a monumental effort that required every team member to step up, to challenge their thinking and to work together in ways they never had before. By embracing blindspotting, fostering a culture of intellectual honesty, curiosity and flexibility, and continually questioning the status quo, Meg and her team accomplished what seemed impossible, turning a potentially overwhelming task into a career-defining success for everyone involved.

Meg's experience provides a compelling example of how leaders can create a workplace culture of blindspotting. Under her leadership, her team embarked on one of the most challenging transformation projects the company had ever faced. The way Meg approached this task illustrates how to incorporate the three mindsets of blindspotting into an organisational culture, enabling her team to see what others might have missed and, as a result, achieve extraordinary results.

From the outset, Meg accepted her intellectual limits, standing before her team and admitting that she did not know how they would accomplish the massive transformation project ahead. 'We were about to undertake one of the largest transformation projects ever attempted, and I had no idea how we were going to do it,' she confessed. Meg's openness about her lack of certainty set the tone for the project, encouraging her team to embrace what *they* didn't know, too, and focus on finding the best solutions rather than pretending to have all the answers from the outset.

Meg's approach highlights the importance of what Adam Grant describes as 'confident humility'.[10] This involves having faith in one's capability while also appreciating that we might not yet have the right solution or even be addressing the right problem. 'I realised what I needed to do was role model the confidence that we could figure it out, as opposed to confidence that I knew the answer,' Meg told me. This mindset helps leaders foster an environment where exploration and learning are valued over certainty, making team members feel safe to voice their own doubts and ask questions.

A key part of creating a culture of blindspotting is disentangling ego from the decision-making process. For Meg, this meant ensuring that her team members were not afraid to admit when they didn't know something or to suggest unconventional ideas. 'I have never been comfortable pretending to have skills that I didn't,' she said. By being transparent about her own gaps in knowledge, Meg modelled the behaviour she wanted to see from her team, allowing them to focus on collective problem-solving rather than on individual performance.

When faced with her team's initial suggestion of migrating one customer at a time to the new cloud infrastructure, Meg recognised it as a bias towards safety and the familiar. 'That idea would have taken fifteen years and a billion dollars,' she recalls. 'We had two years and a fixed budget. We needed a complete rethink and to find a different path.'

Rather than accept the status quo, Meg challenged her team to rethink their approach, continually pushed them to question the underlying assumptions of their proposed solutions. By fostering a mindset of continuous inquiry, Meg helped her team identify potential pitfalls and blind spots that they might have otherwise overlooked.

Blindspotting culture thrives on the search for objective truth and the pursuit of different perspectives. Meg maintained a curiosity mindset throughout Project One Strike, asking her engineers to educate her on what she might be missing. She knew she didn't have all the answers, but she was determined to understand the nuances of the challenge from every angle. 'I am always trying to find how I can get to places that give me more line of sight, more context, a bigger worldview, a bigger understanding,' she explained.

Throughout the project, Meg also demonstrated the ability to read the room to sense the mood, dynamics and unspoken concerns within her team. She understood some team members were anxious about the uncertainty and potential risks involved in such a massive undertaking. Instead of dismissing these concerns, Meg addressed them directly. 'I reinforced that this was an opportunity we had been wanting for a long time, and while it is going to be really hard, it is going to yield so much benefit for us long term that we can feel grateful for the opportunity we are being given to make this leap,' she shared.

By acknowledging the complexity of the task ahead, Meg demonstrated the practice of embracing ambiguity. She was prepared – both emotionally and mentally – for the possibility that the project might not succeed. However, rather than being paralysed by uncertainty, she used it as a catalyst for creativity and problem-solving. 'My entire life has been about parachuting into a context that I was ill-equipped for and then looking around and thinking I need to learn a lot to figure out what works here and why it works here,' Meg reflected. This open-mindedness enabled her to guide her team through the unknown and emerge stronger on the other side.

'If you ask every single member on the team,' Meg said, 'you see their eyes sparkle when they talk about [Project One Strike] because it was the project they were most proud of in their career.' This sense of pride and ownership stems from the fact that her team was encouraged – as modelled by their leader Meg– to navigate uncertainty, challenge norms and ultimately succeed on their own terms.

Meg's leadership offers a powerful example of how to cultivate a culture of blindspotting within a team or organisation. The result of her time at SAP SuccessFactors was not only the successful completion of a complex project but also the development of a more resilient, innovative and engaged team – one that was proud of its work and eager for the next challenge. Her approach proves that leadership is not just about achieving results; it's about fostering a mindset that continuously pushes the boundaries of what is possible.

9

CULTIVATE A BLINDSPOTTING CULTURE

Blindspotting is at its most powerful when it is part of an organisation's values and mission. In this chapter, we'll look at how companies can incorporate blindspotting into their core values – ensuring it becomes a lens through which decisions are made, from the boardroom to the front line. We'll explore examples of companies that have successfully implemented this approach, as well as learning practical tools for aligning corporate values with the principles of blindspotting. This isn't about adding another corporate buzzword to your values statement; it's about building the kind of organisation where blindspotting is practised every day, fostering a culture that can thrive in the face of uncertainty and change.

> **Blindspotting is at its most powerful when it is part of an organisation's values and mission.**

Imagine an organisation where every single employee operates with complete awareness. They navigate challenges with their eyes wide open, spot potential pitfalls before they become crises, and consistently outmanoeuvre competitors by uncovering insights others have overlooked. This is the competitive advantage that comes from fostering a culture rooted in blindspotting – actively seeking out and addressing the unseen biases that can derail effective decision-making. As we have already explored, at the heart of this transformation are Seekers: individuals who operate with mindsets of honesty, curiosity and flexibility, turning blind spots into opportunities for growth.

Blindspotting is not just about identifying flaws or oversights; it's about embedding a culture of proactive discovery. While it is a tool for leaders and teams, the real power of blindspotting unfolds when it reaches critical mass across an entire organisation. This cultural shift enhances agility, fuels creativity, mitigates risks and empowers companies to respond swiftly to market changes. In an age where adaptability is critical for success, organisations that foster a Seeker's mindset at all levels gain a crucial edge over competitors stuck in conventional ways of thinking.

> **Blindspotting is not just about identifying flaws or oversights; it's about embedding a culture of proactive discovery.**

When the Seeker mindset becomes the norm across a workplace, the benefits are transformative. Rather than reacting to problems after they've occurred, companies that embrace blindspotting develop a proactive, forward-thinking mentality. They build trust through honesty and transparency, foster innovation through curiosity, and maintain agility through flexibility. In a world where businesses are constantly tested by new challenges, the organisations that cultivate Seekers will be the ones that consistently thrive.

Blindspotting, when embraced at a cultural level, doesn't only enhance the effectiveness of individual teams or leaders – it becomes the engine that powers the entire organisation.

HOW TO DESIGN A BLINDSPOTTING ORGANISATION
Flatten hierarchies to reduce information silos

In many organisations, hierarchies are designed to establish clear lines of authority and streamline decision-making across the business. While these structures can be efficient, they can also unintentionally create blind spots by reinforcing power dynamics, information silos and groupthink. To successfully mitigate blind spots, organisations need to be intentional in how they structure their hierarchies and foster a culture that promotes open communication, different perspectives and continuous learning. By rethinking their hierarchies, organisations can create an environment where blindspotting becomes a core practice.

One of the most significant risks in traditional hierarchical structures is the formation of information silos. In rigid, top-heavy organisations, communication flows tend to be vertical – moving from the top down or from the bottom up – rather than across departments or teams. This limits the perspectives available to decision-makers, increasing the likelihood of blind spots forming around critical issues such as customer needs, market trends or internal processes.

A flatter hierarchy, where layers of management are minimised, encourages more open and lateral communication between teams. In such a structure, employees at all levels are more empowered to share their insights, and cross-department collaboration is promoted. A flatter hierarchy also tends to democratise decision-making, giving more voices a chance to contribute to important discussions and mitigating the concentration of power at the top, which often leads to authority bias and groupthink. By giving employees a voice and involving them in key decisions, a flatter hierarchy fosters a sense of ownership and accountability at all levels. When people see their ideas shaping outcomes, they feel more invested in the company's success, transforming their roles from passive participants to active contributors. This deeper buy-in not only boosts morale but also drives collective commitment to achieving shared goals.

To promote blindspotting, organisations also need to design structures that encourage upwards and lateral feedback. Feedback loops are essential in any hierarchy to ensure continuous improvement and reduce blind spots. In traditional hierarchies, feedback tends to flow only in one direction – downwards – leaving senior leaders blind to potential challenges, concerns or opportunities that might be obvious to those working closer to the organisation's clients, customers, products or day-to-day operations. Lateral feedback, on the other hand, can be achieved by establishing regular forums where employees at all levels are invited to share their observations, challenges and ideas. When feedback flows in multiple directions, decision-makers will gain a clearer, more nuanced understanding of the company's internal and external environments.

Decision-making transparency
In many traditional hierarchical organisations, a small group of leaders is often perceived to be making decisions behind closed doors, leaving the majority of employees in the dark about the 'why' behind those choices. This lack of transparency is a recipe for disaster – it creates blind spots for leaders who miss critical on-the-ground insights, while employees, feeling disconnected and undervalued, may lose trust and motivation. When decision-making becomes a one-way street, organisations risk poor execution, growing frustration and a culture where innovation and collaboration are stifled.

Promoting transparency in decision-making helps mitigate these risks by ensuring employees at all levels have a clear understanding of how and why decisions are made. It also allows others beyond the leadership team to provide feedback, ask questions and point out blind spots that may have been overlooked by the top-level decision-makers.

HOW TO MAKE BLINDSPOTTING A CORE VALUE
Core values aren't just corporate jargon – they're the compass that guides a company's culture, decisions and priorities. They signal what

truly matters, to employees, stakeholders and customers alike. In a world where change is the only constant – be it economic shifts, technological advancements or social movements – every organisation, from startups to non-profits to local businesses, must adapt to survive. It's no longer enough to focus on profit alone. Companies that align their values with the rapidly evolving world are the ones that will stay relevant in a landscape where standing still means falling behind.

An organisation's values set the tone for everything from hiring practices to customer service and strategic decisions. They form the backbone of the workplace's culture, encouraging ethical behaviour and aligning teams towards common goals. When the three blindspotting mindsets are integrated into a company's DNA, they create an environment that promotes openness, learning and adaptability – essential qualities for long-term success in today's fast-paced world.

> When the three blindspotting mindsets are integrated into a company's DNA, they create an environment that promotes openness, learning and adaptability.

Honesty as a core value

While many companies list integrity and ethical conduct among their core values, in the context of blindspotting the term 'honesty' reflects intellectual honesty rather than honesty in behaviour. Intellectual honesty goes beyond simply telling the truth – it demands a commitment to seeking out and acknowledging facts, even when they challenge preconceived notions, personal biases or corporate interests. In an age where reputation can make or break a company, being intellectually honest is more critical than ever.

In the context of blindspotting, the mindset of honesty is not just about doing the right thing but about having the courage to confront inconvenient truths. An organisation that can be honest with itself ensures decisions are based on reality, not wishful thinking. A company truly guided by intellectual honesty creates an environment where ideas are tested rigorously, decisions are grounded in evidence, and a range of perspectives are genuinely valued. This kind of honesty is what drives innovation, fosters trust and ultimately sets an organisation apart.

> An organisation that can be honest with itself ensures decisions are based on reality, not wishful thinking.

Take **NVIDIA** as an example, the technology giant whose story we explored at the start of this book. Their value of intellectual honesty illustrates how transparency transcends simply telling the truth. They emphasise seeking the truth, learning from mistakes and sharing lessons learnt. NVIDIA states in their Code of Conduct, 'We operate at the highest ethical standards. We seek to accurately know ourselves and our capabilities – acknowledging our weaknesses and learning from our mistakes.'[1] This approach nurtures a culture where mistakes aren't feared but seen as opportunities for growth, creating a transparent and growth-oriented workplace.

Technology company **Intel** incorporates honesty through a focus on 'data-driven decisions with intellectual honesty and constructive debate'.[2] The company encourages employees to challenge each other's perspectives while staying grounded in facts, fostering an environment where honesty, rather than personal agendas, drives decisions. This honesty builds trust internally and also signals to investors and customers that Intel is a company grounded in reality, committed to long-term success.

At the financial services multinational **JPMorganChase**, the emphasis on humility alongside honesty underscores that leaders don't have all the answers, and that's okay. JPMorganChase's values promote fostering 'an environment of openness, trust, and sharing',[3] seeking to create a workplace where employees are encouraged to voice concerns and share different approaches.

One of the core values of food manufacturer **Kellogg's** is to 'have the humility and hunger to learn'.[4] Kellogg's specifies what this looks like for employees, and many of the expectations of this value reflect blindspotting practices:
- Value openness and curiosity to learn from anyone, anywhere
- Seek and provide honest feedback
- Be open to personal change and continuous improvement
- Learn from mistakes and successes in equal measure
- Never underestimate our competition.[5]

Australian hardware distributor **Reece** has a core value of 'Be Humble', and the company lists a number of personal qualities related to humility, such as showing pride without ego. Reece also asks employees to 'Listen first',[6] a quality that reflects blindspotting in action.

Curiosity as a core value

In a rapidly evolving business landscape, curiosity is crucial. Organisations that foster a curiosity mindset are more likely to innovate, adapt to new trends and stay ahead of the competition. Curiosity leads to a deeper understanding of problems, encourages employees to ask tough questions, and enables companies to explore new possibilities.

Computer technology giant **Microsoft** exemplifies curiosity by encouraging employees to respect the thoughts, feelings and backgrounds of others. This value isn't just about kindness; it's about fostering an environment where all perspectives are valued, and an acknowledgement that curiosity about others' ideas leads to better solutions. Microsoft's value of respect promotes inclusivity, and it also drives innovation by encouraging employees to explore and understand different viewpoints.[7]

At **Netflix**, curiosity is woven into the fabric of their corporate culture. They value employees who 'learn rapidly and eagerly' and 'recognise biases and work to counteract them'.[8] This approach not only fosters innovation but also builds a workplace where people are encouraged to question assumptions and think critically about how to improve.

Ford Motor Company goes even further by championing humility through their core value of curiosity. Ford states that they are 'humble enough to know we can learn from every situation and actively question to understand and think critically'.[9] This curiosity, paired with humility, allows Ford to stay competitive by continually evolving and adapting to new challenges.

Mining and resources giant **Rio Tinto** has three core values, one of which is curiosity. The Rio Tinto Code of Conduct describes curiosity at work as 'inviting diverse ideas and collaborating to achieve more together than can be done alone. We are continuously learning, creatively looking for better and safer ways of doing things. We draw inspiration from others and the world around us.'[10]

Virgin Money UK has a core value of 'insatiable curiosity'. Employees are expected to be 'open minded, ask questions and keep on learning. We keep searching for the best ideas, approaches and solutions'.[11] In a constantly changing world, an organisational mindset of insatiable curiosity will transform challenges into opportunities to help ensure long-term success.

Flexibility as a core value

Flexibility is another critical value for organisations, especially in today's fast-paced, uncertain world. Companies that are rigid in their thinking risk becoming irrelevant by failing to adapt to the changing circumstances around them. In contrast, flexibility allows companies to pivot when necessary, embrace new ideas and stay competitive.

It encourages adaptability and openness to change – qualities that are essential for long-term resilience.

American telecommunications company **Verizon** captures flexibility in their value of 'constructive dissent', which encourages employees to voice their opinions, but once a decision is made, everyone rallies around it.[12] This value fosters flexibility in decision-making processes and ensures that a wide range of ideas are heard before reaching a decision. By promoting open dialogue and then committing to a unified direction, Verizon creates an environment where flexibility and decisiveness coexist.

Similarly, **Cisco Systems** encourages its employees to 'open your mind to ideas from everywhere and anywhere' and to 'give your ego the day off'.[13] This promotes flexibility by encouraging employees to embrace ideas from all corners of the organisation, regardless of where they come from. Cisco understands that flexibility isn't just about reacting to external changes but also being open to internal innovation.

From NVIDIA's intellectual honesty to Netflix's curiosity and Cisco's flexibility, blindspotting practices are driving innovation, fostering collaboration and building resilience within organisations. Core values that reflect blindspotting practices empower organisations to uncover hidden biases, adapt to change and make smarter, more inclusive decisions. By embracing the values of honesty, curiosity and flexibility, companies can build cultures that not only withstand disruption but thrive in it, turning blind spots into breakthroughs.

> Core values that reflect blindspotting practices empower organisations to uncover hidden biases, adapt to change and make smarter, more inclusive decisions.

HOW TO BUILD A BLINDSPOTTING BOARD

Boards of directors play a crucial role in shaping the culture, strategy and long-term success of an organisation. However, they are not immune to all the biases, blind spots and fixed mindsets that other teams and individuals often fall victim to. In fact, these dynamics can even be amplified in the boardroom, where power, prestige and group dynamics can overshadow open debate and honest self-reflection. This is why it is vital for boards to engage in blindspotting, actively seeking out and addressing blind spots to foster better decision-making, transparency and accountability.

Boards of directors are the stewards of an organisation's mission and vision, overseeing strategy, ensuring accountability and providing guidance on major decisions. But even if this doesn't reflect your workplace, please keep reading; you don't need a formal boardroom for these ideas to matter. Ask yourself: who acts as your sounding board? Who challenges your assumptions and brings fresh perspectives to the table? It could be a leadership team, trusted advisers or even a group of passionate volunteers or friends. The absence of a board doesn't mean blind spots don't exist; it just means you will need to be intentional about fostering open dialogue and ensuring your decisions are grounded in the collective wisdom of your group. Whether you're running a small business, managing a local sports club or even leading a community group, the principles of blindspotting still apply.

Let's delve into why it is so important for boards to engage in blindspotting, and the practical steps they can take to do so.

Why blindspotting is needed in boardrooms

For boards, blindspotting is especially crucial because their decisions have far-reaching impacts – not just within the company, but potentially across entire industries and communities. If a board is blind to potential risks, emerging trends or different perspectives, it can lead to poor decisions, missed opportunities, or even reputational damage.

When board members are unwilling to admit their own knowledge gaps or biases, it limits the entire organisation's ability to grow and adapt. This blind spot can create a culture of overconfidence, where the board believes past success will translate into future infallibility, ultimately leading to flawed decisions.

> **When board members are unwilling to admit their own knowledge gaps or biases, it limits the entire organisation's ability to grow and adapt.**

As is the case with leaders and their immediate teams, one of the most practical ways boards can engage in blindspotting is by fostering psychological safety in the boardroom. Psychological safety is the belief that one can speak up without fear of negative consequences. When board members and management feel safe to voice concerns, ask difficult questions or challenge dominant opinions, the board becomes more dynamic and less susceptible to groupthink.

The board's Chair is the leader of the board of directors, responsible for setting the tone, facilitating effective discussions and ensuring the board stays focused on its key responsibilities – strategy, oversight and governance. Think of them as the glue that keeps the board aligned and the compass that guides its direction. If a Chair dominates every discussion, it can suppress the voices of other board members, creating a power imbalance. This discourages constructive dissent and reinforces a one-dimensional perspective. Instead, Chairs who actively seek input from quieter members, ask open-ended questions and rethink strongly held assumptions will ensure a full spectrum of viewpoints is considered.

Hold your convictions lightly

Throughout my career, I've spent countless hours inside boardrooms, serving as a company director for large public companies and smaller private organisations. A board director is effectively a team member – albeit a senior one with significant responsibilities and liabilities. Usually alongside up to ten colleagues, also directors, they form the board of directors that helps oversee an organisation's strategy, governance and long-term success. Each director brings differing levels and areas of expertise, but they all have the same mission: to guide the organisation, hold its leadership accountable and ensure its mission and goals are achieved.

I've observed a common thread among the most effective directors: they hold their convictions lightly. This doesn't mean they lack strong views or expertise – quite the opposite. Most board members are appointed for their significant experience, having led large organisations or sectors themselves. They come to the table with well-founded opinions. Yet the best among them understand the importance of keeping their minds open.

In boardroom decision-making, it's crucial to be willing to listen to others, to hear perspectives you might not have considered, and to be open to adjusting your stance based on new information. Holding strong convictions is important, but doing so lightly allows for flexibility and growth, making space for the best possible outcome for the organisation.

Contrary to what you might see on television, real board meetings are generally not dramatic showdowns where decisions are made through heated debates or last-minute votes. In reality, robust discussions in a well-functioning boardroom involve mutual respect and thoughtful conversation. There's a sense of calm but also a sharp focus on critical thinking. Directors might enter the room with a fixed position in mind, but they know that the key to good governance lies in staying open to new ideas and allowing those ideas to influence their final decision.

This willingness to reconsider and evolve their views is what separates an effective board from a dysfunctional one.

Overcoming authority bias

Authority bias is a common blind spot in boardrooms, where the opinions of senior or more influential members carry disproportionate weight. When a board relies too heavily on a single director's experience or viewpoint, it risks ignoring valuable insights from others. A healthy board challenges this bias by ensuring that all directors feel empowered to contribute.

The role of the Chair is pivotal in overcoming authority bias. The Chair must be proactive in encouraging all board members to share their thoughts and ensuring that the board doesn't default to the opinion of the loudest or most senior voice. In situations where authority bias is evident, the Chair can facilitate blindspotting by explicitly asking for dissenting opinions or by posing provocative questions such as, 'What might we be overlooking?'

Fostering inclusion and healthy dissent

The composition of a board is another critical factor in its ability to engage in blindspotting. Homogeneous boards, made up of individuals with similar backgrounds, experiences and perspectives, are more likely to fall prey to groupthink. This can stifle creativity, limit strategic options and lead to overconfidence in decision-making.

A board that values blindspotting actively seeks out diversity in its members – in gender, ethnicity, age, experience and expertise. A diverse board is more likely to challenge initial assumptions, offer fresh insights and identify risks that might not be at all apparent to a more homogeneous group.

Encouraging diversity and inclusion is not just about representation; it is about bringing in a wide range of perspectives that will ultimately enhance decision-making and the organisation's potential for success. But diversity alone isn't enough; it must be paired with healthy dissent. Creating an environment where people feel safe to speak up, question the status quo and disagree respectfully is essential. Healthy dissent fuels better decision-making by exposing blind spots and avoiding groupthink. When everyone thinks alike, mistakes go unnoticed. But when people are empowered to think differently, organisations can tackle challenges more creatively and effectively. Diversity and dissent aren't threats – they're the keys to thriving in a complex, ever-changing world.

> **Diversity and dissent aren't threats – they're the keys to thriving in a complex, ever-changing world.**

Addressing mistakes and learning from failure

As with individual leaders, boards that are willing to admit when they are wrong and that take accountability for their decisions create a culture of learning and improvement. When mistakes are swept under the rug, it fosters a culture of denial and defensiveness, which exacerbates blind spots and makes it harder to learn from failure.

For example, a board should not only celebrate successes but also conduct thorough post-mortems on failures. What went wrong? Why did it happen? What biases might have contributed to the misstep? This reflective approach helps boards become more self-aware and resilient, making them better equipped to handle future challenges.

Blindspotting is not an abstract concept – it is a practical tool boards can use to improve their decision-making processes, foster a culture of openness and navigate complex challenges. By actively searching for blind spots and embracing different perspectives, boards can ensure they are leading their organisations with honesty, humility and curiosity. In doing so, they set the tone for a workplace culture that values transparency, accountability and long-term success.

KEY TAKEAWAYS

- **Blindspotting is a competitive advantage.** Organisations that actively seek out and address unseen biases and assumptions gain a significant advantage by staying ahead of competitors who are stuck in conventional ways of thinking. This mindset transforms blind spots into growth opportunities, fostering adaptability, agility and innovation across the organisation.
- **Seekers are essential to cultivating a blindspotting culture.** Seekers challenge assumptions, identify blind spots and act on discoveries. When a Seeker's mindset is cultivated across an entire organisation, it creates a proactive, forward-thinking culture where blind spots are routinely addressed and new opportunities are uncovered.
- **Flattening hierarchies reduces information silos.** Traditional hierarchical structures often create information silos and reinforce power dynamics, which can exacerbate blind spots. Flatter hierarchies encourage open, lateral communication, which enables employees at all levels to share insights and participate in decision-making.
- **Create psychological safety and room for constructive dissent.** Psychological safety is crucial for blindspotting, especially in boardrooms and leadership teams. When employees and board members feel safe to voice concerns and ask tough questions, organisations become more dynamic and innovative. Encouraging constructive dissent also ensures a range of perspectives are heard, preventing groupthink and promoting better strategic decisions.
- **Foster diversity in leadership teams.** Diverse leadership teams are better equipped to identify and address blind

spots than homogeneous ones. Leaders from a range of different backgrounds and levels of experience bring new and varied perspectives, which can challenge assumptions and encourages a culture of continuous improvement and adaptability, making organisations more resilient in the face of change.

FURTHER READING

Ram Charan, Dennis Carey and Michael Useem, *Boards That Lead: When to take charge, when to partner, and when to stay out of the way* (2014).

Ray Dalio, *Principles: Life and work* (2017).

Amy Edmondson, *The Fearless Organization: Creating psychological safety in the workplace for learning, innovation, and growth* (2019).

Fred Kofman, *Conscious Business: How to build value through values* (2019).

Daniel H. Pink, *Drive: The surprising truth about what motivates us* (2009).

LANDING ON UNCERTAINTY

'Leadership is about knowing you don't have all the answers.'

Robert Denney, Air Vice Marshal, Royal Australian Air Force

As an Air Vice Marshal in the Royal Australian Air Force (RAAF), Robert Denney has faced numerous high-stakes situations throughout his career, but none as life defining as the day the landing gear on his aircraft refused to descend. In the cockpit of an F-111 – a supersonic military jet known for its versatility as a bomber and fighter aircraft – Robert and the test engineer flying alongside him found themselves in a crisis that would demand every ounce of their training, teamwork and mental agility. As Robert guided the fast jet through the sky, he quickly realised landing safely was now becoming a slim possibility – a harrowing reality for any pilot.

Robert and I first met in 1991 on the day we were both recruited as young trainee officers in the RAAF. I was eager to chat with Robert about how far he had come since those early days in his career, and I wanted to get his thoughts on the way blindspotting can make the difference between success and failure in moments of crisis. When you are a fighter pilot like Robert, blindspotting is not just about avoiding catastrophe, but also about role-modelling these behaviours for others, creating an environment where people can think clearly under pressure and find solutions in unexpected places.

It was 2001 when Robert found himself in a situation every pilot dreads: an emergency landing with a malfunctioning landing gear. Robert and his flight test engineer were conducting what was supposed to be a routine test mission in their F-111 fighter bomber. But as soon as the landing gear failed, everything changed. The two men heard a loud '*bang, bang, bang*' and knew immediately that something was wrong. Hydraulic fluid had leaked out into the wheel well, and now the system was failing.

For Robert, this wasn't just about handling a technical failure – it was a test of everything he had learnt throughout his career about decision-making, teamwork and blindspotting. What he didn't know could kill both himself and the engineer beside him, and that was the exact reason why he needed to rely on the team around him. This moment wasn't about him alone – it was about collaborating with others to piece together the best possible solution.

'You're never going to fly the perfect mission,' Robert explained. 'When you think you're on top of it, that's when you're going to get yourself into trouble.'

After going through all his checklists to try to identify the problem, Robert knew he needed a different perspective. He asked a fellow pilot flying nearby in a PC-9 – a lightweight, single-engine turboprop aircraft used for pilot training – to inspect the outside of his aircraft while in the air alongside them. The PC-9 pilot reported back that the F-111's landing gear was not visible, and together they discussed what needed to be done.

Robert knew that even the most seasoned pilots can't see every angle. In leadership, this is a lesson many struggle to accept, especially in corporate environments: no matter how much experience or knowledge we have, we will always need others to help us see the full picture.

As the crisis unfolded, Robert had to balance several competing priorities: land the plane safely, follow procedure and trust his team. In the aviation world, as in the corporate world, structure and process are vital. Robert methodically worked through the checklists designed for emergencies like this one.

These checklists weren't limiting – they were empowering. They provided a foundation that allowed Robert to think clearly and adjust as necessary. Following protocol didn't prevent him from adapting to the situation; rather, it gave him the tools to do so effectively. This is an essential lesson for leaders: structure is not the enemy of flexibility. When used correctly, it can enhance a leader's ability to pivot when the unexpected occurs. As Robert told me, 'Structure provides a strong foundation upon which you can improvise.'

As Robert weighed his options, it became clear that landing without the necessary gear and flaps, which normally slow down an aircraft, would be highly dangerous. He would need to land his aircraft using an arresting cable on the runway – a cable designed to stop planes when their brakes and flaps fail. Robert gave his flight test engineer clear instructions: 'If we miss the cable, pull the handle,' referring to the ejection seat. At this moment, Robert had made the decision on what needed to happen if the cable was missed and now put complete trust in his team. He made sure that if things went wrong, his flight test engineer had the autonomy to make the critical decision to eject them both. Robert wasn't relinquishing control; he was ensuring the best decisions would be made, even if he wasn't the one making them.

As they approached the runway, the pressure mounted. The landing gear had completely malfunctioned, the flaps were still not operational and could not be tested using backup power because Robert was unsure what they might do to the controllability of the aircraft. As a result, the plane was struggling to descend. Without the flaps, it is hard to ensure a steep enough approach to land, and the runway becomes difficult to see over the nose of the aircraft. In the middle of the emergency, Robert had to manually increase the height of his seat to improve his visibility.

Despite the uncertainty, Robert remained calm and focused. He had done everything possible to prepare for this moment. 'I don't remember feeling scared. Afterwards though I was incredibly tired,' he reflected, highlighting the physical and emotional toll of the experience. His ability to remain composed under pressure – while still being open to input from others – was key to landing the plane safely.

Robert's focus wasn't on eliminating all risk – it was on managing it and controlling the risks he needed to take. His approach was a balance of confidence in the procedures and flexibility in the execution, a useful model for leaders who often need to navigate complex and unpredictable environments.

Robert successfully caught the arresting cable, bringing the plane to a stop. It was a moment of immense relief but also one of deep reflection. Robert's ability to model blindspotting behaviours under extreme stress offers a powerful example of how leaders can create a culture where others are encouraged to do the same.

It's a timely reminder that leadership isn't about having all the answers or always being in control. It's about recognising your blind spots, creating a team culture where all perspectives are valued, and trusting others to make decisions when it matters most. Whether in the cockpit or the boardroom, the ability to lead with humility, curiosity and flexibility is what ensures long-term success.

CONCLUSION

As you turn the final pages of this book, it's important to recognise that blindspotting is not a destination – it's a journey. It's the continuous practice of seeing beyond the obvious, embracing what we don't know and challenging our assumptions.

Blindspotting is about becoming acutely aware of the limitations in our thinking and remaining humble enough to admit that no matter how much we learn or achieve, there will always be more to uncover. It's a lifelong practice that calls for intellectual honesty, curiosity and flexibility.

To truly grasp the depth and utility of blindspotting, it's crucial to understand that this isn't just a skill or a framework we apply once and forget. The journey never really ends. Even as you finish this book, you are merely at a new beginning.

What you've read so far has equipped you with the mindsets, practices and tools to identify the cognitive traps that hold us back. Throughout this book, we have encountered the wisdom of leaders and thinkers who have mastered the art of blindspotting in their respective fields. These individuals, from Wendy McMahon to Safi Bahcall, David Epstein to Julie Inman Grant, and so many more,

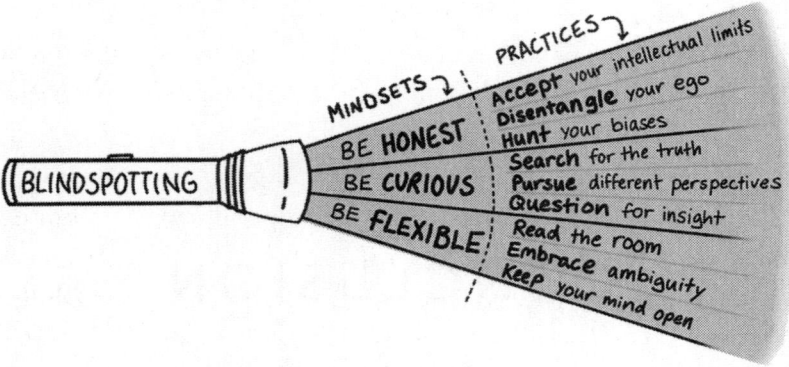

have generously shared their personal insights and stories, each revealing that the journey towards knowledge and understanding is never complete. Their experiences are a testament to the fact that blindspotting is a lifelong practice – a continuous pursuit of intellectual honesty, curiosity and flexibility.

Yet, as inspiring as their stories are, blindspotting isn't only about learning from others – it's about putting these principles into practice in your own life. Every leader, every individual, has blind spots. The question is: are you willing to confront yours?

> Every leader, every individual, has blind spots.
> The question is: are you willing to confront yours?

BE HONEST

It's fitting to begin where all great leadership starts: with honesty. The honesty you show others, and the honesty you show yourself.

The blindspotting mindset of honesty involves recognising that no one has all the answers. True intellectual honesty requires us to confront our limitations head-on, accepting that there will always be gaps in our knowledge. When we acknowledge these intellectual limits, we free ourselves from the pressure of pretending to know it all and we open the door to deeper learning and growth. This vulnerability allows us to invite others in, strengthening our decisions with fresh perspectives and insights. Being honest with ourselves and others not only builds trust but also encourages a culture where curiosity and exploration are valued over certainty.

But honesty doesn't stop there. To fully embrace this mindset, we must disentangle our ego from our ideas. When we become too attached to being right, we close ourselves off to new possibilities, letting our biases and assumptions cloud our judgement. Instead, when we seek out and challenge our biases – deliberately hunting them – we create space for greater objectivity and clearer thinking. By questioning our assumptions and listening openly to feedback, we position ourselves to make smarter, more inclusive decisions. This approach sharpens our thinking and signals to our teams that we value growth and adaptability over rigid certainty.

BE CURIOUS

The blindspotting mindset of curiosity is rooted in a relentless pursuit of the objective truth, even when it challenges our beliefs. At its core, this mindset requires us to go beyond surface-level assumptions and dig deeper into the complexities of every situation. By seeking the objective truth, we move away from confirmation bias and the comfort of familiar ideas, instead embracing a mindset of constant discovery. Curiosity pushes us to ask, 'What am I missing?' and compels us to actively seek out facts that paint a more complete picture, regardless of whether or not they support our initial viewpoint.

However, the true power of curiosity lies in the ability to pursue different perspectives and ask questions for insight. When we approach problems with a spirit of inquiry, we don't just look for answers – we seek to understand the reasoning behind them. By welcoming different viewpoints, we open ourselves to new angles and solutions that might otherwise remain hidden. This practice of asking questions for insight transforms simple discussions into meaningful explorations, where deeper understanding can emerge. We don't settle for the first explanation or the most convenient conclusion – we dig deeper, continuously refining our understanding and ultimately driving smarter, more innovative decisions.

BE FLEXIBLE

The blindspotting mindset of flexibility thrives on our ability to read the room, adapting to the dynamics and needs of the moment. We recognise that every situation is fluid, and rather than clinging to a fixed approach, we remain attuned to the changing environment around them. This skill allows us to adjust our style, strategy and decisions based on the unique context we're facing, ensuring that our response is as effective as possible. By reading the room, we can sense when it's time to push forward with confidence or when a more reflective, collaborative approach is needed. Flexibility isn't about abandoning our convictions – it's about knowing when to shift gears in the pursuit of better outcomes.

Embracing ambiguity is central to flexibility – being comfortable when clear answers are not immediately available. When we practice this mindset, we understand uncertainty is often part of the process, and rather than being paralysed by it, we use it as an opportunity to explore new possibilities. Keeping an open mind is essential in these moments. When we let go of rigid thinking and allow ourselves to consider multiple options, we invite innovation and adaptability. A flexible mindset ensures we remain agile, continuously evolving as new information or perspectives emerge, and willing to rethink our approach to find the best path forward.

STAY VIGILANT

Of course, no matter how much we practice blindspotting, we will always be at risk of falling into cognitive traps. The curse of expertise, for instance, can make us blind to new information because we think we know all there is to know. Hubris can lead us to overestimate our abilities, causing us to dismiss important viewpoints. And the illusion of knowledge can make us believe we have a full understanding of something when, in reality, our grasp of it is superficial at best.

This is why blindspotting is a continuous practice. It requires us to stay vigilant, to constantly practise self-awareness and reflect on our thinking, and to seek out feedback from others. Don't assume that because you've succeeded in the past, you'll succeed again in the same way. Stay honest, stay curious and stay flexible.

> **Blindspotting is a continuous practice.**

Hubris, as we've seen through the stories of corporate failures included in this book, blinds us to the feedback we desperately need to hear. In organisations where hubris reigns, any dissenting opinions are stifled, and the leader's vision becomes the only path forward – no matter how flawed it may be. The challenge is to recognise when we're letting pride cloud our judgement, and to practice intellectual humility instead.

COLLECTIVE TRANSFORMATION

While blindspotting begins with the individual, its true power lies in its potential for collective transformation. When entire teams and organisations commit to the principles of blindspotting, innovation flourishes. Wendy McMahon and Meg Bear both highlighted the importance of creating cultures where intellectual honesty, curiosity and flexibility are woven into the fabric of an organisation. In these environments, different perspectives are not only welcomed but encouraged.

Sukhinder Singh Cassidy's leadership offers a clear blueprint for how organisations can cultivate this culture. By prioritising diversity and ensuring that leadership teams are reflective of the broader world, Sukhinder has shown that blindspotting isn't just about identifying cognitive biases – it's about recognising the social and structural blind spots that prevent us from seeing the full picture. Inclusive leadership is one of the most powerful ways to ensure that organisations remain adaptable, innovative and ahead of the curve.

Fostering a culture of blindspotting within organisations leads to better decision-making, greater innovation and more inclusive environments. When teams are encouraged to question assumptions, challenge the status quo and approach problems from multiple angles, they become more resilient and adaptable.

In this book, we've explored how to build teams and organisations that practise blindspotting. This includes creating psychologically safe environments where people feel comfortable speaking up, admitting they don't know something and challenging dominant narratives. It means rewarding Seeker behaviours – those that exemplify curiosity, open-mindedness and the pursuit of knowledge. And it means celebrating blindspotting as a core value, embedding it throughout an organisation through leadership development, performance metrics and everyday practices.

CHALLENGE FOR THE FUTURE

Blindspotting allows you to see what others miss, because you're willing to admit what you don't know. It's about maintaining intellectual honesty, staying curious and being flexible enough to change your mind when new information arises. It's about building teams and cultures that value these traits, and understanding that the journey towards better thinking and better leadership never really ends.

> **Blindspotting allows you to see what others miss, because you're willing to admit what you don't know.**

By embracing blindspotting, you're recognising that every time you think you've got something figured out, there's still more to learn. It means you have the humility to admit that even the most brilliant ideas can be improved, and the courage to confront the cognitive traps that might be holding you back.

Blindspotting is a tool that can transform your leadership, your team and your organisation. But it requires commitment – a commitment to lifelong learning, constant self-reflection and the willingness to change when new information arises.

As you walk away from this book, I hope you take with you the lessons you've learnt from these leaders, but more importantly, I hope you take the lessons you've learnt about yourself. The most powerful legacy will be left by leaders who are willing to embrace blindspotting, to see beyond the obvious, and to challenge their assumptions. Will you remain open to what you don't know? Will you seek out new perspectives, challenge your assumptions, and stay flexible in the face of change?

The future belongs to those who can see what others miss. The question is: will you be one of them?

EPILOGUE

When Jensen Huang co-founded NVIDIA in 1993, his vision was grand, and his confidence was soaring. Little did he know that the defining success of NVIDIA wouldn't be its technical innovations alone, but also its mindset built around intellectual honesty, curiosity and flexibility. The foundation that led NVIDIA to become one of the most valuable companies in the world by 2024 was formed through a series of near-catastrophic failures, punctuated by a relentless pursuit of truth – even when that truth was uncomfortable.

In the late 1990s, NVIDIA revolutionised the gaming world with the release of the GeForce 256, a graphics processing unit (GPU) that far exceeded the expectations of PC gamers. Huang and his team hadn't just released another product – they'd created a whole new category, positioning the GPU as a vital piece of gaming hardware. Gamers could now experience 3D rendering with unprecedented detail and speed.

The GPU was NVIDIA's first major success, but as Huang understood well, success is fragile. In the tech industry, companies live and die by their ability to innovate and stay ahead of the competition, and Huang knew he needed to continue pushing boundaries to keep NVIDIA at the forefront. Yet, the journey forward would be anything but smooth.

In 1999, NVIDIA's rise seemed unstoppable, but the seeds for their next great leap were sown by an unexpected player: a graduate student named Ian Buck. In 2000, Buck, who was studying computer graphics at Stanford, became fascinated with the processing power of NVIDIA's GPUs. He hacked together a supercomputer in his dorm room using NVIDIA's GeForce cards to play the first-person shooter game Quake, but his curiosity soon led him to an unexpected realisation. The GPUs he was using for gaming had the potential to perform high-speed mathematical calculations in parallel time – an application far beyond gaming experience.

Huang soon learnt about Buck's unique approach and recognised the potential in his work. Soon, Buck was working at NVIDIA, and his discovery would lead to the development of Compute Unified Device Architecture (CUDA), a proprietary programming platform that allowed engineers to harness the full power of NVIDIA GPUs for purposes far beyond gaming.

CUDA wasn't an instant hit. In fact, it was met with scepticism both inside and outside NVIDIA. Investors were focused on short-term profitability, and few believed that a programming language designed for parallel computing would have a wide enough market to justify the investment. The stock price of NVIDIA fell by 50 per cent between 2008 and 2013, and downloads of CUDA declined.

But Huang remained steadfast in his belief. 'Creating a new computing model is incredibly hard and rarely done in history,' he told students at a university address in 2023.[1] 'The cost of CUDA was very high for NVIDIA – we suffered many years of poor performance. Our shareholders were sceptical, but we persevered. We believed the time for accelerated computing would come.'[2]

This was intellectual honesty at work. Huang recognised that CUDA wasn't delivering immediate results, but he didn't shy away from the truth. Instead, he confronted it with patience and curiosity, trusting that the future would reward those who stayed the course.

That patience paid off. Today, CUDA drives the entire suite of NVIDIA products and is taught to software engineers around the world. What began as a risky gamble has since become the backbone of the AI revolution.

While NVIDIA was refining CUDA, thousands of miles away at the University of Toronto, three researchers were working on a project that would inadvertently secure NVIDIA's place at the forefront of the AI revolution. Geoffrey Hinton, a scientist and professor often referred to as the 'Godfather of AI', was using CUDA to train a neural network that could recognise human speech. Hinton had long believed in the potential of neural networks, but it wasn't until two of his students – Alex Krizhevsky and Ilya Sutskever – came along that the technology would reach its full potential.

In 2012, Krizhevsky and Sutskever entered a global competition called ImageNet, which tasked teams with creating algorithms capable of classifying images from a massive database. With a tight budget and a desire to prove their theory, the two students purchased two GeForce GPUs from Amazon and began training their neural network, which they named AlexNet.

The results were nothing short of astounding. While researchers at Google had needed 16,000 CPUs to train a neural network to recognise cats, Krizhevsky and Sutskever were able to achieve even better results using just two NVIDIA GPUs. Their neural network outperformed competitors by a staggering 10.8 per cent, shaking the foundations of the AI research community.

AlexNet marked the beginning of the deep learning craze, and it became clear that GPUs were uniquely suited to the demands of artificial intelligence. Suddenly, the technology NVIDIA had spent years developing for gaming was repurposed as the foundation for the AI revolution.

For Huang, this was a profound moment. 'The fact that they can solve computer vision, which is completely unstructured, leads to the question, "What else can you teach it?"' he wondered.[3] With the success of AlexNet, Huang realised that the future of NVIDIA was not in graphics alone. It was in artificial intelligence.

In 2012, following AlexNet's success, Huang made a decision that would define NVIDIA's future. Over the course of a single weekend, he transformed NVIDIA from a graphics company into an AI company.

As NVIDIA executive Greg Estes recalls, 'Huang sent out an email on Friday evening saying everything is going to be deep learning, and that we were no longer a graphics company. By Monday morning, we were an AI company. Literally, it was that fast.'[4]

This is intellectual flexibility at its best. Huang didn't cling to NVIDIA's past successes in gaming or graphics. He recognised that the real opportunity lay in AI, and he wasn't afraid to change the company's direction overnight to adapt to the changing environment around them.

The decision wasn't without risk. Investors were still wary, and the long-term profitability of AI was far from certain. But Huang had seen enough to trust that deep learning was the future, and he bet everything on it.

NVIDIA began to design every chip with artificial intelligence in mind. Within four years, Huang personally delivered NVIDIA's first supercomputer, the DGX-1, to the offices of OpenAI, where it would be used to power cutting-edge AI research. Ilya Sutskever, one of the co-creators of AlexNet, was now OpenAI's chief scientist, helping lead the charge in developing AI technology that would reshape industries.

Fast forward to 2024, and NVIDIA's market share of the AI chip industry is estimated to be up to 95 per cent.[5] When OpenAI's ChatGPT exploded in popularity in 2022, breaking records as the fastest-growing consumer application in history, it was powered by NVIDIA's chips. Today, NVIDIA's technology underpins everything from self-driving cars to virtual reality, from cryptocurrency mining to the generative AI tools that are reshaping how we work and live.

The stakes couldn't be higher. NVIDIA's latest chips, such as the Blackwell series, can perform quadrillions of calculations per second, providing the computational power needed to drive the next wave of AI advancements. The company's dominance in AI is so complete that it briefly became the most valuable company in the world in 2024, with a market valuation exceeding $3.35 trillion.[6]

Yet, none of this success came without risk – and none of it would have been possible without the blindspotting mindsets of intellectual honesty, curiosity and flexibility.

Throughout NVIDIA's journey, Huang demonstrated a remarkable ability to confront hard truths. When NVIDIA's early products failed, he didn't shy away from admitting mistakes. When CUDA struggled to gain traction, he stayed the course because he believed in its potential, even when others doubted.

As Huang himself puts it, 'You have to reinvent yourself over time. And if you want to reinvent yourself, you need to have great people. Without intellectual honesty, you can't have a culture that is willing to tolerate failure, because people cling too much to an idea that likely will be bad or isn't working.'[7]

This willingness to call a spade a spade, to recognise when something isn't working and to change course accordingly, has been the driving force behind NVIDIA's success.

Huang's story is also one of relentless curiosity. When Ian Buck discovered that NVIDIA's GPUs could be used for parallel computing, Huang didn't dismiss it as a distraction from the company's core mission. Instead, he embraced the opportunity to explore new possibilities. That same curiosity drove the pivot to AI when the potential of deep learning became clear.

Huang's curiosity extends to his leadership style as well. 'People love teaching people who are great students. I dedicate myself a lot to being a good student,' he says.[8] By remaining open to new ideas and continually learning from those around him, Huang has fostered a culture of innovation at NVIDIA that encourages exploration and experimentation.

Finally, NVIDIA's success is a testament to the power of flexibility. Huang has repeatedly demonstrated a willingness to change course when necessary, whether that meant abandoning NVIDIA's early graphics architecture, pivoting from gaming to AI, or overhauling the company's entire product development strategy. This flexibility has allowed NVIDIA to stay ahead of the competition and continually push the boundaries of what's possible. By embracing change rather than resisting it, Huang has positioned NVIDIA to lead not just the AI revolution, but also whatever technological breakthroughs come next.

As we step into a future increasingly shaped by AI, the practice of blindspotting will become more crucial than ever. While AI can analyse vast amounts of data and offer insights beyond human capability, it cannot replace the uniquely human ability to be honest, curious and flexible, especially in the face of uncertainty. The algorithms we build will always reflect the biases and blind spots of those who create them, making it essential for us to remain vigilant.

The true power of AI lies not in its ability to replace human thinking, but in its potential to challenge us to see what we're missing. As leaders, thinkers and innovators, it's our responsibility to keep asking: 'What don't we know?' In this era of unprecedented technological growth, the greatest advances will come not from knowing all the answers, but from our willingness to constantly seek them.

APPENDIX: BLINDSPOTTING SELF-ASSESSMENT TOOL

You can complete the Blindspotting Self-Assessment Tool by visiting **blindspotting.com.au**. It only takes five minutes to complete, and you will receive your free, personalised assessment, which also compares your results to others'. This tool will help you understand where to best focus your efforts as you endeavour to become a better Seeker. But remember, there is no perfect score: everyone will have different areas of strength.

METHODOLOGY

In conjunction with organisational psychologist and psychometrician Dr Ben Searle, I developed the Blindspotting Self-Assessment Tool to help you assess your current perceptions of how well you engage in blindspotting. This includes the three key mindsets – Be Honest, Be Curious and Be Flexible – and the nine blindspotting practices contained within them. The self-assessment tool is a set of twenty-six questions that have been empirically tested and validated across each of the nine practices of blindspotting. The full set of questions are outlined at the end of this appendix.

PILOT STUDY

In developing the tool, a pilot study sample group of 560 participants was recruited through social media. Of these 455 (81 per cent) identified as female, 100 (18 per cent) as male, one person identified as 'other', and four people did not disclose their gender. Participants came from twenty-three countries around the world, including Australia, New Zealand, the United Kingdom and the United States.

Data analysis

For the pilot study, we used a version of the Blindspotting Self-Assessment Tool that contained fifty-four questions in total, six per blindspotting practice. The pilot study sample group was asked to respond to each question using a Likert scale from 1 (Strongly Disagree) to 7 (Strongly Agree).

Responses to these questions were examined using an iterative series of confirmatory factor analyses, with questions retained or rejected based on the strength of factor loadings and other indications of suitability for the appropriate practice, along with reviews of question wording and the meaning of each practice. Factor structure tests were conducted, for example, by including a single generic factor to assess the effect of positive response bias, but all results converged in the same way. Practices were also checked for convergent and divergent validity as well as reliability. The result was a model that used the best three questions for eight of the nine practices, and one practice that used the best two questions.

The table below provides the means, standard deviations and reliabilities for all nine practices, as well as correlations between the nine practices.

Blindspotting Practice	Mean	Standard deviation	Cronbach's alpha	Correlations							
				1	2	3	4	5	6	7	8
1. Accept your intellectual limitations	6.11	0.77	.67								
2. Disentangle your ego	5.17	1.00	.77	.45							
3. Hunt your biases	5.14	1.03	.83	.20	.29						
4. Search for truth	5.15	0.99	.71	.19	.21	.39					
5. Pursue different perspectives	5.75	0.81	.76	.38	.42	.32	.36				
6. Question for insight	5.11	1.23	.66	.21	.25	.18	.27	.26			
7. Read the room	5.39	0.84	.69	.20	.28	.26	.27	.28	.28		
8. Embrace ambiguity	5.52	1.15	.87	.23	.28	.17	.11	.36	.12	.31	
9. Keep your mind open	5.87	0.70	.71	.36	.37	.31	.28	.45	.18	.30	.30

Table 2 – Blindspotting Self-Assessment Tool Data Analysis

APPENDIX: BLINDSPOTTING SELF-ASSESSMENT TOOL 279

Questions

The final questions used in the Blindspotting Self-Assessment Tool are shown on the following page.

Anyone can complete this self-assessment. We all lead in our families, our communities and in our roles so this scale is relevant to everyone.

Please answer each question based on how you believe you would react, not how you think you should react. It may help to think about situations you have been in recently where you have been challenged by someone on something you feel strongly about or when you had to make an important decision. Reflect on how you felt and behaved.

Please respond to each statement with how strongly you agree or disagree with each statement.

	Strongly disagree	Disagree	Somewhat Disagree	Neither Agree nor Disagree	Somewhat Agree	Agree	Strongly Agree
If I'm asked a question, and I don't know the answer, I find it easy to say so							
I value constructive criticism of my ideas – it reveals where I may need to rethink assumptions							
I find it valuable to talk to people whose opinions differ from mine							
I understand how to adapt my thinking to suit whatever situation I find myself in							
Before I share an opinion, I consider whether it might be influenced by bias							
I would rather seize a chance to learn than pretend to know things I don't							
I can think of several times when I changed my mind and it led to a better outcome							
I'm comfortable taking on projects that have a lot of unknowns							
I can listen to someone disagreeing with me without feeling defensive							
I take time to investigate new claims, no matter whether I think they are true or false							
I never ask questions as a way to indicate I think someone else is wrong							
I believe I can cope well in situations where important details are unclear							
I regularly think about how my biases might impact the decisions I make							
Before I make a big decision, I seek the opinion of people who see things differently from me							
I am not afraid to ask questions, even if this reveals I have misunderstood something							
I always ask questions as a way to understand others rather than to win arguments							
Even when I believe one approach is superior, I'm willing to consider alternatives							
When I get feedback that rejects my ideas or my thinking, I don't take it personally							
I can tell when the situation calls for a different way of thinking							
I am cautious when I discover new information, even when it aligns with my opinions							
I can always tell if my approach is working or if I need to change tactics							
I value ambiguous situations as they provide freedom to explore options and find novel solutions							
I actively seek to understand the biases I hold and how they may impact my thinking							
I am always ready to rethink my assumptions when new evidence appears							
When making decisions, I prioritise examining all the available data and evidence							
I put time and effort into seeking different perspectives because it leads to better outcomes							

Table 3 – Blindspotting Self-Assessment Tool

NOTES

Throughout this book you will find extensive references to academic literature as well as interviews and internet resources. I have also included a list of books at the end of each chapter which you may find of interest as you dive deeper into any of the areas of research.

Most of the quotes in this book have come from individuals who graciously offered their time to be interviewed for this book. Where any quotes have been used from another available source, I have endeavoured to reference them as such.

PROLOGUE

1 'NVIDIA: An overnight success story 30 years in the making', *Crucible Moments*, episode 8, Sequoia Capital; sequoiacap.com/podcast/crucible-moments-nvidia/
2 ibid.
3 'Jensen Huang NVIDIA CEO National Taiwan University commencement speech', YouTube, 27 May 2023; youtube.com/watch?v=__Ewkal7s3g
4 Ben Cohen, 'The 84-year-old man who saved NVIDIA', *Wall Street Journal*, 18 May 2024.
5 ibid.
6 'Jensen Huang NVIDIA CEO National Taiwan University commencement speech', YouTube, 27 May 2023; youtube.com/watch?v=__Ewkal7s3g
7 ibid.

8 Adam Bryant, 'I'm prepared for adversity. I waited tables', *New York Times*, 5 June 2010.
9 ibid.
10 ibid.
11 Emily Rella, 'Mark Zuckerberg says this CEO is the "Taylor Swift" of tech', *Entrepreneur*, 8 March 2024.

1 SEE WHAT OTHERS MISS
1 'Kettering gives key to progress', *New York Times*, 15 November 1938.
2 ibid.

2 DISCOVER SEEKERS AND KNOWERS
1 Josh Taylor, 'Elon Musk's X v Australia's online safety regulator: untangling the tweet takedown order', *Guardian*, 23 April 2024.

3 UNMASK YOUR THINKING TRAPS
1 'Ex-Fujitsu boss admits calling Horizon "Fort Knox"', *BBC*, 23 January 2024.
2 Nick Wallis, *The Great Post Office Scandal*, Bath Publishing Ltd, Oct 2022.
3 Michael Fitzpatrick, 'Sub-postmasters have wrongful convictions quashed', *BBC*, 23 September 2024.
4 Michelle Rimmer, 'Inside the UK's Post Office scandal and the years-long fight for justice', *ABC News*, 1 February 2024.
5 Katie Strick, 'Post Office scandal: from suicides to jail time with child killers – the heartbreaking stories of the postmasters', *Standard*, 10 January 2024.
6 Andrew Head and Tim Robinson, 'Post Office lied and threatened BBC over Horizon whistleblower', *BBC*, 12 January 2024.
7 'Evidence from Paula Vennells – former Group Chief Executive Officer of Post Office Ltd', 24 May 2024; postofficehorizoninquiry.org.uk/hearings/phases-56-24-may-2024
8 Matthew Fisher and Frank C. Keil, 'The curse of expertise: when more knowledge leads to miscalibrated explanatory insight', *Cognitive Science*, 40(5), 2015, pp. 1251–69.
9 Shih-Wei Wu, Johnnie E. V. Johnson and Ming-Chien Sung, 'Overconfidence in judgements: the evidence, the implications and the limitations', *Journal of Prediction Markets*, 2(1), 2008, pp. 73–90.

10 Brian Resnick, 'Intellectual humility: the importance of knowing you might be wrong', *Vox*, 5 January 2019.
11 Erik Angner, 'Epistemic humility – knowing your limits in a pandemic', *Behavioural Scientist*, 13 April 2020.
12 Adam Grant and David Dunning, 'Explaining the Dunning-Kruger effect and overcoming overconfidence', *Worklife with Adam Grant*, TED Audio Collective; podcasts.apple.com/us/podcast/explaining-the-dunning-kruger-effect-and/id1346314086?i=1000661578914
13 Erik Angner, 'Epistemic humility – knowing your limits in a pandemic', *Behavioural Scientist*, 13 April 2020.
14 Brian Resnick, 'Intellectual humility: the importance of knowing you might be wrong', *Vox*, 5 January 2019.
15 Nathan Ballantyne, 'Epistemic trespassing', *Mind*, 128(510), 2019, pp. 367–95.
16 Mohammad Ali Saghiri and Julia Vakhnovetsky, 'Epistemic trespassing into uncharted territory', *Advances in Human Biology*, 13(2), 2023, p. 227.
17 Nathan Ballantyne, 'Epistemic trespassing', *Mind*, 128(510), 2019, pp. 367–95.
18 Liz Wiseman, 'The power of not knowing', Brigham Young University (BYU) forum address, 26 January 2016; speeches.byu.edu/speakers/liz-wiseman/
19 Duncan Mavin, *The Pyramid of Lies: Lex Greensill and the billion-dollar scandal*, Macmillan, 2022.
20 Henry A. Kissinger, 'The 100 most influential people: Elizabeth Holmes', *Time*, 16 April 2015.
21 Carol Krucoff, 'Daniel Boorstin and his love affair with books', *Washington Post*, 28 January 1984.
22 Steven Sloman and Philip Fernbach, *The Knowledge Illusion: The myth of individual thought and the power of collective wisdom*, Macmillan, 2017.
23 Steven A. Sloman and Nathaniel Rabb, 'Your understanding is my understanding: evidence for a community of knowledge', *Psychological Science*, 27(11), 2016, pp. 1451–60.

4 BE HONEST

1 Voltaire, 'Letter to Frederick the Great', 28 November 1770, *Voltaire in His Letters*, ed. Evelyn Beatrice Hall, G. P. Putnam's Sons, 1919.

2 Bruce Grierson, 'Certainty is a psychological trap and it's time to escape', *Psychology Today*, 5 July 2023.
3 Brian Resnick, 'Intellectual humility: the importance of knowing you might be wrong', *Vox*, 5 January 2019.
4 Rick Famuyiwa, *They Call Me Magic*, Apple, 2022; tv.apple.com/au/show/they-call-me-magic/umc.cmc.67518fzfnhcjcajidzbpff8i5
5 Scott Barry Kaufman, 'The pressing need for everyone to quiet their egos', *Scientific American*, 21 May 2018.
6 Warren Berger, 'Are you intellectually humble?', *Psychology Today*, 18 March 2021.
7 Jim Collins, *Good to Great: Why some companies make the leap and others don't*, HarperBusiness, 2001, p. 21.
8 Max Rollwage, Alisa Loosen, Tobias U. Hauser, Rani Moran, Raymond J. Dolan and Stephen M. Fleming, 'Confidence drives a neural confirmation bias', *Nature Communications*, 11(1), 2020, p. 2634.
9 Emily Pronin, Daniel Y. Lin and Lee Ross, 'The bias blind spot: perceptions of bias in self versus others', *Personality and Social Psychology Bulletin*, 28(3), 2002, pp. 369–81.

5 BE CURIOUS

1 Mark Leary in conversation with Sara Ivry, 'What is intellectual humility?', *JSTOR Daily*, 24 January 2024.
2 Daniel Kahneman, *Thinking, Fast and Slow*, Farrar, Straus and Giroux, 2011.
3 Rishi Iyengar, 'Taylor Swift says the dress is black and blue', *Time*, 26 February 2015.
Billboard Staff, 'Justin Bieber, Taylor Swift, Lady Gaga, Demi Lovato and more weigh in on #thedress', *Billboard*, 27 February 2015.
4 Billboard Staff, 'Justin Bieber, Taylor Swift, Lady Gaga, Demi Lovato and more weigh in on #thedress', *Billboard*, 27 February 2015.
5 Rosa Lafer-Sousa, Katherine L. Hermann and Bevil R. Conway, 'Striking individual differences in color perception uncovered by The Dress photograph', *Current Biology*, 25(13), 29 June 2015, pp. R545–6.
6 Daniel Kahneman, 'Don't blink! The hazards of confidence', *New York Times Magazine*, 19 October 2011.
7 L. Festinger, *A Theory of Cognitive Dissonance*, Stanford University Press, 1957.

8   Pia Lauritzen, *Questions*, Johns Hopkins University Press, 2023.
9   Indra Nooyi, 'Indra Nooyi teaches leading with purpose', *Masterclass*; masterclass.com/classes/indra-nooyi-teaches-leading-with-purpose?ref=journeymatters.ai
10 Indra Nooyi on stage at WOBI Sydney, World Business Forum, 11–12 October 2023, shared by Chris Stanley, WOBI Global Content Director; linkedin.com/posts/christopherstanley1_wbfsyd-wbfny-leadership-activity-7200272334006435840-t2YQ?utm_source=share&utm_medium=member_desktop
11 ibid.

6 BE FLEXIBLE

1   Carol S. Dweck, *Mindset: The new psychology of success*, Ballantine Books, 2008.
2   Dan W. Grupe and Jack B. Nitschke, 'Uncertainty and anticipation in anxiety: an integrated neurobiological and psychological perspective', *Nature Reviews Neuroscience*, 14, 2013, pp. 488–501.
3   Howard Marks, 'The folly of certainty', Oaktree Capital, 17 July 2024; oaktreecapital.com/insights/memo/the-folly-of-certainty
4   Daniel Kahneman, 'Don't blink! The hazards of confidence', *New York Times Magazine*, 19 October 2011.
5   Tenelle Porter, Abdo Elnakouri, Ethan A. Meyers et al., 'Predictors and consequences of intellectual humility', *Nature Reviews Psychology*, 1, 2022, pp. 524–36.
6   Mark Lilla, 'No one knows what's going to happen', *New York Times*, 22 May 2020.
7   ibid.
8   Annie Duke, *Thinking in Bets: Making smarter decisions when you don't have all the facts*, Portfolio, 2018.
9   ibid.
10 Howard Marks, *The Most Important Thing: Uncommon sense for the thoughtful investor*, Columbia University Press, 1 May 2011.
11 ibid.
12 'Professor tells students to open minds to truth', *Blytheville Courier News*, 27 January 1940, p. 2.
13 Bruce Grierson, 'Certainty is a psychological trap and it's time to escape', *Psychology Today*, 5 July 2023.

14 Hulda Thórisdóttir and John T. Jost, 'Motivated closed-mindedness mediates the effect of threat on political conservatism', *Political Psychology*, 32(5), 2011, pp. 785–811.
15 Bruce Grierson, 'Certainty is a psychological trap and it's time to escape', *Psychology Today*, 5 July 2023.
16 Erik Dane, 'Reconsidering the trade-off between expertise and flexibility: a cognitive entrenchment perspective', *Academy of Management Review*, 35(4), 2010, pp. 579–603.
17 Daniel Kahneman, *Thinking, Fast and Slow*, Farrar, Straus and Giroux, 2011.
18 Beyoncé, Instagram post, 13 December 2013; instagram.com/p/h2YFO6P-w1d/?utm_source=ig_web_copy_link&igsh=MzRlODBiNWFlZA==
19 Anita Elberse and Stacie Smith, 'Beyoncé', Harvard Business School Case 515-036, August 2014 (revised October 2014); hbs.edu/faculty/Pages/item.aspx?num=47985

7 BECOME A BETTER SEEKER

1 Ethan Kross and Igor Grossmann, 'Boosting wisdom: distance from the self enhances wise reasoning attitudes and behavior', *Journal of Experimental Psychology: General*, 141(1), 2012, p. 43.
2 Tenelle Porter, Abdo Elnakouri, Ethan A. Meyers et al., 'Predictors and consequences of intellectual humility', *Nature Reviews Psychology*, 1, 2022, pp. 524–36.
3 Luis Velasquez, 'When asking too many questions undermines your leadership', *Harvard Business Review*, 22 July 2024.
4 Edgar Schein, *Humble Inquiry: The gentle art of asking instead of telling*, Berrett-Koehler, 2013.
5 Shane Snow, 'A new way to become more open-minded', *Harvard Business Review*, 20 November 2018.
6 Imani Perry, 'A lesson in intellectual humility', *The Atlantic*, 20 October 2022.
7 ibid.
8 ibid.
9 Mark Twain and Brander Matthews, *The Innocents Abroad*, New York and London, Harper & Brothers, 1911; loc.gov/item/15022628/
10 Safi Bahcall, *Loonshots: How to nurture the crazy ideas that win wars, cure diseases, and transform industries*, New York, St. Martin's Press, 2019.

11 Evan Nesterak, 'Remembering Daniel Kahneman: a mosaic of memories and lessons', *Behavioral Scientist*, 11 April 2024.
12 John A. Bargh, Mark Chen and Lara Burrows, 'Automaticity of social behavior: direct effects of trait construct and stereotype activation on action', *Journal of Personality and Social Psychology*, 71(2), 1996, p. 230.
13 Stephen Doyen, Olivier Klein, Cora-Lise Pichon and Axel Cleeremans, 'Behavioural priming: it's all in the mind but whose mind?', *PLOS One*, 7(1), 2012.
14 Fritz Strack, Leonard L. Martin and S. Stepper, 'Inhibiting and facilitating conditions of the human smile: a nonobtrusive test of the facial feedback hypothesis', *Journal of Personality and Social Psychology*, 54(5), 1988, pp. 768–77.
15 Ulrich Schimmack, 'Reconstruction of a train wreck: how priming research went off the rails', Replication Index, 2 February 2017; replicationindex.com/2017/02/02/reconstruction-of-a-train-wreck-how-priming-research-went-of-the-rails/
16 Daniel Kahneman, 'Adversarial collaboration: an EDGE lecture', *Edge*, July 2022; edge.org/adversarial-collaboration-daniel-kahneman
17 John A. Bargh, 'Nothing in their heads', *Psychology Today*, 5 March 2012.
18 Susan T. Fiske, 'Mob rule or wisdom of crowds?', *APS Observer*, in press; datacolada.org/wp-content/uploads/2016/09/Fiske-presidential-guest-column_APS-Observer_copy-edited.pdf
19 Daniel Kahneman and Amos Tversky, 'Subjective probability: a judgment of representativeness', *Cognitive Psychology*, 3(3), 1972, pp. 430–54.
20 Daniel Kahneman, 'Adversarial collaboration: an EDGE lecture', *Edge*, July 2022; edge.org/adversarial-collaboration-daniel-kahneman

8 BUILD TEAMS OF SEEKERS

1 Satya Nadella, Greg Shaw and Jill Tracie Nichols, *Hit Refresh: The quest to rediscover Microsoft's soul and imagine a better future for everyone*, New York, NY, HarperBusiness, an imprint of HarperCollinsPublishers, 2017.
2 Marieke Funck, Slawa Tomin and Rudiger Kabst, 'The importance of intellectual humility in new venture teams', Working Papers Dissertations 116, Faculty of Business Administration and Economics, University Paderborn, 2023; ideas.repec.org/p/pdn/dispap/116.html
3 Markus Baer and Greg R. Oldham, 'The curvilinear relation between experienced creative time pressure and creativity: moderating effects of

openness to experience and support for creativity', *Journal of Applied Psychology*, 91(4), 2006, p. 963–70.
4 Amy C. Edmondson, *The Fearless Organization: Creating psychological safety in the workplace for learning, innovation, and growth*, John Wiley & Sons, 2018.
5 Thomas L. Friedman, 'How to get a job at Google', *New York Times*, 22 February 2014.
6 ibid.
7 Adam Bryant, 'I'm prepared for adversity. I waited tables', *New York Times*, 5 June 2010.
8 ibid.
9 Stephen Witt, 'How Jensen Huang's NVIDIA is powering the AI revolution', *New Yorker*, 27 November 2023.
10 Adam Grant, *Think Again: The power of knowing what you don't know*, Viking, 2021.

9 CULTIVATE A BLINDSPOTTING CULTURE

1 'Code of Conduct', NVIDIA, accessed 20 December 2024; chrome-extension://efaidnbmnnnibpcajpcglclefindmkaj/https://images.nvidia.com/aem-dam/en-zz/Solutions/about-us/NVIDIA-Code-of-Conduct-External.pdf
2 'At Intel, our values define us', Intel, accessed 20 December 2024; intel.com/content/www/us/en/corporate-responsibility/our-values.html
3 'Our business principles', JPMorganChase, accessed 20 December 2024; jpmorganchase.com/about/business-principles#:~:text=Our%20firm%20is%20defined%20by,culture%20and%20approach%20to%20service
4 'Our values', Kellogg's, accessed 20 December 2024; kelloggs.com/en-in/who-we-are/our-values.html
5 ibid.
6 'Purpose and values', Reece Group, accessed 20 December 2024; group.reece.com/who-we-are/purpose-values
7 'Our corporate values', Microsoft, accessed 20 December 2024; microsoft.com/en-us/about
8 'Netflix culture – the best work of our lives', Netflix, accessed 20 December 2024; jobs.netflix.com/culture
9 'Be curious', Ford, accessed 20 December 2024; corporate.ford.com/about/culture/be-curious.html

10 'The way we work – our Code of Conduct', Rio Tinto, accessed 20 December 2024; riotinto.com/en/about/suppliers/working-with-us
11 'Values, culture and behaviour', Virgin Money UK, accessed 20 December 2024; virginmoneyukplc.com/our-people/values-culture-and-behaviour/
12 'Our Code of Conduct', Verizon, accessed 20 December 2024; verizon.com/about/our-company/code-conduct
13 'What makes Cisco's culture unique?', Cisco, accessed 20 December 2024; cisco.com/c/en/us/about/careers/we-are-cisco/conscious-culture.html

EPILOGUE

1 'Jensen Huang NVIDIA CEO National Taiwan University commencement speech', YouTube, 27 May 2023; youtube.com/watch?v=__Ewkal7s3g
2 ibid.
3 Stephen Witt, 'How Jensen Huang's NVIDIA is powering the AI revolution', *New Yorker*, 27 November 2023.
4 ibid.
5 Kif Leswing, 'NVIDIA dominates the AI chip market but there's more competition than ever', *CNBC*, 2 June 2024.
6 'NVIDIA Corporation common stock (NVDA)', Nasdaq, accessed 13 December 2024; nasdaq.com/market-activity/stocks/nvda
7 Jensen Huang, 'Vision versus perspective', Stanford Technology Ventures Program, Stanford University, 8 April 2009; stvp.stanford.edu/videos/vision-versus-perspective/
8 Jensen Huang and Joel Hellermark, 'On Leadership', Sana AI Summit, Stockholm, 31 May 2023; youtube.com/watch?v=h5xY_kRKHxE

ACKNOWLEDGEMENTS

While writing is a solitary endeavour, the ability for any piece of writing to truly resonate depends on a collective response, which is well out of the hands of the writer. That is one of the joys too – the unknown every writer jumps into when they find the courage to share their work with others.

Writing and publishing a book relies on the support of many, and I am incredibly grateful to everyone in my life who makes my writing possible.

First and foremost, nothing I do is possible without the love of my husband, Glen. We have been together for three decades, and throughout that time Glen has been unflinching in his unconditional support of everything I do. This book, and all that might follow, are because of Glen.

My daughters Emily and Zoe are two of the most emotionally intelligent, whip smart and all together brilliant women I know. They are also the two people in the world I am most proud of. I am so lucky to be their mother, and the world is damn lucky to have them in it.

Having neighbours who are like family feels similar to winning the lottery of life. Tessa and Allan, thank you for being the best neighbours anyone could hope to have. Your constant support, encouragement and friendship are valued by us all, including, of course, Huey.

This book has been able to come to life because of the fabulous team at Penguin Random House Australia. Huge thanks to Sophie Ambrose for the original vision and Meredith Curnow for shepherding this book through to completion. Importantly, my eternal gratitude is extended to editor extraordinaire, Shané Oosthuizen. Her sharp eyes, curious mind and aversion to repetition have benefitted readers on every page of this book.

Thank you to my Australian literary agent, Fiona Inglis at Curtis Brown and my international literary agent, Esmond Harmsworth at Aevitas Creative Management. Without you both, my writing career would look very different.

I want to thank the incredible Adam Grant – a true giver – for his ongoing support and guidance to an Aussie on the other side of the world. Adam, your generosity is legendary, and I am full of gratitude for simply being in your orbit. I am also thrilled you were able to introduce me to Reb Rebele.

It is not an exaggeration to say this book could not have been written without the remarkable Reb Rebele. When Reb and I first spoke about my idea for this book, I told him I felt like I had 'the twisties', Simone Biles's description of what caused her to withdraw from the 2020 Tokyo Olympics. I felt lost in the air and not quite sure how to land. Reb is not only responsible for helping me land safely, but also for helping me land in a much better position than even I imagined was possible. Reb, your ability to synthesise ideas, your way with words and language, and your vision for inspiring me to see what I might otherwise have missed was invaluable. I feel honoured to know you and to be able to benefit from your expertise.

Luisa McIlvride has been my right hand for many years now, and she makes sure my life and work come together seamlessly. Luisa manages everything that readers of this book do not see behind the scenes. My life would grind to a halt without her beside me. Thank you, Luisa, and I hope you know how much I value all you do.

Thank you also to Victoria Brown, who has drawn the fantastic images in this book. Victoria has a knack for taking a half-baked idea I send her in a poorly written email and turning it into a diagram that captures the precise essence of what I want to convey. Victoria, your art and creativity is a skill that goes hand in hand with what I try to do with words; I am so grateful to work with you.

I would like to thank Dr Ben Searle, who I collaborated with to develop the Blindspotting Self-Assessment Tool. I am much better with words than I am with numbers and statistics, so partnering with an expert like Ben is imperative. I am grateful to him for his help in developing the scale, analysing the data and helping me introduce to the world a tool everyone can benefit from.

Finally, thank you so much to the many people who have taken the time to speak to me for this book. I know you all have incredibly busy lives, so thank you for choosing to spend a small fraction of that time with me. In alphabetical order, thank you to Safi Bahcall, Meg Bear, Richard Bistrong, Marcus Collins, Robert Denney, David Epstein, Chris Havrilla, Cindy Hook, Julie Inman Grant, Pia Lauritzen, Duncan Mavin, Wendy McMahon, Marlene Poynder, Megan Reitz, Ulrich Schimmack and Sukhinder Singh Cassidy.

INDEX

accolades 63, 78, 79
acknowledging what you do not know
 23, 24, 28, 33, 54–5, 73, 75, 85, 89,
 94, 177, 188–9, 212
 empowering others 55, 94, 96, 97
 fostering a culture of 39
 strength, as 55, 93–4
active listening 56
adaptability 9, 12, 28, 39, 55, 56, 58,
 74, 147, 164
 changing mind with new data 39, 55,
 116, 170, 208–9
 interview questions to test for 234–5
 unwillingness to adapt with new
 evidence 62
admitting and confronting mistakes 4,
 5, 70, 82, 181
advantage blindness 137–8
alternatives
 always considering 187–8
 failure to investigate 61, 63, 99, 114
 openness to 123
ambiguity 43, 46, 57, 151
 creativity, as a source 167–8

embracing 153–4, 163–8, 174, 175,
 241, 266
growth mindset, cultivation 163–4
humility, fostering 168
open-mindedness, fostering 168, 241
resistance to 164, 166
artificial intelligence (AI) 8, 11, 152
 ChatGPT 273
 NVIDIA 272–5
assumptions, challenging 7, 10, 28, 29,
 33, 55, 66, 73, 109, 112, 115, 132,
 187, 224, 265
 evidence contradicting 115–16
audience, understanding 179–80
authority bias 255
automation 152
aviation industry 65, 260–1

Bahcall, Safi 15, 145–9, 203, 263
 *Loonshots: How to nurture the crazy
 ideas that win wars, cure diseases
 and transform industries* 147, 203
Ballantyne, Nathan 64
Bankman-Fried, Sam 67

Bear, Meg 15, 238–42, 267
beginner's mindset 65, 75
Beyoncé 177, 179–82
biases, hunting 89–90, 103–9, 224, 236, 265
  acknowledging 86, 88, 105
  alternatives, seeking 104
  benefits of hunting biases 108–9
  challenging, actively 104, 212
  cognitive biases 43, 46, 103, 104, 132
  distortion of perception 104
  encouraging others to see their own 86
  feedback *see* feedback
  inability to see our own 105
  leading by example 109
  mitigating before making decision 108–9
  'red team' exercise 224
  reflect on your own 195–6
  stress and emotion, impact 107–8
  unseen biases 59
Bistrong, Jacob 78
Bistrong, Richard 15, 77–82
blame 102, 138, 139
blindness to new insights 44, 63
blindspotting
  actively seeking out blind spots 185
  benefits 29–30
  biases, hunting 89–90, 103–9, 224, 236, 265
  calibration, not hesitation 27
  collective transformation, power for 267–8
  concept of 9, 22
  confidence 28–9, 91–2, 187–8
  continuous practice, as 263–4, 267
  curiosity *see* curiosity
  ego, disentangling 57–8, 86, 88, 89, 99–103, 110, 240, 265
  encouraging in others 56
  failure to practise 11

flexibility *see* flexibility
fosters inclusive, innovative environments 24, 25
honesty *see* honesty
key mindsets 9–10, 25–7, 264
leaders, benefits for 30–1
limitations, recognising 7, 9, 13, 33, 86, 88, 90–9, 263, 264
organisations and teams, benefits for 31–2
practice of 22, 24, 25, 36, 53, 55, 185–6
practices 10, 86–109, 264
transforms how we think about ourselves 24
vigilance, need for 266–7
what it is not 27–9
blindspotting culture, fostering 220, 221–31, 235–6, 239, 242, 243–4, 268
  board of directors 252–6
  collaboration over competition 222
  competitive advantage 244, 257
  core values 246–52
  hierarchies, flattening of 222, 245–6, 257
  proactive, forward-thinking 244
  Seekers, recognition, reward, recruitment and promotion of 221, 257
Blindspotting Self-Assessment Tool 211, 276–80
  methodology 276
  pilot study 277–8
  website 211, 276
Blockbuster 66, 67
board of directors
  authority bias 255
  blindspotting, how to build 252–6
  Chair, role of 255
  convictions, hold lightly 253–4
  dissent, healthy 255–6, 257

INDEX

diversity of members 255, 257
homogeneous, when 131, 255
knowledge gaps, failure to admit 253
mistakes, addressing and learning from 256
need for blindspotting by 252–3
psychological safety in 253
role 252
willingness to reconsider 254
Bock, Laszlo 231
Boorstin, Daniel J. 71
breaking down large goals 57, 98
Buck, Ian 271, 274
Buss, Jerry 95

calibrate confidence 91–2, 187–8, 212
Cassidy, Sukhinder Singh 15, 54–8, 267–8
certainty 63, 90, 115, 123, 164
  false certainty 166–7
  human need for 165–6
  illusion of 123–4
  people who project, attraction of 165
change 158
  see also adaptability
  openness to 159, 170
  resistance to, reasons for 171–2
changimg mind with new data 39, 55, 116, 170, 208–9
  see also adaptability
Chenault, Kenneth 95
Cisco Systems 251
closed-mindedness 11, 66, 171
Cobb, William G. 23
cognitive dissonance 130, 172
cognitive rigidity 62, 158–9
cognitive traps 59, 61, 63, 66, 73, 74, 75, 263, 266
collaboration 8, 24, 29, 30, 31–2, 36, 87, 88, 91, 103
  accountability and ownership, fostering 142

culture of 193
different perspectives, by seeking 133, 170, 174
prioritising over competition 220, 222
Seekers and 220–1, 236
valuing 94
collective inquiry 142
collective power 220
collective wisdom, gathering 56
Collins, Jim
  Good to Great 100
Collins, Marcus 15, 177–81
communication
  all levels, fostering dialogue across 206, 245–6
  availability and accessibility 206
  between team members 206
community, power of 180–1
  working with 181
'community of knowledge' 72
competing priorities, balancing 260–1
complacency 32, 68, 118
composure under pressure 262
confidence mistaken for competence 68
'confident humility' 240
confirmation bias 73, 125, 129, 159–60, 265
continuous inquiry 241
continuous learning 30, 31, 32, 33, 73
  questions encouraging 141–2
continuous reassessment of skills 65
contributions of others
  all levels, fostering dialogue across 206, 245–6
  empowering people to make 39, 58, 86, 88, 97
  encouraging others to speak up 56–7, 87, 129, 133, 169, 170, 174
  valuing 24, 29, 30, 31, 90, 98, 133, 169, 170, 174

convictions
  balancing with flexibility 170, 174
  hold lightly 169, 209–11, 253–4
  proportional to evidence 28
  rooted in reality 27
core beliefs in ourselves 100
core values, corporate 246–50
  blindspotting practices, reflecting 251
  curiosity as 249–50
  flexibility as 250–1
  intellectual honesty 247–9
corporate collapses, recent 67, 75
corporate corruption, victims 79–80
corporations
  innovation replaced by politics and personal advancement, where 148
  systems changing behaviour 148
corrupt behaviour 79–81
  isolation and 81
'crazy ideas', nurturing 203–4
creativity 8, 12, 24
  ambiguity as source of 168
  open-mindedness as inspiration for 173
critical thinking 25, 52, 125, 129, 224, 230
culture, corporate
  blindspotting culture, cultivating 219–20
  building teams of Seekers 219–36
  continuous improvement, of 193
  flexibility, promoting 176
  know-it-all culture 220
  toxic 70
  understanding 204–5
curiosity 6, 7, 9–10, 24, 25, 27, 29, 37, 58, 61, 71, 85–6, 117–20, 145, 187, 265–6
  core value, as 249–50
  'crazy ideas', nurturing 203–4

different perspectives, seeking 10, 22, 24, 28, 29, 33, 55, 70, 75, 98, 120, 128–9, 132, 143, 265
discovery, driver of 143
foundation of learning, innovation and adaptability 119
how to be 197–205
interview questions to test for 234–5
journalists mindset, adopt 197–8
key mindset of blindspotting 9–10, 25, 85, 118, 187
new possibilities, opens to 118
objective truth, seek out 198–200, 265
practices 119–20
questions to gain insight 120, 134–142, 143, 200–1, 265
stopping, effects 117–18
world view, expand 202

data
  gathering 55
  source of, reliability 199
data-driven decision-making 37, 56, 116, 248
de Mestral, George 173
decision-making
  blindspotting see blindspotting
  evidence, grounded in 88
  hierarchical 8
  incomplete information, with 55, 112
  informed and balanced 134
deductive learners 56
defensiveness 99, 102, 234
Denney, Air Vice Marshal Robert 15, 65, 101–2, 259–62
Diercks, Dwight 234
different perspectives, seeking 10, 22, 24, 28, 29, 33, 55, 70, 75, 98, 120, 128–9, 132, 143
  better decision-making, fostering 133–4

cognitive dissonance 130, 172
collaboration, sparking 133, 174
critical evaluation 129
dissent and diversity, opportunities for 206, 224
encouraging others to speak up 56–7, 87, 129
groupthink 130–2, 255
innovation, creating space for 133, 169, 173
learning from 129–30
valuing different opinions 30, 87, 98, 129, 131, 132, 170, 174
disconnect between perception and reality 81
'disprove yourself' 187
disruptors, identifying 205
dissent 256
constructive dissent 224, 251, 255–6, 257–8
opportunities for, creating 206, 224
diversity 206, 255, 257
doubt
doubt as a strength 23, 90–1
failure to have 61, 64
due diligence 72
Duke, Annie 167, 168
Dunning, David 63–4
'Dunning-Kruger Club' 63–4
Dweck, Carol 163–4

echo chambers 73, 130, 159
groupthink 130–1, 255
ego, disentangling 57–8, 86, 88, 89, 99–103, 110, 240, 265
allows us to see more 102–3
concept of 99
difficulty 100–2
ego as a defence mechanism 100
purpose not ego, driven by 100
Einstellung effect 66
emotional resilience 31

emotional triggers, recognising 191–2
self-distancing techniques 193–4
emotional wellbeing 34
'epistemic trespassing' 64–5
Epstein, David 15, 112–16, 263
The Sports Gene 112, 113, 115
eSafety Commissioner
digital safety regulator 215, 216, 217
X (Twitter) and 214–18
Estes, Greg 273
evidence
aligning beliefs with 28
changing direction with new 55, 74, 170
contradicting assumptions 115–16
decisions grounded in 88
source of, reliability 199
existing beliefs, clinging to 99, 123–5, 169, 173, 174, 175
experiences
learning from 13, 30, 153
past, reliance on 67, 68, 75, 80, 158, 172
experiment, willingness to 38, 153
expertise, the curse of 59, 63–7, 71, 74, 75, 79, 82
barrier to open-mindedness, as 172
experts 63, 64
closed to new possibilities, when 66, 75, 172
'epistemic trespassing' 64–5
overconfidence and 63, 64

Facebook 5, 179
fail, willingness to 38
fairness 127, 196
'fake it till you make it' 93
familiarity, comfort of 125, 130
fear of being wrong 57, 203
fear of judgment 29, 31, 33, 93, 222
fear of retribution 31, 204, 253

feedback 30, 30, 70, 101
　all levels, seeking from 206, 245–6
　critical evaluation of 129
　inviting 106
　reaction to 107
　regular loops, establish 224, 246
　role 106
　safe to give 106
Ferguson, Dr Kirstin, AM
　awards vii
　career and education vii, 13
　Head & Heart: The art of modern leadership 26
　leadership roles 13
　RAAF 13
Fernbach, Philip
　The Knowledge Illusion 72
financial markets
　banana markets 148–9
　Picasso markets 149
Fleming, Alexander 173
flexibility 6, 7, 10, 24, 25, 27, 29, 38, 56, 58, 61, 71, 86, 147, 150–4, 174, 175, 187, 266
　all levels, fostering dialogue across 206, 245–6
　ambiguity, embracing 153–4, 163–8, 174, 175, 241, 266
　balancing with our convictions 170, 174
　change mind, willingness to 39, 55, 116, 170, 208–9
　cognitive 26, 56, 116, 167
　convictions, hold lightly 169, 209–11
　core value, as 250–1
　corporate culture, as 176
　dissent and diversity, opportunities for 206, 224
　external forces, awareness of 205–6
　how to be flexible 204–11
　key mindset of blindspotting 9–10, 25, 85, 150, 187

open mind, keeping 154, 165, 174
organisational culture, understanding 204–5
practices 153
'reading the room' 26, 49, 153, 154–62, 174, 175, 204, 266
relational dynamics, reading 206–7
societal changes, recognise 205–6
stagnation, counteracts 152
trends, monitoring industry and market 205
Ford Motor Company 250
forecasting 166–7, 168
Fujitsu UK 59–63

Galbraith, John Kenneth 166
General Motors (GM) 23
genetics and athletic performance 113–14
Google 54, 231, 272
Grant, Adam 240
Grant, Julie Inman 15, 214–18, 263
Greensill, Lex 68
Greensill Capital 68, 73, 75
group identity 171
groupthink 130–2, 255
growth mindset, fostering 190–1, 220
'gut-data-gut' decision-making 56

Havrilla, Chris 15, 125–7
Head & Heart Leader Scale 26
　8 key attributes of modern leadership 26
Head & Heart: The art of modern leadership 26
help, seeking 5, 81–2, 95–6, 98, 101, 260
hierarchical organisations 93
　flattening of hierarchies 222, 245–6, 257
　information silos 245
　lack of transparency 246

INDEX

Hinton, Geoffrey 272
Holmes, Elizabeth 67, 69, 73
honesty 9, 25, 26, 27, 29, 58, 61, 71, 74, 86–90, 187, 264–5
see also intellectual honesty
  admit what you do not know 188–9
  biases, reflect on 195–6
  calibrate confidence 91–2, 187–8, 212
  core value, as 247–9
  emotional triggers, recognise 191–2
  growth mindset, foster 190–1
  honest with others 86, 265
  honest with ourselves 86, 265
  how to be 187–97
  key mindset of blindspotting 9–10, 25, 85, 110, 187
  practices 88
  self-distancing techniques 193–4
  stereotypes, challenge 196–7, 212
Hook, Cindy 15, 97–8
Horizon accounting software 59–63
hospitality industry 209–10
Huang, Jensen 1–6, 233, 270–1, 274–5
  NVIDIA, pivoting to AI 273, 274
hubris 59, 67–70, 71, 74, 75, 81, 82, 266–7
humility 4, 16, 26, 82, 86, 88, 98, 193, 231
  definitions 16
  modern leadership attribute 26
  tool for growth, innovation and adaptation 16
  weakness, often seen as 16, 115
hypothesis, forming and testing 56

identify known unknowns 225–6
illusion of knowledge 59, 65, 71–4, 75, 82, 188, 267
'illusion of validity' 124
inclusivity 31–2, 98, 268

inconvenient truths 248
infallibility, sense of 68, 80, 91, 253
information
  assessing new 26, 28
  information overload 160–1
  recalibrating when receiving new 28
innovation 12, 33
  acknowledging limitations as a catalyst to 96–7
  creating space for 169, 173
  culture of innovation 23, 32, 97
  different perspectives, by seeking 133, 169, 170, 173, 174
inquiry, culture of 119
instinctive learners 56
instincts 28, 56, 68, 203, 204, 210
Intel 248
intellectual arrogance 75, 92
intellectual curiosity 26, 29
intellectual honesty 5, 17, 24, 29, 36, 38, 69, 70, 75, 85, 110, 265–6
  acknowledging what you do not know 23, 24, 73, 85, 89, 94, 177, 188–9, 212
  core value, as 247–9
  distinct from intellectual humility 17
  interview questions to test for 234–5
  limitations, recognising 7, 9, 13, 33, 86, 88, 90–9, 263, 264
  overlap with intellectual humility 17
  practice of 189
  strength, as 115
intellectual humility, theory of 16, 26
  intellectual honesty and 17
  tool for growth, innovation and adaptation 16
intellectual limitations, acknowledge 7, 33, 86, 88, 89, 90–9, 110, 177, 188–9, 212, 240
  benefits of 94–9
  difficulties with 93
  doubt as a strength 90–1

intellectual limitations, acknowledge *continued*
  empowering teams, as a tool for 55, 94, 96, 97, 239, 240
  finding the sweet spot 92–3
  freedom to learn, provides 95–6, 103
  innovation, as a catalyst for 96–7
  signalling commitment to growth 98–9
  trust with others, fosters 96
intellectual servility 92
interpersonal relationships 29, 30–1
invincibility, sense of 67, 79
Irimajiri, Shoichiro 3

Johnson Junior, Earvin 'Magic' 95–6
journalists, mindset of 37, 197–8
JPMorganChase 248–9

Kahneman, Daniel 124, 165, 172, 208
Kalanick, Travis 67, 70
Kellogg's 249
Kettering, Charles F. 22, 23, 24, 33
know-it-all culture 220
Knowers 41–2, 45–8, 71
  asset, circumstances where 46, 49
  balance with being a Seeker 52
  coach, don't punish 228–9
  defensiveness 46
  mindset 49, 52
  overestimation of intellectual strength 46
  questionnaire 47–8
  recognising context to be and not be 49, 50–1, 52
knowledge
  'community of knowledge' 72
  confirmation bias 73, 125, 129, 159–60
  gaps in, as learning opportunities 190–1, 212

  overestimation of one's own 63, 64, 71
  the illusion of 59, 65, 71–4, 75, 82, 188, 267
Knowles, Mathew 179
Kotschnig, Professor Walter 170
Krizhevsky, Alex 272

Lauritzen, Pia 15–16, 136–7, 139
leaders
  'all-knowing and wise' mindset 94
  critically assess before acting 30
  effective 9, 12
  effective decision-making 30
  expectations of, implicit 7
  intellectual limitations, recognising 7, 33, 86, 88, 89, 90–9
  interpersonal relationships, strong 30
  leadership capabilities, enhanced 30
  levels of, descriptions 100
  moments of impact 11–12
  purpose not ego, driven by 100
leadership 262
  leadership experience 28
  traditional approaches to, inadequacy 8
learning
  freedom to learn 95–6, 103
  openness to 8, 9, 12, 85
life satisfaction 29, 30, 34
Lilla, Mark 167
limitations, recognising 7, 9, 13, 33, 86, 88, 90–9, 263, 264
  fostering a culture of 38, 86
  Seekers 44
listen, willingness to 12, 55, 133, 169, 170, 174
'listening tours' 55

McMahon, Wendy 15, 35–40, 263, 267
Malachowsky, Chris 1

INDEX

market, misjudgment 2, 3, 193
marketing 179–80
  marketing orthodoxy 180
  traditional channels, by-passing 181
  trends, monitoring industry and market 205
Marks, Howard 164–5, 166, 168
Mavin, Duncan 15, 67–8, 70, 131
  The Pyramid of Lies: Lex Greensill and the billion-dollar scandal 68
Microsoft
  core values 249–50
  DirectX 2, 4
  Windows 95 2
mistakes
  admitting and confronting 4, 5, 70, 82, 102, 172, 181, 192
  encouraging others to freely admit 193
  learning opportunity, seeing as 6, 102, 212
  normalise making 192
'moral fading' 79
Musk, Elon 214, 216

Nadella, Satya 220
needs of others 29, 161
Netflix 66
  core values 250, 251
Neumann, Adam 67
new ideas, rejection of 65, 122
new information, actively seek 73
new opportunities, failure to recognise 66
new possibilities, openness to 39, 118
  curiosity, through 118
Nooyi, Indra 140–1
NVIDIA 1–5, 233, 270
  AI and 273–5
  Code of Conduct 248
  CUDA 271–2
  GPU 270–1, 272

intellectual honesty as core value 233, 248, 251
reinvention 273, 274, 275

objective truth 43, 121, 122–3, 143, 241
see also truth, search for
  creative connections, make 199
  data and evidence 199
  logic and reasoning 198
  seek out 198–200, 265
  source, consideration of reliability 199–200
one-on-one meetings 55
open-mindedness 154, 165, 168, 169–75, 241
  balancing beliefs and flexibility 170
  benefits of 173–5
  concept of 169
  creativity, inspires 173
  expertise as a barrier to 172
  innovation, creates space for 169, 173
  new ideas, invites 175
  resistance to change, reasons for 171–2
  seeking and listening to other opinions 169, 170
  self-reflection questions 210–11
open to being wrong 73
openness, culture of 29, 87
optimism bubble 137
organisations
  all levels, foster dialogue across 206, 245–6
  benefits of blindspotting 31–2
  building teams of Seekers 219–36
  core values 246–9
  culture of, strengthening 32, 94
  morale 206
  relational dynamics, reading 206–7
  understanding the organisational culture 204–5
  unspoken rules 204

overconfidence 63, 64, 65, 72, 74, 75, 82, 165, 187
  aviation industry, in 65
overestimation of one's knowledge 46, 63, 64, 71, 72, 266–7

passion, interview questions to test for 234–5
past achievements 67, 68, 75, 80, 158, 172
patterns, observing 55, 88
Pauling, Linus 64
peer connection 205, 206
Perry, Imani 202
perspective, modern leadership attribute 26
pivot, ability to 5, 9, 39, 56, 147, 170
Post Office Limited (UK) scandal 59–63
  Post Office Horizon IT Inquiry 2024 62
Poynder, Marlene 15, 209
Priem, Curtis 1
problem-solving
  collaborative 32, 91, 98, 120, 142, 143, 174, 192, 240
  creative 32, 133, 152, 236
problems
  seeking the true nature of 126, 140–1
  truth-seeking perspective, approaching from 122, 127, 128
process over outcome 230–1, 236
protocol, following 261
psychological safety, culture of 29, 30, 33, 102, 193, 222–3, 236, 257
  board room, in 253

questions
  asking questions to win 138–40
  believe we know the answer already 139
  benefits of using to learn 140

  calibrate confidence by asking 188, 212
  challenging assumptions by 135–6
  context for asking 201
  continuous learning, promotes 141–2
  difficulty in asking questions for insight 136–8
  discovery, framing for 135
  insight, questioning for 120, 134–142, 143, 200–1, 265
  intent behind 134–5
  interview questions to identify Seekers 232–3
  open-ended 120, 135, 138, 141, 143, 212
  power dynamic and 137–8
  right questions, asking 67, 86, 87, 139
  specific outcomes, link to 201
  tone of 143
  too many, asking 201
  who we ask and who we fail to ask 137
  willingness to 23

'reading the room' 26, 49, 153, 154–62, 174, 175, 204, 266
  benefits of 161–2
  biases hindering context recognition 159–60
  calibrating response to the context 162
  concept of 154
  context 155
  external signals 162
  information overload 160–1
  internal signals 162
  prioritising 161
  resistance to 158–61
  self-reflective questions to assess skills 207

specificity of conversation 156–7
uncertainty, when to admit 155–6, 162
'red team' exercise 224
Reece 249
Reitz, Megan 15, 94, 137–8, 195
reputation, seeking to protect 63
resilience 30, 130, 164
Richards, Kevin 113
right, need to be 74, 89, 102, 103
right questions, asking 67, 86, 87, 138, 139
rigidity in thinking 32, 52, 151
  cognitive rigidity 158–9
Rio Tinto 250
risks
  managing and controlling 262
  weighing 167
risk-taking 69
  calculated risks 168
  reckless 69

scientific validation of technology, insufficient 73
Searle, Dr Ben 276
second-hand information, relying on 72
Seeker 41–5, 71, 186, 187
  balance with being a Knower 52
  becoming a better Seeker 186–7
  blindspotting culture, fostering 220, 221–31, 235–6
  collaboration and 220–1
  identify known unknowns 225–6
  interview questions to identify 232–3
  mindsets 49, 52, 186, 187
  objective truth 43
  questionnaire 44
  recognising context to be and not be 49, 50–1, 52
  recognition, reward, recruitment and promotion of 221
  teams of *see* Seeker teams

Seeker teams
  attracting 221, 236
  biases, encourage hunting of 224–5, 236
  blindspotting culture, fostering 220, 221–31, 235–6, 257
  building teams of 219–36
  coach, don't punish Knowers 228–9
  collaboration and 220–1, 222, 236
  encourage different perspectives 229–30
  hiring Seekers 231–5
  interview questions to identify 232–3
  passion, adaptability and intellectual honesty, testing for 233–5
  process over outcome 230–1, 236
  psychological safety, culture of 29, 30, 33, 102, 193, 222–3, 236, 257
  publicly reward Seeker behaviours 226–7
  recognition, reward, recruitment and promotion of 221
Sega America 3–4, 5
self-awareness 73, 82, 87–8, 267
self-distancing techniques 193–4
self-reflection, capacity for 47, 53, 70
self-worth 89, 99
setbacks, absorbing 30
shared ownership, culture of 92
shared problem-solving 91
'shoshin' 65, 75
Shulz, Kathryn 171, 172
simplicity, need for 124–5
Sloman, Steven 72
The Knowledge Illusion 72
social media engagement 180
social-media platforms
  laws to protect online users 214
societal changes, recognise 205–6
startups 93
stereotypes, challenge 196–7, 212
strategies, refining 30

stubborness 52
success
  allure of 67, 68, 75, 80
  familiarity, mistaking for 117
superiority illusion 137, 138
suspending judgment until evidence is gathered 56
Sutskever, Ilya 272
system failure 63

Tait, Duncan 59
Theranos 67, 69, 73, 75
Thinkers50 177
threatened, feeling 99, 171
Time magazine 100 most influential people 5
top-down approach 180
transparency, culture of 32, 57, 93–4, 222, 246
trends, monitoring industry and market 205
Tripadvisor 54
trust 93
  focusing on objective truth 128
  with others, building 94, 96, 192
truth, search for 74, 119–20, 121–8, 143
  certainty, the illusion of 123–4
  fairer decisions 127
  objective truth 121, 122–3, 143
  reshaping our understanding 125, 127
  seeking out the objective truth 198–200
  subjective truth 121, 122, 126
Twain, Mark 202
Twitter (now known as X) 214–18
  harmful online material 215

Uber 67, 70
uncertainty 54, 57, 153, 164, 165, 168, 241
  fear response 166
  knowing when to admit 155–6, 162, 212
  navigating 164, 241, 242
unethical behaviour 79–81
  isolation and 81
United Kingdom (UK) Post Office Limited scandal 59–63
  Post Office Horizon IT Inquiry 2024 62
unlearn, ability to 9, 147
unwillingness to adapt with new evidence 62
unwillingness to admit fault 61, 62, 89, 172
user-centric thinking 37

Van Tongeren, Daryl R. 91
Velasquez, Luis 201
Vennells, Paula 59–63
Verizon 251
video games graphics 1, 2
Virgin Money UK 250
visionary leadership
  blind arrogance and 69
Voltaire 90
vulnerability 86, 88
  modelling 106

warning signs, overlooking 65, 73, 75
WeWork 67
Wiseman, Liz
  Multipliers 65–6
world view, expand your own 202

X (formerly Twitter) 214
  eSafety Commissioner and 214–18
  harmful online material 215
Xero 54, 55, 57

Zuckerberg, Mark 5

Powered by Penguin

Looking for more great reads, exclusive content and book giveaways?

Subscribe to our weekly newsletter.

Scan the QR code or visit penguin.com.au/signup